The Sustainable Learning Community

The Sustainable Learning Community

One University's Journey to the Future

JOHN ABER, TOM KELLY,

AND BRUCE MALLORY,

EDITORS

University of New Hampshire Press

Durham, New Hampshire

Published by

University Press of New England

Hanover and London

KH

University of New Hampshire Press
Published by University Press of New England,
One Court Street, Lebanon, NH 03766
www.upne.com
© 2009 by University of New Hampshire Press
Printed in the United States of America
5   4   3   2   1

Library of Congress Cataloging-in-Publication Data
The sustainable learning community : one university's journey to the future /
John Aber, Tom Kelly, and Bruce Mallory, editors.
     p.   cm.
Includes index.
ISBN 978-1-58465-771-2 (pbk. : alk. paper)
1. University of New Hampshire. 2. Sustainable living — New Hampshire.
3. Universities and colleges — Environmental aspects — New Hampshire.
4. College facilities — Environmental aspects — New Hampshire. I. Aber,
John D. II. Kelly, Tom, 1956– III. Mallory, Bruce L.
LD3779.N43S87   2009
378.742'5 — dc22   2009000995

Cover image courtesy of artist Dennis Balogh and the UNH Foundation, Inc.

12/1/10

To the Hubbard family for their timely and creative vision for, and
support of, sustainability as a campus-wide CORE value
at the University of New Hampshire, and to
Bill Mautz and Peter Lamb, who saw the
big picture from the beginning.

Contents

Editor's Preface JOHN ABER xiii

Acknowledgments xvii

Chapter 1. Sustainability as an Organizing Principle for
Higher Education TOM KELLY 1

Chapter 2. Teaching and Learning Sustainability: Curriculum
and Pedagogy JOHN CARROLL, editor 54

Curriculum: Biodiversity and Ecosystems 58
Engaging Students in the Sciences, GEORGE HURTT /
59; How Does a Local Master of Public Health Program Address Global Emerging Infectious Disease?
ROSEMARY CARON / 61; Sustainable Science and Engineering, KEVIN GARDNER AND NANCY KINNER /
64; UNH-EcoQuest and Sustainability in New Zealand — Te Rarangahau Taiao, RIA BREJAART, KIM
BABBITT, AND DONNA DOWAL / 66

Curriculum: Climate and Energy 68
ESCI 405: Global Environmental Change, CAMERON
WAKE / 69; The Energy Waste Watch Challenge and Stu-
dent Energy Captains, MICHELE HOLT-SHANNON AND
SARA CLEAVES / 72; Organizing a Curriculum on the
Environment — Inclusiveness or Security? JOHN ABER /
75; Science, Politics, and Policy from Global to Local in
an Undergraduate Seminar, STACY VANDEVEER / 77

Curriculum: Food and Society 79
Dual Major in EcoGastronomy, JOANNE CURRAN-
CELENTANO / 79; Integrating Sustainability into the

Professional Development of Dietetic Interns, JOANNE
BURKE / 83; "The Real Dirt," JOHN E. CARROLL / 86;
UNH CREAM, DREW CONROY AND PETER ERICK-
SON / 87

Curriculum: Culture and Sustainability   90
The Promise of the Sun, TOM KELLY / 90; Artistic En-
gagement — Discovering and Developing a Theatri-
cal Response to Sustainability, DAVID KAYE / 94; The
University Dialogue and a Sense of Place, JOANNE
CURRAN-CELENTANO / 97; How the Sustainable Liv-
ing Minor Came to Be, ROBERT ECKERT AND BERT
COHEN / 99

Chapter 3. Practicing Sustainability: Campus Operations   101
DOUGLAS BENCKS, editor

Operations: Biodiversity and Ecosystems   104
Landscape Master Plan, DOUGLAS BENCKS / 105; Land
Use Committee, TOM LEE / 108; The MUB Meadow,
JOHN L. HART / 112

Operations: Climate and Energy   117
It's Risky Business Doing the Right Thing — The Co-
Gen Plant and EcoLine, PAUL CHAMBERLIN AND
MATT O'KEEFE / 118; Transportation and Land Use,
STEVE PESCI / 123; The UNH Greenhouse Gas In-
ventory, BRETT PASINELLA / 128; The Energy Task
Force — A Cross-Campus Collaboration to Address
Climate Change, SARA CLEAVES / 129

Operations: Food and Society   132
The UNH Compost Program — From Waste to Com-
post, ELISABETH FARRELL AND RICK MACDONALD /
133; Acting Locally — The UNH Local Harvest Initiative, ELISABETH FARRELL AND RICK MACDONALD /
136; Innovative Dining Hall Hours and Plate Waste,
RICK MACDONALD / 139

Operations: Culture and Sustainability   141
Developing Our Sense of Place — The Role of the Committee for Campus Aesthetics, VICKI C. WRIGHT / 142;

Sustainable Building Design, DOUGLAS BENCKS / 145;
Moving the Kingsbury Mural, DOUGLAS BENCKS / 149;
Sustainable Buildings — Do You Want Fries with Your
Building? No Thank You! DOUGLAS BENCKS / 151

Chapter 4. Creating the Intellectual Basis for Sustainability: 153
Research and Scholarship
JOHN ABER AND CAMERON WAKE, editors

Research on Biodiversity and Ecosystems   157
Cooperative Institute for Coastal and Estuarine Envi-
ronmental Technology, RICH LANGAN AND DOLORES
LEONARD / 158; The History of Marine Animal Popu-
lations, ANDREW ROSENBERG, JEFF BOLSTER, KAREN
ALEXANDER, AND BILL LEAVENWORTH / 161; The
Stormwater Research Center, TOM BALLESTERO / 163;
Oyster Restoration — Planning, Research, and Imple-
mentation in New Hampshire, RAY GRIZZLE / 164

Research on Climate and Energy   166
The Institute for the Study of Earth, Oceans, and Space,
DAVID S. BARTLETT / 166; The Environmental Research
Group, KEVIN GARDNER AND TAYLOR EIGHMY /
169; Multidisciplinary Design Competition, JENNA
JAMBECK AND KEVIN GARDNER / 171; Regional Cli-
mate Assessments — Supporting Informed Public Pol-
icy, CAMERON WAKE / 173

Research on Food and Society   175
The UNH Organic Dairy Research Farm, JOHN E. CAR-
ROLL AND TOM KELLY / 175; The Atlantic Marine Aqua-
culture Center, RICH LANGAN AND DOLORES LEON-
ARD / 179; The UNH Community Food, Nutrition, and
Wellness Profile, JOANNE BURKE / 182; From Campus
Farm to Dining Hall, JOHN MCLEAN / 183

Research on Culture and Sustainability   185
The Undergraduate Research Conference — A Key In-
gredient in the Sustainable Learning Community, EL-
EANOR ABRAMS / 185; The Carsey Institute — Building
Knowledge to Support Opportunity for Families in

Sustainable Communities, MIL DUNCAN / 188; The Growing a Green Generation Project, JOHN NIMMO / 192

Chapter 5. Sustaining the Larger Community: Engagement   195
JEFFREY A. SCHLOSS, editor

Engagement in Biodiversity and Ecosystems   198
The New Hampshire Lakes Lay Monitoring Program — A Sustainable Model for Engaging Citizens, JEFFREY A. SCHLOSS / 199; Forest Watch — Enhancing Pre-College Understanding of Biodiversity and Ecosystems, BARRY ROCK / 202; The UNH Marine Docent Program, MARK WILEY / 204; Students Without Borders, JENNA JAMBECK AND KEVIN GARDNER / 206

Engagement in Climate and Energy   208
Collaboration for a Low-Carbon Society — Carbon Solutions New England, CAMERON WAKE / 209; The New Hampshire Carbon Challenge, CHRIS SKOGLUND, DENISE BLAHA, AND JULIA DUNDORF / 212; WildCAP Discount Program, BRETT PASINELLA / 215; Informing Public Policy — Engagement on Climate with the State of New Hampshire, CAMERON WAKE / 217

Engagement in Food and Society   219
The New Hampshire Farm to School Program, ELISABETH FARRELL AND LYNDA BRUSHETT / 219; Cooperative Fisheries Research — The Innovative Fisherman, KEN LAVALLEY / 223; The Organic Garden Club, REBECCA GRUBE / 226; New Hampshire Center for a Food Secure Future, ELISABETH FARRELL / 227

Engagement in Culture and Sustainability   230
Deliberation in the Civic Sector — The Role of Higher Education in Sustaining Democracy, BRUCE L. MALLORY / 230; Building a Sustainable Community of Engaged Scholars — The UNH Outreach Scholars Academy, JULIE E. WILLIAMS, ELEANOR ABRAMS, AND CHRISTINE SHEA / 233; Portsmouth Black Heritage Trail, VALERIE CUNNINGHAM / 237; *Four Hands, One*

Heart—Ed and Mary Scheier Documentary and Exhibit, TOM KELLY / 238

Chapter 6. How the Sustainability Ethic Developed at UNH,   241
and the Next Phase of Our "Journey to the Future"
SARA CLEAVES, TOM KELLY, AND JOHN ABER

Contributors   251
Index   255

Editor's Preface

Sustainability has exploded onto our collective campus consciousness. For most of the last decade, the national conversation in the United States ignored the accumulating evidence for rapid and directional change in climate, biodiversity, food and energy security, and quality of life. Distracted by foreign adventures and ideological politics, the nation, and to some extent the universities as well, fell out of step with most of the rest of the developed world, and ignored the growing need to address critical cultural, resource and environmental issues.

The turnaround has been dramatic. Whether it was Katrina, *An Inconvenient Truth*, escalating energy and food prices, or (most probably) a combination of these and a number of other drivers, the national focus is now riveted on a different set of issues. The current generation of students reflects this change; the alteration in their values is as dramatic as the change in national direction. Their energy and voice play no small role in leading universities to sustainability. Reflecting their concerns, almost every university website has something to say about sustainability and environmental awareness.

But what does it mean for a campus to be "sustainable"? A new cultural term, especially one with such high marketing value, tends to be defined loosely and can be recast to fit the goals of the user. Variations on the theme appear quickly and can be interpreted in many ways. For example, "carbon neutral" has a nice ring to it, and you see it on a lot of university websites, but achieving actual neutrality is an incredibly challenging task, and — short of purchasing credits (which also remain poorly defined in the United States) — has not been achieved by any major U.S. institution of higher learning.

So there is a need to define sustainability in the campus context and to present examples that might be of value to other institutions. National structures are beginning to emerge that will provide guidelines and metrics for determining and enhancing sustainability on campuses (for example AASHE — the Association for the Advancement of Sustainability in

Higher Education). These will put some teeth and credibility into claims of "sustainability."

At the same time, it may be of value to present a detailed case study of one campus that has long valued environmental initiatives and has been a leader in establishing sustainability as a supported and effective program. That is the purpose of this book.

The reader will find many different voices here, but some constant themes. We have enlisted more than sixty different authors from all parts of the campus, from academics to operations to engagement (or extension). This has been purposeful. No one voice can speak for a complex issue like sustainability in an enterprise as complex as a university. Progress comes as the concept becomes embedded in the fabric of the place, as individuals from all sectors feel drawn to the goal and rewarded for the effort. Similarly, there is no one solution. We like to say that high energy prices, or resource challenges in general, place a high premium on creativity and innovation. Universities should be good at this, not just through the creation of knowledge, but by creating an environment that recognizes and responds to good ideas wherever they arise.

Two constants across all of the chapters and stories in this book are a feeling of excitement generated by innovation and a sense of forward progress. The sustainability program, and especially its director, have emphasized that sustainability is not about giving things up and "freezing in the dark." Rather, it is about enhancing the quality of life by improving environmental quality, developing a better system of food production and delivery, and enhancing cultural values and awareness. A key aspect of the program, as it has developed at the University of New Hampshire (UNH), and as described in the first chapter by Tom Kelly, is that *all* of these functions need to be enhanced simultaneously. Sustainability is not about reducing your carbon footprint if it means damaging the food system (the example of corn-based ethanol will be raised in later chapters). Sustainability is about making life better, while ensuring that what we do today does not reduce the options and opportunities for the generations that follow.

Sustainability at UNH, then, is about being clever and creative; about doing many things at once; about finding synergistic solutions to a number of issues in all sectors; and mostly, about involving everyone across campus. What you will encounter in the more than five dozen stories that make up the heart of this book is a multiplicity of creative solutions that enhance the quality of the living, working, and learning experience on campus, while reducing our environmental footprint.

The stories here, and the changes they represent, take many forms. In the classroom, topics range from climate change, to health and nutrition, to the role of the arts in creating a culture of sustainability. At a more fundamental level, the basic premise of education is shifting, emphasizing discovery and engagement, or student-initiated, research-based learning that encompasses experiences in the field with practitioners. The same can be said for research and scholarship — with "outreach scholarship" expressing a new paradigm that brings potential users of the results of a research project into that project at the very beginning. Campus operations are a key component, and here at UNH creative and somewhat risky investments in infrastructure have been made to reduce environmental impacts, while also saving a considerable amount of money and providing grist for classroom exercises and student research. Closing the food cycle by involving local producers (including students utilizing university lands) and recycling and composting wastes, is another operational area where gains can be made. Finally, the activities of the university take place in an architectural and artistic setting that can enhance or reduce a sense of place and enduring values and commitment to aesthetics.

These four areas of activity — teaching, research, operations and engagement — define the core chapters of the book. One challenge in creating this structure has been the widely interdisciplinary nature of many of the stories. The line between teaching and research blurs when undergraduates perform the experiments. Research and engagement become inseparable when stakeholders become part of the research team. Operations and culture are entwined completely in the design and construction of buildings. In this way, our book reflects the fundamental interdisciplinarity and interconnectedness of sustainability initiatives.

Tom Kelly, the Director of the University Office of Sustainability (UOS) and Chief Sustainability Officer, begins the volume with an overarching introduction to the "big idea" that is sustainability, and what it means to be a sustainable learning community. Drawing on national and international efforts and declarations, long-term trends in educational and environmental philosophy, and the major issues facing the world in the twenty-first century, he shows how these relate directly to the structure of the programs developed by the UOS and the topics presented in the chapters that follow.

Those next four chapters are structured to reflect the four major areas of activity on campus: Curriculum, Operations, Research, and Engagement (or CORE as defined by Tom Kelly). Within these areas, each chapter has four sections that capture the major initiatives within the Sustainability program that Dr. Kelly and his team have created: Biodiversity and Ecosystems, Climate and Energy, Food and Society, and Culture and Sustainability. In each section, a general introduction to activities on campus is followed by three to five case studies.

The concluding chapter summarizes how this broad and deep commitment to sustainability developed on the UNH campus, and the role that the University Office of Sustainability and other campus entities have played in catalyzing new structures and programs

Because of this structure, the book can be approached in two different ways. A straight-through reading will give an overview of the kinds of actions that individuals and groups on campus have taken to contribute to the fabric of sustainability on campus, and also show the pattern of the fabric created. The book also can be treated as something of a reference. The structure of stories placed within the context of the CORE activities and the four initiatives allows direct access to template programs that may be directly adaptable by faculty, students, and staff working in specific parts of other institutions.

So, these many stories, told with more than sixty voices, present at least one example of what it takes to bring sustainability to life on a campus and make it real. What emerges from the cross-campus conversation that these voices represent is one university's definition of a sustainable campus: a general and shared commitment to living well, but within our means, and leaving the place better than we found it.

JA
Durham, N.H.
July 2008

Acknowledgments

This book by itself is an acknowledgment of all the effort made by several generations in the UNH community to link scholarship and practice with the challenges and opportunities of sustainability. From the global to the local and the long-term to the short-term, they have worked to sustain our past, present, and future. We thank the many authors of this volume who have given voice to that vision, and all those who have created a sustainability culture on campus.

Phyllis Deutsch, at University Press of New England, gave life to this book by encouraging the editors to pursue the project, and by helping shape its size, scope, and structure. Peter Fong and the editorial staff at UPNE were instrumental in assuring the quality of the final product.

We also thank in a special way Elisabeth Farrell and Sara Cleaves, who occupy a central role in the sustainability effort on campus, and who gave generously of their time and talent in bringing this volume to completion.

The Sustainable Learning Community

CHAPTER 1

Sustainability as an Organizing Principle for Higher Education

Tom Kelly

Sustainability is a big idea, a very big idea. When taken at its full measure, it presents a challenge to individual and institutional cooperation that tests our imagination and culture on a scale unique in human history. Sustainability is a contested idea: a plural concept like democracy and justice that must be owned and made sense of by communities of diverse perspectives, conflicting values, and particular ecological and cultural settings. Sustainability is a practical idea that must be worked out on the ground, concretely and in synch with the rhythms of day-to-day life. Sustainability is a cosmopolitan idea; it is global, international, and intergenerational in outlook. Sustainability is fundamentally about education because it continually presents questions of value and practice by asking what is best and why, for the long run. The questions to which this book offers provisional answers is: How do we in higher education make our work fundamentally about sustainability? What kinds of questions do we need to ask and address? How does sustainability relate to our other core values and our mission? How does sustainability relate to the most pressing problems of our institutions and the broader society they serve? What can sustainability offer to scholars, practitioners, and students, some already pressed to do more with less, and others who have adequate resources but lack a broader creative culture that cultivates and rewards responsive interdisciplinary scholarship? And, what can scholars, practitioners and students offer to sustainability given their experience with big ideas, diverse perspectives, and the liberal arts?

In telling our story of the University of New Hampshire's journey to the future, we are introducing the "sustainable learning community" as an educational model for integrating sustainability into the fabric of an institution of higher learning to achieve the educational goal of cultivating a critical and creative global sustainability outlook. We begin by recognizing that our overarching effort is a variation on a much older and abiding cultural concern: clarifying what it means to be educated. Our approach to this concern weaves together ancient insights and modern necessities in a set of perspectives that we believe are responsive to the extraordinary challenges and opportunities of sustainability and that aim to empower and inspire students in all fields to advance sustainability in their civic and professional lives. The sustainable learning community model focuses on four key systems that underpin the ability of a community or society to define and pursue quality of life: biodiversity and ecosystems, climate and energy, food and society, and culture and sustainability. These are integrated as educational initiatives focused on institutional practices across what we refer to as the core functions of the university: curriculum, operations, research, and engagement (CORE). Together, the four systems and the CORE create the basis for building a global sustainability outlook by supporting educational innovations that cultivate perspectives that we have defined as "Earth system," "citizen of the world," "public health practitioner," and "engaged intellectual." The argument or experiment of the sustainable learning community is that by cultivating these perspectives in all students through a shared commitment to sustaining the foundations of a good quality of life for everyone, they will take a critical and creative global sustainability outlook into their civic and professional lives regardless of their area of specialization.

Many of these ideas are not new, though they are integrated with other ideas in what for some readers may be novel or unorthodox ways. The sustainable learning community draws heavily on the classical Western approach to liberal education, an education that "liberates the mind from the bondage of habit and custom, producing people who can function with sensitivity and alertness as citizens of the whole world."[1] What is new is the world our students are inheriting. During the lifetime of today's fifty-year-old, a wave of modernization and globalization has combined with startling demographic trends and technological developments to transform the earth system at an unprecedented rate.[2] Economically, extraordinary levels of wealth have been achieved but at extraordinarily high costs. Reflecting on the transition from the twentieth to the twenty-first century in 2000, then–United Nations Secretary General Kofi Annan observed that while there was much to be grateful for,

Sustainable Learning Community

FIGURE 1.1. The four initiatives each are engaged in projects or interventions across the CORE functions of curriculum, operations, research, and engagement. All initiatives and CORE functions are overlapping and interactive. Sustainability entails sustaining the integrity of all four systems simultaneously. Together, the four initiatives and the CORE create the basis for building a global sustainability outlook by supporting education innovations that cultivate perspectives that we have defined as "earth system," "citizen of the world," "public health practitioner," and "engaged intellectual." *Adapted from Tom Kelly, "Building a Sustainable Learning Community at the University of New Hampshire," The Declaration 6.2 (November 2003), www.ulsf.org/pub_declaration_ othvol62.htm*

there are also many things to deplore, and to correct. The century just ended was disfigured, time and again, by ruthless conflict. Grinding poverty and striking inequality persist within and among countries even amidst unprecedented wealth. Diseases, old and new, threaten to undo painstaking progress. Nature's life-sustaining services, on which our species depends for its survival, are being seriously disrupted and degraded by our own everyday activities.[3]

In terms of pressing societal problems, the next generation is inheriting a set of ecological and cultural challenges within our communities and across the globe that will shape the world of university students for generations to come, and against which we will continuously assess the responsiveness of our university community and the education it provides. As represented in figure 1.1, the sustainable learning community model is an interpretation of the principles of sustainability articulated in agreements and declarations by the international scientific, political, and cultural communities beginning in the second half of the twentieth century. It is focused on sustaining the integrity of the four key systems within a learning community that teaches and learns through all of its actions.

In their current state, most universities and colleges could point to disparate academic programs, courses, research projects, and policies that relate directly and indirectly to the principles of sustainability. But as we will see, the key to sustainability is that it requires that all four systems (biodiversity, climate, culture, and food) be sustained *simultaneously* in order for overall integrity to be sustained; and that requires a different kind of scholarship that systematically focuses on *interactions* in a comprehensive and purposeful way.

For example, any approach to addressing carbon reduction and energy issues within the climate system, such as with biofuels, must be consistent with the integrity of the other systems if it is to be sustainable. In other words, to be sustainable, a biofuel must not only produce energy with a dramatic decrease in related greenhouse gas emissions — or even while functioning as an emissions sink — but must do so while not in any way undermining the integrity of ecosystems or the food and culture systems. The importance of attending to interactions is fundamental to sustainability and the cultivation of an outlook that focuses on those interactions is fundamental to the sustainable learning community. Accordingly, at UNH we are concerned with how best to draw out those interactions as part of a common experience for all students. The global sustainability outlook we seek to cultivate is not understood as a specialized outlook associated only with certain disciplines or professions, but rather is a shared outlook that forms the foundation of critical thinking, interpretation, and creativity across all disciplines; that shared outlook is rooted in the set of perspectives referenced above.

Our effort to build a common conception of sustainability is taking place within a university community that is being shaped continually by the large and impersonal forces of demography, culture, technology, political economy, and ecology; but our community is also being shaped by the immediate, personal forces of its own choices and the countless individual and collective decisions that are being made on a daily basis. These individual and collective decisions add up to an expression of identity and core values, an articulation of how we see and understand ourselves and our place in the world. As that identity and its values are internalized and upheld or overturned by successive generations of students, faculty, administrators, and staff, a learning community results, whether by intention and design or not; and that learning community constitutes a powerful educational force that teaches, whether by intention and design or not. This is where a common conception of sustainability comes in. As faculty, staff, and students, we inherit an institutional identity that we collectively interpret and either sustain or overturn for what we think is better. The sustainable learning community, then, is presented as an educational reform project, an intentional effort to assess critically the complex web of relations that constitute our learning community and, where our interpretation of sustainability leads us to alter those relations, in and across our curriculum, operations, research, and engagement (the CORE), to do so.

Building the sustainable learning community begins by reformulating the question "what is sustainability" to "what sustains us?" This reformulation neutralizes, at least temporarily, the problem of sustainability as a term of jargon that often elicits a narrowly focused response about the environment or an inert, memorized phrase or fragment approximating the triad of economy, ecology, and equity or a variation on the definition from *Our Common Future*.[4] When asked what sustains human communities, responses encompass everything from the basic necessities of air, water, food, and shelter to beauty and love as well as livelihoods, education, religion, and healthcare. The question elicits a genuine sense of the breadth and inclusiveness of sustainability without reference to any particular report or international agreement. This intuitive or common-sense grasp of sustainability is fundamental to building a common purpose because common sense reflects common values that provide a foundation for dialogue, critical reflection, and collaboration. It also aligns with the idea of "quality of life" as a rich, complex tapestry that shapes "what people are able to do and to be," a profound concept that goes far beyond a country's gross national product or measurements of individual economic utility.[5]

The sustainable learning community is built upon the principle of integrity. Integrity must be sustained within and across the four systems in order for the integrity of the community and quality of life to be ensured. Integrity here is defined from its Latin root *integritas*, which described an unimpaired condition, soundness, and health as well as uprightness.[6] Accordingly, the health, wholeness, and soundness of each of the four systems need to be sustained, for it is the long-term integrity of the climate, biodiversity, food, and culture systems that sustains human communities now and in the future. Put directly, then, in a world of interconnectedness and interdependence, where integrity entails patterns of interaction among many different processes across the blurred boundary of culture and nature, the job of sustainability is to nurture and restore the integrity of key systems that sustain the community of life and quality of life. As a critical and creative outlook, sustainability requires an adequate understanding of these systems and their interactions and highlights the need to weave together the arts, sciences, and humanities that only together can provide the range of perspectives and outlook that we are trying to cultivate in all students.

The collection of case studies that are presented in the subsequent chapters involve faculty, staff, students, and administrators working across the CORE in an increasingly coordinated fashion. Their stories are practical, concrete, and in synch with the rhythms of day-to-day life on and beyond the campus, but in the end they are all about the big idea of sustainability; about a critical and creative global sustainability outlook taking root within all of our students; about a community of learning in which this plural, contested, cosmopolitan idea is continually being worked out in practical terms on the ground, and thereby in the consciousness of all members of the community.

The fundamental place of community in sustainability cannot be overstated. Collective reflection on the overarching impact of all these efforts is a vital part of the sustainable learning community and a formative experience in the give and take of community life. Not only is the community the focus of what is to be sustained, it is also the basis for the ongoing *process* of sustainability. As noted above, sustainability is a contested, plural idea that has to be worked out continuously by communities of diverse perspectives, conflicting values, and particular ecological and cultural settings.

At the same time, sustainability is a universal idea that can be recognized *across* the diverse community settings where it is lived, a transcultural point of reference that can provide a basis for criticizing and reforming localized interpretations.[7] It is far too easy, and in fact likely, to lose sight of the big idea of sustainability in the many details of the CORE. But to lose that big idea is to undermine the sustainable learning community and the critical dialogue between the detailed particulars of one community and the general principles of sustainability for all human communities.

The remainder of this chapter will provide background for connecting the big idea with its practical applications. It begins with the contemporary origins of the concepts of sustainability and sustainable development in the collective aspirations and "great values" of the post–World War II era; the resulting institutions, principles, and norms of modernization form the most immediate and familiar layer of our cultural inheritance and the setting in which the transition to sustainability takes place. A common understanding of the origins and evolution of this very big idea serves the sustainable learning community by providing grounding for dialogue, argument, and persuasion to develop a shared interpretation of sustainability and its implications for the CORE. Following the review of this background, we briefly review salient trends and projections within and across the four key systems and the significance of the four educational perspectives that underpin the critical and creative global sustainable outlook that the sustainable learning community works to cultivate in all learners.

Defining Sustainability

In a contemporary sense, the principles, practices, and science of sustainability originate in the concept of sustainable development. "Sustainable development" is a term often used interchangeably with "sustainability." Sustainable development grew from a series of international agreements on actions to advance the health and well-being of the world's diverse communities in the face of unprecedented threats. These agreements emerged from debate and discussion within the international scientific community as well as through international political frameworks under the auspices of the United Nations and in manifold consultations in civil society. This is not to say that these principles, or more precisely the motives or intentions behind them, are not contested. On the contrary, plenty of contention surrounds sustainable development, particularly with regard to the authenticity of commitment to its stated principles by nations and organized interests, but also with its basic conception of "development" and the political, economic, and cultural assumptions upon which it is built; and as we will see, the questions of what is to be sustained by whom, for whom, and how it is undertaken are, and must be, the continual focus of sustainability initiatives.[8]

The international principles of sustainable development are articulated in reports such as *Our Common Future*, Agenda 21, and related documents resulting from decades of international discussion in the post–World War II period.[9] The resulting documents underscore the all-encompassing breadth of sustainable development and the depth of transformation, collaboration, and coordination required to incorporate its values and principles into the world's diverse cultures and institutions.[10] A concise summary by Kates, Parris, and Leiserowitz points to the creative ambiguity of what they conclude is the most widely accepted definition of sustainable development: "Humanity has the ability to make development sustainable — to ensure that it meets the needs of the present without compromising the ability of future generations to meet their own needs."[11] This definition, which is from the Brundtland Commission, they argue, provides the "malleability to allow programs of environment or development; places from local to global; and institutions of government, civil society, business and industry to each project their interests, hopes, and aspirations onto the banner of sustainable development." That is both the good news and the bad. Sustainability cannot mean all things to all people; and the malleability of this definition enables calls for both radical and incremental change or continuation of the status quo to claim it as their cause, and advance what can be mutually exclusive approaches to defining and pursuing a quality of life.[12] As noted earlier, development is a highly contested concept and indeed one framing of the issue is that resolution of this conflict requires a search not for developmental alternatives but for alternatives to "development," such as making quality of life the goal of international politics.[13]

Identifying the antecedents of sustainability in the common concerns and aspirations for peace, freedom, development, and the environment expressed in the international dialogue of the post–World War II period, Kates and his colleagues trace these core themes to the World Commission on Environment and Development (WCED) that was formed in 1982 and issued its report, *Our Common Future*, in 1987. Throughout the forty-year period leading up to the WCED, a series of international commissions and conferences endeavored to "link together the aspirations of human kind — demonstrating how the pursuit of one great value [peace] required [the simultaneous pursuit of] the others [freedom, development and environment].[14] This interdependence of great values is a critical and basic principle of sustainability and accounts for its consistent emphasis on the need to coordinate the interactions of culture and nature in very diverse settings. However, the emergence of sustainable development was also a response to a series of struggles by nongovernmental organizations and peasant and indigenous groups against an international development system that was driving a growing gulf between rich and poor countries, and between populations within countries, as well as environmental degradation and competition over natural resources. In the midst of these struggles, the United Nations called for a conceptual and political re-examination of development.[15]

While the general principles of sustainable development were refined and endorsed at the 1992 Earth Summit in Rio de Janeiro and reinforced ten years later at the 2002 World Summit on Sustainable Development, held in Johannesburg, South Africa, the inconsistency between principles and rhetoric on the one hand, and the worsening facts on the ground on the other, were inescapable; over the ten-year period from 1992 to 2002, conditions for the majority of the world's poor worsened along with local, regional, and global ecological systems.[16] At the same time, the underlying assumptions and objectives of sustainable development as conceived by the wealthiest and most powerful nations were criticized for an unceasing advance of free trade and privatization in the name of continual economic growth as the only means to development. The United States and other Western nations were seen to be exercising their hegemony within the international order to impose a libertarian free-trade agenda through bilateral and multilateral mechanisms such as the General Agreement on Tariffs and Trade (GATT), the World Trade Organization, the International Monetary Fund, and the World Bank at the expense of social justice and ecological and cultural integrity.[17] The continued wave of privatization and globalization, many developing countries argued, was resulting in the disempowerment of millions of the world's citizens through a shift in power from "national and local political agendas to global centers of economic power," and all in the name of sustainable development.[18]

This sense of a shift away from national and local control raised serious political and cultural questions about the goals of "development" and the international political processes devised to pursue it. Throughout the 1980s and 1990s, "culture" began to emerge as a critically important consideration in development and within the movement to rethink development. The United National Education, Scientific and Cultural Organization's (UNESCO) World Decade for Cultural Development was initiated in 1988 in response to the "dual need for a radical review of conceptions of development and for a reshaping of practices" that had made the 1980s what many experts characterized as a "lost decade" for development.[19] One of the principle undertakings of the Decade initiative was the work of the World Commission on Culture and Development. The introduction by the Commission's president, Javier Perez de Cuellar, to its 1995 report *Our Creative Diversity* articulated concerns over what had become the orthodox and institutionalized values of development:

> When our Commission began its work [in 1992], it had long been clear that development was a far more complex undertaking than had been originally thought. It could no longer be seen as a single, uniform, linear path, for this would inevitably eliminate cultural diversity and experimentation, and dangerously limit humankind's creative capacities in the face of a treasured past and an unpredictable

future. This evolution in thinking was largely the result of global political eman-
cipation, as nationhood had led to a keen awareness of each people's own way of
life as a value, as a right, as a responsibility and as an opportunity. It had led each
people to challenge the frame of reference in which the West's system of values
alone, generated rules assumed to be universal and to demand the right to forge
different versions of modernization. It had led peoples to assert the value of their
own cultural wealth, of their manifold assets that could not be reduced to measurement in dollars and cents, while simultaneously to seek the universal values
of a global ethics.[20]

In considering the role of culture in individual and collective well-being, the
commission drew directly from the experience of integrating environment
and development and declared that "the time had come to do for culture and
development what had been achieved for environment and development" by
the 1987 Brundtland report. The commission focused on policy recommendations as part of a broad call to action rooted in the recognition that economic and political rights could not be realized separately from social and
cultural rights any more than peace could be pursued independent of consol-
idating democratic values: These were all "indivisible goals." It was time, they
said, "to move culture to the center stage of development."

Recognizing the central role of culture in development draws the International Covenant on Economic, Social and Cultural Rights and the closely
related International Covenant on Civil and Political Rights into sustainability. Together, these two international covenants articulate a set of commitments in support of universal human rights that provide a basis for defining
the integrity of the cultural system, and that are ultimately inseparable from
climate, biodiversity, food systems, and quality of life.[21] This is extremely
important for grasping the cosmopolitan nature of sustainability and it has
very concrete and practical implications on the ground for universities. As was
noted earlier, questions of development were central to the post–World War
II international order, including the establishment of the United Nations; and
human rights, understood as encompassing economic, civil, cultural, political, and social rights were being discussed, debated, and negotiated along with
the charters for the World Bank, International Monetary Fund, and GATT.[22]
In other words, the international financial institutions through which the
free trade, economic growth, and globalization approach to development has
been conducted, were part of the same post–World War II order that gave rise
to universal human rights, including cultural rights, that challenge the growth
and consumption definition of development in favor of diverse perspectives

on modernization and quality of life. So, the plural and contested nature of development, and therefore sustainable development and ultimately sustainability, literally was built into the international order through treaties, declarations, and institutions that have helped shape the post–World War II era.

Two final international articulations need to be mentioned to bring this very brief history of sustainability to the present: First, the Millennium Development Goals (MDGs) were adopted in September 2000 to reaffirm the collective faith in the United Nations and its charter as "indispensable foundations of a more peaceful, prosperous and just world." The MDGs present a series of quantifiable goals based on the same interdependent set of values of earlier agreements including freedom, equality, solidarity, tolerance, respect for nature, and shared responsibility.[23] A set of specific goals in areas such as poverty reduction were adopted to make concrete progress on social and environmental factors of development by 2015. The other articulation of sustainable development is the Earth Charter, an international, grassroots effort to develop "a declaration of fundamental principles for building a just, sustainable and peaceful global society in the 21st century."[24] The Earth Charter initially was undertaken in preparation for the 1992 Earth Summit as a response to the Brundtland Commission's call for a new charter setting new norms to guide the transition to sustainable development. While agreement among governments could not be reached on the charter at the Earth Summit, its advocates felt that it had received very strong support from international nongovernmental groups. In 1994, it was relaunched as a civil society initiative that now provides a well-grounded and widely endorsed approach to sustainability based on a survey and analysis of ethical principles embodied in more than fifty international legal documents and a six-year participatory review process involving thousands of written comments from around the world.

The significance of the Earth Charter lies, at least partly, in its alternative interpretation of sustainable development. Based upon articulated international ethical principles and broad input from international civil society, it calls for a concept of development that is about "being more, not having more" once basic needs have been met. We will look at this in more detail in our review of the cultural system, but for now, the key point is that the Earth Charter brings the plural nature of sustainability to its ethical foundations and focuses on quality of life — being more, not necessarily consuming more — as the goal of sustainable development. Understanding quality of life as a *culturally determined* collective goal rather than a single, uniform, linear path measured by economic growth means that sustainability arrives at our institutions of higher education as a work in progress with its plural, contested nature intact; and because culture is the only means we have to interpret sustainability and work it out on the ground, it is extremely important that it be incorporated explicitly into a shared concept of sustainability.[25] Cultural self-understanding is an integral part of the citizen of the world and engaged intellectual perspectives and a full appreciation of the cosmopolitan outlook of sustainability would be impossible without it. Without cultural self-understanding, it is impossible to understand cultural rights as a part of basic human rights, human development, and quality of life; without cultural self-understanding, the big idea of sustainability is inaccessible to interpretation and utterly lost. And without cultural self-understanding, the ultimate significance of the interactions of the climate, biodiversity, and food systems and their relationship to sustaining quality of life for everyone, long-term, is also lost.

As noted previously, current and future generations of our students are inheriting a complex set of ecological and cultural challenges against which we should assess the responsiveness of the education we provide and the kind of scholarship we undertake. Toward that end, the University of New Hampshire introduced a set of perspectives that we believe form the foundation of a critical and creative global sustainability outlook and that when combined with the skills and knowledge of particular disciplinary majors will empower and inspire all graduates to advance sustainability as citizens and as professionals. The trends and interactions of the climate, biodiversity, food, and culture systems that we now will review briefly provide a grounded basis for thinking critically about the kinds of awareness, knowledge, skills, and commitments we need to cultivate in our sustainable learning community and thereby in our students. We have stressed the plural and contested nature of sustainability and we also have said that it cannot mean all things to all people and still have meaning; we also have argued that sustainability requires the integrity of all four systems to be sustained simultaneously at all scales: This means that a very complex set of interdependencies constrain and enable the cultural choices that we make about quality of life as we interpret sustainability and the universal ethical principles it seeks to uphold.

The Four Key Systems and the UNH Education Initiatives

Biodiversity and Ecosystems

As noted at the outset, the rate and degree of transformation of the Earth system during the lifetime of today's fifty-year-old is unprecedented. Indeed, that is precisely one of the principle findings of the Millennium Ecosystem Assessment (MA), a five-year study modeled on the Intergovernmental Panel on Climate Change, conducted under the auspices of the United Nations, and involving more than thirteen hundred scientists from 95 countries: "Over the past 50 years, humans have changed ecosystems more rapidly and extensively than in any comparable period of time in human history." The MA notes that these changes were the result of humanity's approach to meeting "rapidly growing demands for food, fresh water, timber, fiber and fuel." However, it also notes that the result of these rising demands and our collective approach to meeting them has resulted in large-scale, irreversible loss in the diversity of life on Earth. Moreover, our approach to meeting these rapidly growing demands for ecosystem services has resulted in striking inequalities in which many regions and populations have been harmed in the process. Those who have suffered most from this process are the poor and disenfranchised.[26] The MA presents us with an extraordinary set of facts and a profound choice: Either we reverse the degradation of ecosystems while meeting rapidly increasing demands for their services, or continued and accumulating loss of biodiversity could overwhelm incremental efforts to sustain ecosystem services and trigger large-scale irreversible change. For scholars and educators, this presents a critical question: What does it mean to be educated in a biosphere that is suffering ecological degradation at a rate that is unparalleled in human history at a time when demand for ecosystem services is growing rapidly? We asked the parallel question for the climate system, and indeed the MA also noted that the impacts of climate change could surpass agriculture and land use as the dominant driver of global biodiversity loss by the end of this century.[27]

The significance of biodiversity is that it is a vital sign for the health of ecosystems. Human communities are absolutely dependent upon healthy functioning ecosystems for their basis of survival and cultural flourishing; if the integrity of those ecosystems is corrupted, and declining biodiversity tells us that it is, then we are undermining the source of what sustains present and future generations.[28] A summary of global trends in ecosystem degradation is dramatic and disturbing. Large-scale transformation of the surface of the planet is resulting in irreversible changes to the diversity of life on Earth. Globally, the number of species on the planet is declining, as are the population size and geographic range of the majority of species across a range of taxonomic groups, and regions are becoming more homogenous as globalization inadvertently spreads flora and fauna species.[29] The MA reports that human activities have "increased the species extinction rate by as much as 1,000 times over background rates typical over the planet's history," with somewhere between 10 and 30 percent of mammal, bird, and amphibian species currently being threatened with extinction. Coral reefs have been reduced by 20 percent with another 20 percent degraded, and mangroves that buffer coastal communities from storm surges and rising sea levels as well as providing critical habitat for thousands of fish species have suffered losses of approximately 35 percent.[30] The amount of freshwater impounded behind dams has quadrupled since 1960 and water taken from rivers and lakes has doubled in the same time, with 70 percent of it going to agriculture. As will be discussed in greater detail in the subsequent section on the food system, industrial agriculture has also resulted in a doubling of nitrogen and tripling of phosphorus coursing through the biosphere. Human activities have been established as the principal driver of ecosystem degradation and the critical uncertainties largely are focused on the collective actions of humanity in the coming one to four decades. The MA assessment brings the challenge of mitigating ecosystem degradation to society and higher education.

Mitigation of ecosystem degradation must also share center stage with the challenges of ongoing impacts of that degradation at regional scales as well as the adaptive capacity and vulnerability of populations to the accumulating loss of ecosystem services. The MA describes a scale of ecosystem degradation and loss of their life-sustaining services that is affecting billions of people. For example, the following ecosystem services are in a continuing state of degradation: capture fisheries, water supplies, waste treatment and detoxification, water purification, natural hazard protection, and the regulation of air quality, erosion, and local climate. Both capture fisheries and freshwater supply are characterized as being degraded well beyond levels that can be sustained and as much as one-quarter of global freshwater use is being met through "engineered water transfers or overdraft of groundwater supplies, including for irrigation, because water use exceeds long-term, accessible supplies." A 2003 report by the United Nations Environment Program concluded that freshwater scarcity was affecting a billion people in 2003, and will affect 4 billion people by 2050. The report also concluded that, as of 2003, adequate sanitation facilities are lacking for 2.4 billion people, about 40 percent of humankind, and that half of all coastal regions, where 1 billion people live, have degraded through overdevelopment or pollution.[31]

Those who are the most vulnerable to continuing ecosystem degradation are the poor and disenfranchised. The MA cites the persistence of extreme poverty and the critical observation that ecosystem degradation will exacerbate poverty and widen inequities and disparities. In other words, the MA observed that ecosystem decline is having a disproportionate impact on the world's poorest people while acknowledging that it is also at times a principal factor causing poverty. Ecosystem degradation is taking the patterns of poverty and inequity that modern development models have helped create and is making them worse. The results include burdens of disease being borne by the poorest and most vulnerable: The MA notes that half the urban population in Africa, Asia, Latin America, and the Caribbean suffers from one or more diseases associated with inadequate water and sanitation and more than approximately 1.7 million people — more than the entire population of the state of New Hampshire and Vermont combined — die each year as a result of inadequate water, sanitation, and hygiene. That the crisis of biodiversity is largely the result of altering ecosystems to produce food and fiber for human benefit is without question; notwithstanding the astonishing levels of production that have been achieved over a fifty-year period, "levels of poverty remain high, inequities are growing, and many people still do not have a sufficient supply of or access to ecosystems services."[32]

Biodiversity loss is a cumulative process in the biosphere. Educationally, the Earth system perspective makes clear that this is a global issue not simply because it is happening all over the globe, but because the drivers and the impacts are all connected: Continuing loss of biodiversity in the Amazon Basin affects all parts of the planet; we are all part of a single biosphere. When we consider sensitivity and adaptive capacity to biodiversity loss on a global scale, then poverty and vulnerability to the collapse of freshwater sources and fisheries, for example, take on gargantuan proportions affecting hundreds of millions of people. The public health practitioner perspective understands the vital importance of strengthening adaptive capacity to reduce vulnerability, the citizen of the world perspective cultivates solidarity and a shared sense of community with communities and cultures throughout the biosphere, and engaged intellectuals bring all of their capabilities to bear on this challenge. In order to frame the challenge that we face in the immediate and longer-term future, the MA developed four plausible future scenarios of human activities, including approaches to economic development, international relations, and governance.[33] The subsequent analysis found that, even under the most optimistic assumptions, the combined challenge of reversing ecosystem degradation while meeting increasing demands for ecosystem services could be only met partially; and even that outcome would entail "significant changes in policy, institutions and practices that are not currently underway."[34] In other words, partial success will require a reversing or redirecting of a suite of policies, institutions, and practices that are driving the problem.

Examples of near-term actions required to respond include "significant investments in environmentally sound technology, active adaptive management and proactive action to address environmental problems before their full consequences are experienced." It also calls for "major investments in public goods (such as education and health), strong action to reduce socio-economic disparities and eliminate poverty, and expanded capacity of people to manage ecosystems adaptively."[35] The political economy of making such changes will require all of the reason and persuasion that can be mustered, and then some. The stakes could not be higher: As the MA points out, continued degradation of ecosystems will exacerbate rather than address growing levels of poverty, hunger and food insecurity, child mortality, and disease.

More than a billion people lack access to improved water supplies and more than twice that lack access to improved sanitation. In 2004, approximately a billion people survived on less than $1 per day of income and nearly 3 billion on less than $2 per day.[36] And as noted by the World Bank, "poverty makes people vulnerable to economic shocks, natural disasters, violence, and crime. They are often denied access to education, adequate health services, and clean water and sanitation."[37] This syndrome of poverty and ill-health is a major concern for public health; as succinctly stated by the World Health Organization, poverty breeds ill-health, and ill-health keeps poor people poor.[38] What the MA makes clear is that this syndrome includes ecosystem degradation, meaning that loss of ecosystem services breeds and exacerbates poverty, which breeds ill-health, and ill-health keeps people poor and can lead to further loss of ecosystem services. Clearly, the adaptive capacity of nearly half of the world's population living in the grips of poverty is highly constrained, which means that they are the most vulnerable to ecosystem degradation. Pointing to patterns of "winners" and "losers" associated with ecosystem changes, the MA observes that it is the poor, women in poverty, and indigenous communities that have been harmed most by ecosystem changes and their lack of political and economic power combined with greater dependence on ecosystem services will result in their bearing the brunt of continued degradation.

So the challenge of mitigation of ecosystem degradation must be addressed in parallel with regional impacts and adaptation. As framed by the MA, the challenge of reversing ecosystem degradation on a global scale must be pursued while meeting increasing demand for those same ecosystem services.

The heightened vulnerability of almost half of the world's people to loss of ecosystem services, and those impacts combined with climate change, must be addressed if the integrity of the four systems are to be upheld simultaneously and sustainability is to be realized. The scale of the undertaking is vast and proportional to the unprecedented magnitude of the degradation of ecosystems. The implications for the citizen-professionals graduating from our institutions of higher education over the coming decades is inescapable: If they are to be responsive to this challenge, they will need the knowledge, awareness, skills, and commitment to affect an unprecedented level of institutional change domestically and internationally in order to reverse ecosystem degradation and reduce the vulnerability of those most affected by its impacts; the challenge very likely could grow more urgent and complex. The MA notes that the long-term sustainability of actions to mitigate ecosystem degradation are uncertain due to the potential of continuing loss of biodiversity to cause irreversible loss of ecosystem services. The MA states that there is "established but incomplete evidence that changes being made in ecosystems are increasing the likelihood of nonlinear changes in ecosystems including accelerating, abrupt and potentially irreversible changes." Such changes will have a broad range of direct and indirect impacts on human well-being.[39]

The challenge of mitigation and adaptation to declining biodiversity and ecosystem services presents an immediate need for responsive curriculum, operations, research, and engagement on college and university campuses. How do we prepare the next generation of graduates to confront this challenge with critical and creative thinking and a commitment to action? How can we connect the Earth system, public health practitioner, citizen of the world, and engaged intellectual perspectives to empower and inspire graduates in all fields to advance ecosystem integrity? Here again, the sustainable learning community at UNH looks to continuity across the CORE. In the case of biodiversity, our large undergraduate course on global biological change (described in chapter 2) provides the Earth system perspective, while the Campus Master Plan described in chapter 3 provides a concrete example of ecosystem management in a mixed-use landscape. The plan includes a forest ecosystem reserve on the main campus with specific projects and management mechanisms that involve students, faculty, and staff, described in case studies in chapter 3 on the MUB Meadow and the Land Use Committee described. The Earth system and engaged intellectual perspectives come together in an innovative research initiative on the History of Marine and Animal Populations and the Stormwater Research Center described in chapter 4 and the Lakes Lay Monitoring Program described in chapter 5.

In terms of biodiversity and ecosystem degradation, the challenge for our sustainable learning community is to cultivate the same Earth system perspective with particular emphasis on the biosphere and ecosystems and how human activities function within that system. This perspective combines a grasp of both the climate system and the biosphere as complex systems in and of themselves that are components of the larger Earth system. It also includes a clear understanding of the interdependence of human communities and ecosystems for sustaining mutual integrity, and the inescapable need to reverse ecosystem degradation on a global scale. We can symbolize this perspective by the Apollo 11 image of the Earth from space, the fragile, beautiful, and complex system that sustains our community of life. An international perspective is crucial here, because an unprecedented level of international cooperation is urgently required to reverse the degradation of ecosystems while meeting increasing demands for their services. When combined with the Earth system outlook, the cosmopolitan perspective cultivated in the citizen of the world engenders a respect and appreciation for the unity and diversity of nature and culture and their perpetual interactions that make our world. This "United Nations" outlook in turn supports the public health practitioner perspective that recognizes that divergent political, economic, social, and ecological conditions combine to render some populations, regions, and nations extremely vulnerable to ecological degradation. The resulting alertness to vulnerability can then awaken a sense of social justice and a call to action that is refined and put into action through the engaged intellectual perspective cultivated through experiences gained in our immediate community and region that nurture a cosmopolitan yet place-based orientation, or what has been referred to as a "rooted cosmopolitanism." From this grounded experience, a grasp of complex systems is integrated with respect for cultural and ecological diversity and a commitment to public health and human rights that propel the inspired imagination, effective action and persuasive advocacy.

Climate and Energy

As of the writing of this book, the fourth assessment report (AR4) of the Intergovernmental Panel on Climate Change (IPCC), a collective scientific undertaking spanning more than two decades and involving thousands of scientists from around the world, has presented us with an extraordinary set of facts that have given rise to a profound choice: Either we reduce greenhouse gas emissions by at least 80 percent below 1990 levels by 2050, or we introduce "dangerous levels" of human-induced climate change.[40] As familiar as these numbers have become, scholars and practitioners must stop and fully grasp the enormity of this collective choice and its implications for higher education: What does it mean to be educated in a climate system that we now understand to be without precedent? The latest IPCC assessment observes that global atmospheric concentrations of carbon dioxide, methane, and nitrous oxide far exceed the natural range of concentrations over the last 650,000 years, and indeed some scientists suggest that carbon dioxide concentrations are without precedent in the last 25 million years.[41] The AR4 also observes that the *rate of increase* of the climate impact, or radiative forcing of these rising concentrations, is unprecedented in the last ten thousand years and that the warming of last half-century is unusual in at least the previous thirteen hundred years.[42]

The evidence of change surrounds us: From rising global average land and sea surface temperatures, accelerating warming trends, and the heating up of the global ocean to melting glaciers and rising sea level, the warming of the climate system is well underway, and the primary role of human activities in driving that change is beyond scientific dispute. As with biodiversity, the critical uncertainties that remain mostly have to do with what collective actions are taken or not taken by humanity over the next one to four decades: How will human societies respond to the climate crisis with respect to energy, land use, agriculture, and culture? Human responsiveness is the key variable and education, science, and philosophy are critical factors in shaping that responsiveness. As science continues to improve its understanding and predictive capability of regional impacts and adaptation, including the magnitude of warming in response to continued accumulation of greenhouse gases in the atmosphere, the focus finally has shifted from proving human-induced climate change to responding to it.[43] Another challenge of *mitigation* — reducing greenhouse gas emissions by at least 80 percent below 1990 levels by 2050 — joins the mitigation of ecosystem services at center stage in cultural responsiveness, including higher education: What kind of education and scholarship are called for?

As with biodiversity, the climate and energy challenges that we face include more than mitigation: The AR4 also analyzed the interactions of a changing climate with human and ecological systems and their adaptive capacity and vulnerability. The challenge of vulnerability is understood as a function of how sensitive a system or population is to climate change and the degree to which it can buffer its sensitivity through adaptation — whether it be levees along the Mississippi River or access to air-conditioned spaces for large urban populations. Adaptive capacity is the key to managing vulnerability and it is a direct result of economic, cultural, and political factors. For example, in 1995, a heat wave in Chicago resulted in more than seven hundred deaths in one week; a disproportionate percentage of those were poor and African Americans who, along with other residents, "died alone, behind locked doors and sealed windows, out of contact with friends, family, and neighbors, unassisted by public agencies or community groups."[44] The most vulnerable, those with the least capacity to adapt, suffered the greatest harm. Similarly, in August 2003, nearly fifteen thousand deaths were attributed to a heat wave in France, 60 percent of which were people aged 75 or older;[45] and in 2005, Hurricane Katrina played out in real time a scenario that emergency managers had planned for yet resulted in failures in emergency response at the local, state, and federal levels as well as in the social support systems for the poor, giving rise to a social catastrophe that overwhelmingly affected poor minority populations.[46]

Questions of adaptive capacity and vulnerability apply globally as well as locally in settings such as Chicago and New Orleans. Climate change is a global phenomenon, so sustainability must address these questions on a global scale. In 2007, twelve out thirteen "flash appeals" — urgent requests by the United Nations for international financial and material aid for disasters — were weather-related. Flooding from Central and South America to Asia, where more than 60 million people were displaced, led the emergency relief coordinator of the United Nations to declare that a climate change "mega disaster" is upon us.[47] When we consider sensitivity and adaptive capacity to climate change on a global scale, then poverty and vulnerability to storms, floods, droughts, and heat waves take on gargantuan proportions where population growth, urbanization, and poverty combine with other factors to place hundreds of millions of people in highly vulnerable conditions. Educationally, an "earth system" perspective makes clear that climate change is a global issue; a "public health practitioner" perspective points to the importance of enhancing adaptive capacity to reduce vulnerability. The "citizen of the world" perspective cultivates solidarity with the multitudes of geographically remote vulnerable populations as well as with those in our own communities; and the "engaged intellectual" works as a citizen and as a professional to respond concretely to these challenges.

The *Stern Review*, a widely read and discussed economic analysis of climate change mitigation, impacts, and adaptation conducted by the British government in 2006, expressed the complexity of the challenge this way: Measures to help people adapt to an already-changing climate are essential, and "the less mitigation we do now, the greater the difficulty of continuing to adapt in the future." In other words, we have to address the impacts of an already-changing climate in the name of humanity and moral responsibility as evidenced by the United Nations' "flash appeals" of 2007; but we must simultaneously reduce greenhouse gas emissions on a dramatic scale. The political economy of such an undertaking will require all of the reason and persuasion that can be garnered and then some. The *Stern Review* concluded that the "benefits of strong, early action [to shift to a low-carbon economy] considerably out-weigh the costs"; but from a political point of view, it also noted the long lead times of such actions: "What we do now can have only a limited effect on the climate over the next 40 or 50 years. On the other hand what we do in the next 10 or 20 years can have a profound effect on the climate in the sec-ond half of this century and in the next." But can we democratically conclude that we are responsible and have an obligation to act now for the benefit of future generations? Science has made clear that the risks of serious, irrevers-ible impacts of climate change increase strongly as concentrations of green-house gases in the atmosphere rise, and the economic analysis of the *Stern Review* concluded that taking aggressive short-term action is economically rational. But will these arguments persuade us to make the changes that must be made?

The challenge of mitigation, reducing global levels of greenhouse gas emissions by at least 80 percent below 1990 levels by 2050, must be linked to regional impacts and adaptation if, as an international society, we are to sustain the integrity of the community of life and the basis of quality of life as sustainability requires. Accordingly, if the citizen-professionals graduating from our institutions of higher education over the next two decades are to be responsive to the crisis and opportunities of climate change, they will need the knowledge, awareness, and skills to affect an unprecedented level of insti-tutional change to stabilize the climate system while reducing vulnerability to an already-changing climate. This is an enormous task. Indeed, it is propor-tional to the problem that our graduates are inheriting from us; and they will need every insight, inspiration, and vision that their culture has produced in order to meet that challenge. Moreover, as politically and culturally complex as that challenge is, it likely could become even more complex. The dynamics of the Earth system could lead to abrupt and irreversible changes of climate in the near-term on regional scales and the potential impacts could devastate the most vulnerable systems and populations along with the basis for inter-national cooperation that mitigation and adaptation requires.

Under such conditions, would enlightened self-interest lead the United States and other wealthy nations to invest in the adaptive capacity of the most vulnerable nations? Could the desire to maintain order actually result in benefits for the most disenfranchised? Or would the wealthiest nations fortify their respective borders and consolidate control of resources to minimize their own vulnerability as "survival rather than religion, ideology, or national honor" drive political alliances?[48] If the recent past is prologue, then there is reason for deep concern: Climate change has already begun, as have the impacts of changing patterns of precipitation, wind, and extreme weather from warming; in addition, existing greenhouse gas concentrations already ensure that greater climate change and associated impacts in the coming years are unavoidable due to the long lifespan of carbon dioxide already in the atmosphere.[49] Impacts are already cascading across key systems and affecting basic needs, including freshwater, food, fiber and forest production, coastal settlements, and the integrity of estuarine ecosystems that contribute to fisheries and buffer flooding from tropical storms. The direct and indirect impacts on public health are projected to affect hundreds of millions of people through malnutrition, exposure to extreme events and water, vector and airborne disease, and pollution. Social institutions including industry and government will face economic impacts that could threaten their viability. Yet, in the face of these challenges, we are failing to respond proportionally, when we respond at all.[50]

The AR4 notes that current levels of adaptation are inadequate to reduce vulnerability to future climate change; at the same time, emissions increases and therefore future concentrations of greenhouse gases are accelerating as "fast-growing economies invest in high-carbon infrastructure" and demand for energy and transportation grow.[51] What is both hopeful and discouraging is that a significant amount of the knowledge, technology, and strategies for successful mitigation and adaptation already exist but are not being employed. The AR4 states that "formidable environmental, economic, informational, social, attitudinal and behavioral barriers" stand in the way of implementation. It is precisely these barriers that we and the graduates of our higher education institutions will have to overcome.

Higher education has some important questions to answer. How do we prepare the next generations of citizen-professionals to respond to these challenges in an effective manner? What knowledge, awareness, and skills are required to balance parochial and global interests and short-term desires and needs with long-term equity while mitigating and adapting to climate change? What educational experiences are capable of inspiring and empowering the critical and creative problem-solver as scientist, legislator, entrepreneur, designer, clergy, parent, and citizen? From the perspective of sustainable learning community, the answers lie in a continuity of experience that purposefully links the classroom with the research lab or study site and the broader community; and this is where the case studies that follow come in. The co-generation power plant combined with the landfill methane gas line described in the Climate and Energy section of chapter 3, on campus operations, provides students with a concrete example of an energy policy and infrastructure that saves money, reduces greenhouse gases, and enhances energy security. When presented as part of a general education science course on Global Environmental Change, described in the same section in chapter 2, students studying the Earth system and sustainability analyze its impact on overall university community emissions, and build upon it to identify and recommend specific ways to aggressively reduce emissions further. Those student recommendations are then integrated into the policy deliberations of the Energy Task Force described in chapter 3, and in some cases forwarded as recommendations to the UNH president and cabinet. Stated simply, the sustainable learning community model assumes that the only way to ensure that we are preparing *responsive* citizen professional in all fields, is to ensure that we act as a *responsive community*, comprehensively and systemically, in our day-to-day lives as a university community.

With respect to the climate system, that means cultivating an Earth system perspective based upon a clear understanding of how climate and human activities function within that system, gaining a full appreciation, for example, of how human activities both affect and are affected by the climate and recognizing that there are worse and better ways to configure human societies to sustain the integrity of our interdependent climate and cultural systems. In responding to the challenge of climate change, the Earth system perspective is the best perspective that modern science can provide and is perhaps best symbolized by the Apollo 11 image of the Earth from space; an image that reminds us that we are all citizens of this Earth system. This perspective also reminds us that humanity, in our aggregate numbers and transformative activities, now affects the planetary system like a force of nature, leading scientists to refer to a new geological epoch, the Anthropocene Era, in which human activities are not only influencing but dominating the system.[52]

But as vital as the Earth system perspective is, it is only one part of the educational challenge of climate change. The *Stern Review*, referred to above, takes what it calls "an international perspective." Noting that "climate change is global in its causes and consequences, and that international collective action will be critical in driving an effective, efficient and equitable response on the scale required," it points to the absolute necessity for "deeper international cooperation." This international perspective must compliment and be informed by the Earth system perspective while recognizing the profound complexity of the international cultural landscape. We refer to this as the "citizen of the world" perspective, one that nurtures a cosmopolitan rather than a parochial outlook and that cultivates a sense of solidarity with the rest of humanity, who, of course, are also citizens of the world. This perspective is part of our cultural inheritance from the philosophy of ancient Greece and will be discussed in greater detail in the final section of this chapter.[53] Given the urgent need for international cooperation, we could symbolize the citizen of the world perspective by the official emblem of the United Nations, a projection of the Earth framed in olive branches representing the interdependent great values of peace, freedom, and respect for nature and human rights.[54]

The citizen of the world perspective not only needs to be informed by the Earth system perspective, but also by what we refer to as a "public health practitioner" perspective. This perspective recognizes the dynamics of the sensitivity, adaptive capacity, and vulnerability framework introduced earlier: While human populations share broad physiological sensitivities to climate variability and the cascading direct and indirect impacts it has for public health, factors such as poverty, social isolation, and political disenfranchisement reduce or effectively eliminate adaptive capacity and leave some populations much more vulnerable than others; this is the case whether they are in a city like Chicago or New Orleans in the United States, or in the rural areas of Uganda. A public health practitioner perspective also serves as a powerful bridge between the impacts of environmental degradation resulting from global change and violations of human rights. Recognition of how human rights affect health and vulnerability, how public health policies affect human rights, and how their synergistic interactions shape the ability of a community to sustain a desired quality of life form an important part of the global sustainability outlook that we are working to cultivate in our learning community and students in order to strengthen our responsiveness to climate change.[55]

With the public health practitioner perspective, the Earth system and citizen of the world outlooks are integrated in the UNH curriculum within a framework that understands human health and integrity as emergent properties of a complex set of continual interactions operating from the local to the global scale and from the past and present out into the future. The public health practitioner perspective also bridges this complex systems and human rights outlook to an action-oriented commitment that characterizes what we refer to as the "engaged intellectual" perspective. The engaged intellectual continuously looks to the application of knowledge, creativity, and insight to advance sustainability. The engaged intellectual also continually tests the soundness of conventions such as laws, theories, or practices and with the foundation of the other perspectives, attends to the interactions of culture and nature in a nuanced and alert way.

Food and Society

In the 2008 film documentary *Killer at Large*, the Surgeon General of the United States from 2002 to 2006, Dr. Richard Carmona, was asked what the most pressing issue was in America. He responded, "Obesity. Because obesity is a terror within. It is destroying our society from within and unless we do something about it, the magnitude of the dilemma will dwarf 9/11 or any other terrorist event that you can point out."[56] Carmona's predecessor, Dr. David Satcher, also had recognized this public health crisis and issued a call to action in 2001 that declared an epidemic of overweight and obesity and an appeal for preventive action.[57] Satcher was reacting to national trends that included a doubling of overweight children and a tripling of overweight adolescents in the previous twenty years. In an October 2000 letter to the editor in the *Journal of the American Medical Association*, the director of the Centers for Disease Control and Prevention, commenting on growing prevalence rates of obesity in the United States including a 60 percent increase in adult obesity rates since 1991, stated that "as a nation, we need to respond as vigorously to this epidemic as we do to an infectious disease epidemic." In his *Call to Action*, Surgeon General Satcher pointed to the "tragic results" of the epidemic, including approximately 300,000 deaths a year associated with overweight and obesity. "Left unabated," he observed, "overweight and obesity may soon cause as much preventable disease and death as cigarette smoking."[58]

But the need for action is not just in the United States. In 2002, the World Health Organization published the findings of one of its largest-ever research initiatives: *The World Health Report 2002 — Reducing Risks, Promoting Healthy Life*. The report was a collaborative effort of health experts from around the world and it focused on a select number of what they considered to be the most important risks to human health identified by the burden of disease they are associated with.[59] The goal of the analysis was to project the global health benefits of *continuously reducing* these same risks over the next few decades. The analysis of the actual causes of major diseases produced a prioritized top-ten list of risk factors that could be targeted for reduction, and if successful, positively affect an extraordinary number of lives through reducing the burden of disease. This list of ten, which follows, accounted for more than one-third of all deaths worldwide: underweight; unsafe sex; high blood pressure; tobacco consumption; alcohol consumption; unsafe water, sanitation, and hygiene; iron deficiency; indoor smoke from solid fuels; high cholesterol; and obesity. As can be seen, literally half of this list — underweight, unsafe water, sanitation, and hygiene, iron deficiency, high cholesterol and obesity — are all directly connected to our food system; and of the remaining five risk factors, high blood pressure and indoor smoke are at the very least indirectly linked to the food system as well.[60]

Under the heading of "enemies of health, allies of poverty," the report notes how the risk-factor findings emphasize the alarming global gap between rich and poor and the degree to which global disease burden is the result of undernutrition among the poor and of overnutrition among those who are better-off, *wherever they live.* Some quantities illustrate what the report calls the "shocking" contrast: "At the same time that there are 170 million children in poor countries who are underweight — and over three million of them die each year as a result — there are more than one billion adults worldwide who are overweight and at least 300 million who are clinically obese. Among these, about half a million people in North America and Western Europe die from obesity-related diseases every year." As striking as these contrast are, the report has even more troubling conclusions for the world's most vulnerable: risk factors including high blood pressure, cholesterol, tobacco, alcohol, and obesity were previously understood as risks of affluence largely associated with so-called industrialized countries. But findings of the 2002 report demonstrated that these risks have increased in developing nations, thereby creating a "double burden" of risk as they combine with the continuing infectious diseases threats still endemic to much of the world's populations to increase the overall risk among the poorest and most vulnerable populations in the world.

The report makes a profound observation about a globalizing culture of recklessness, stating that "in a number of ways, then, this report shows that the world is living dangerously — either because it has little choice, which is often the case among the poor, or because it is making the wrong choices in terms of its consumption and its activities."[61] This is a point that will be discussed in more detail under the next section on culture, but it is worth noting that the evidence of the report suggests that a kind of "risk transition" is taking place in which patterns of living associated with affluence, consumerism, and chronic rather than infectious disease are taking root in many parts of the world. Developing countries are experiencing marked increases in over-weight and obesity among children, adolescents, and young adults and the same threefold increase in obesity that has taken place in the United States since 1980 also has occurred in Eastern Europe, the Middle East, the Pacific Islands, Australia, and China. So the challenge of nutritional health clearly comes to center stage of sustainability and the need for cultural responsive-ness. But, as was the case with the climate system and ecosystems, mitiga-tion of our collective nutritional health crisis presents multiple challenges. The WHO report points to a critical link to the larger food system, noting that "changes in food processing and production and in agricultural and trade pol-icies have affected the daily diet of hundreds of millions of people."[62] Recog-nition of this same link to the larger food system had been articulated clearly in 1996 in the goals and plan of action resulting from the World Food Sum-mit in Rome, as well as in the 2008 World Development Report by the World Bank and the 2008 International Assessment of Agricultural Knowledge, Sci-ence and Technology for Development (IAASTD).[63]

The World Bank's focus on agriculture in its 2008 World Development Report, its first focus on agriculture in more than 25 years, could represent a genuine turn-around of how agriculture is viewed and prioritized by the inter-national development community. Over the previous 25 years, agriculture became a low-priority economic activity for the international development field; under the dominant view of development that advanced a uniform path of modernization, agriculture was an activity that was supposed to recede in national importance as development progressed. The results of this were concrete and devastating for the world's poorest countries: Development assistance for agriculture from foreign governments and international finan-cial institutions decreased by 50 percent between 1980 and 2002; "a neglect" as one analysis observes, "that is all but incomprehensible given that three-quarters of the world's population living below the $2 per day poverty line live in rural areas, most of them directly or indirectly dependent on agriculture for their survival."[64] This disinvestment in agriculture was also manifest in the budget of the FAO, the convening organization of the 1996 World Food Sum-mit. The FAO's program and operating budget fell by 31 percent and its total staffing by 25 percent between 1994 and 2005.[65] These cuts occurred at the same time that the FAO was charged by UN member nations with increas-ing the access of all people at all times to sufficient nutritionally adequate and safe food; achieving a 50 percent reduction of chronically undernourished people by 2015; and achieving this goal by integrating sustainable agriculture and rural development while working to support sustainable utilization of natural resources including land, water, forest, fisheries, and genetic resources for food and agriculture.[66]

Domestically, the link to agriculture and the larger food system is also well-recognized. The findings of a summit of food and nutrition experts on childhood obesity concluded that agricultural policies have a profound impact on the food system. Citing subsidy policies under the U.S. Farm Bill that have stimulated the overproduction of corn, they trace the impacts of those subsidies to decisions by the food industry to expand the use of cheap corn as livestock feed and as a sweetener. The report cites USDA data showing that "over the last four decades, the real prices of energy-dense foods, such as meats, fats, oils and processed foods, have decreased, while the price of fresh fruit and vegetables has skyrocketed." Consequently, energy-dense foods became more affordable than foods such as nutrient-dense fresh produce leading to the inescapable conclusion that "public health goals have not been considered in the design of agricultural policies." A responsive food system, they argued, should ensure that available foods are healthy and that includes the "systems designed to produce and distribute them." The results of a responsive system would benefit the "economic vitality and physical health of farmers, consumers and their communities."[67]

Not surprisingly, these same agricultural policies are directly affecting agriculture, which means farmers, soils, and communities across the country. The result has been a polarizing force that is wreaking havoc on U.S. farmers as well as farmers across the globe. An analysis by the University of Tennessee Agricultural Policy Analysis Center found that a shift in U.S. farm policy from market stabilization to what is referred to as "decoupled" programs and trade liberalization have had dramatic results particularly since 1996:

> U.S. crop exports have remained flat or declined, farm income derived from the marketplace has fallen dramatically, government payments to farmers have skyrocketed, and consolidation and corporate integration of farm assets in ag sectors such as livestock have reached record levels. The consequences of the policy shift have been global, making American ag policy a lightening rod for governments and producers around the world. Since 1996, world prices for America's four chief farm exports — corn, wheat, soybeans and cotton — have plunged more than 40 percent. In their wake, farmers from the U.S. to Peru, from Haiti to Burkina Faso have harvested poorer incomes, hunger, desperation and migration. Today, global agriculture faces a crisis.[68]

The complex web of unrestricted production levels of highly subsidized commodity crops in the United States and other industrialized nations, combined with international finance and trade policies that demand that developing countries liberalize their agriculture markets, has created disastrous results for small-scale farmers in the developing world producing for domestic and often very local markets. A sustainability perspective focused on the food system highlights the fact that the U.S. Farm Bill, a multibillon-dollar legislative policymaking mechanism, "directly affects trade, subsidies, [export] dumping, food aid, market concentration and public health" globally.[69]

In the United States, one of the results has been growth in the extremes of agricultural enterprises: Very small farms that sell directly to customers through farmers' markets and other direct-marketing settings, often on a part-time basis, are flourishing, while mega-agribusinesses that have consolidated an unprecedented level of control over agriculture, processing, and marketing are growing significantly. This pattern of agricultural development has had a disastrous effect on independent family farmers that has led to what is being referred to as a "disappearing agriculture of the middle."[70] The "middle" refers to the market place between very small-scale direct marketing, which includes many part-time farmers, and vertically integrated commodity markets that reach around the globe. The agriculture of the middle represents the farm enterprises that provide fulltime livelihoods for large family farms. These farms also manage the largest percentage of farm land in the country, which they steward in anticipation of their offspring continuing to farm for generations to come; they also play a key role in sustaining rural communities through their unique contributions to the economic, ecological, and cultural foundations that sustain those communities. As a result of a loss of the agriculture of the middle, farm diversity has decreased and vulnerability has increased across rural America.

So the challenge of advancing a sustainable food system requires responsiveness to the interdependence of agriculture, trade, rural development, and nutrition. It also requires that mitigation and adaptation to climate change be addressed while sustaining the integrity of the ecosystems that form the foundation of agriculture.[71] As noted in the previous section on ecosystems, agriculture is the principle driver of habitat change, which itself is the most important direct driver of biodiversity loss globally. With cultivated systems now covering a quarter of the Earth's land surface and projections of still greater conversions of grasslands and forestland to cultivation in the coming decades — along with associated nutrient runoff and water withdrawals for irrigation — the challenge of sustaining the integrity of food systems as well as the ecosystems upon which we all depend has never been greater.[72] While organic agriculture's capacity to meet the growing demand for food is debated, the policy and scholarly community have argued that an ecological approach to agriculture — including Integrated Pest Management and Conservation Agriculture, which pursues higher production rates with significantly lower inputs of chemical fertilizers and pesticides — is required for sound ecosystem management.[73]

In fact, a 2007 study that compared productivity of conventional and organic and sustainable agricultural production systems found that "current scientific knowledge simply does not support the idea that a switch to organic and sustainable agriculture would drastically lower food production and lead to hunger." On the contrary, the study concluded that "even under conservative estimates, organic agriculture could provide almost as much food on average at a global level as is currently produced," and that under more "realistic" estimates organic agriculture could actually increase global food production.[74] The debate over production systems is part of a larger political struggle over who decides what development paths, including programs to reduce hunger and poverty, are to be taken. Within this larger debate, the concept of "food sovereignty" emerged in the 1990s as an "umbrella term for particular approaches to tackling the problems of hunger and malnutrition, as well as promoting rural development, environmental integrity and sustainable livelihoods."[75] Developed by nongovernmental and civil society organizations including farmers, food sovereignty is being advanced as "a counter-proposal to the mainstream development paradigm built on liberalized international agricultural trade, trade-based food security, and industrial agriculture and food production by well-resourced producers that are seen as lacking respect for or that support the interests and needs of smallholder farmers, pastoralists and fisherfolk and the environment."[76]

So the challenge of mitigating under- and overnutrition, or hunger and obesity, must be linked to agriculture and trade if the international community is to achieve the goals of the World Food Summit, the Millennium Declaration, and sustainability. It also will have to incorporate agroecological approaches to farming, including organic and sustainable agriculture, across the diverse ecological, cultural, and political settings of the world's populations, and it will have to ensure that agriculture and trade policies do not undermine local and regional agricultural enterprises and food sovereignty. In addition, it will have to incorporate mitigation and adaptation to climate change and loss of ecosystem services. This broad and integrated approach was called for by the 2008 International Assessment of Agricultural Knowledge, Science and Technology for Development (IAASTD), an international assessment process initiated in 1992 by the World Bank, the Global Environmental Facility, and UN agencies. Based upon broad, international stakeholder consultations, the IAASTD issued findings and recommendations on how agricultural knowledge, science, and technology can best be developed and deployed to meet the need for "food and livelihood security under increasingly constrained environmental conditions from within and outside the realm of agriculture and globalized economic systems."[77]

As with climate change and biodiversity, the knowledge, awareness, and skills to reorient institutions across the food system in order to advance public health and food sovereignty on both a local and global scale, while sustaining the integrity of ecosystems and adapting to climate change and loss of ecosystem services, are to be found in a continuity of experience across the curriculum, operations, research, and engagement (CORE) functions of the university that models a sustainable food system. For example, the case study on the New Hampshire Center for a Food Secure Future described in chapter 4 provides a research and engagement complement to the dual major in EcoGastronomy described in chapter 2. Both are rooted in a food systems outlook that integrates sustainable agriculture, food entrepreneurship, and economics with nutrition and public health. When these scholarly efforts are presented as part of the annual Local Harvest dinner that also features produce from the student Organic Garden Club described in chapter 3 and a poster on the Organic Dairy Research Farm described in chapter 4, students, faculty, staff, and the broader community experience the integrated and systemic response of the sustainable learning community to the challenges and opportunities of the food and agriculture system. In other words, at UNH we are working to inspire and empower all graduates to advance sustainability in the food system by embodying the principles of a sustainable food community across the CORE.

The IAASTD concluded that "business as usual is not an option" and that to meet food-related development and sustainability goals, a "fundamental shift in agricultural knowledge, science, technology, policies, institutions, capacity development and investment" is required. To build a global sustainability outlook on the food system, the Earth system perspective provides an understanding of the ecological foundations of agricultural production systems and their direct and indirect interactions with climate and biodiversity; it also emphasizes the interdependence of energy, biogeochemical cycles, ecosystem services, resilience, and vulnerability. The Earth system perspective enables students to appreciate ecological interdependencies from a continuum of vantage points encompassing the Apollo 11 image of the Earth to their own watershed and those that are a half a world away. The goals of the Plan of Action of the World Food Summit, the recommendations of the IAASTD, and the broader Millennium Development Goals clearly require the same unprecedented level of international cooperation called for by both the climate and biodiversity challenges and therefore require the nuanced international outlook of the citizen of the world perspective. This includes a grasp of the demographic patterns of burgeoning population growth and urbanization in the developing world, the significant impacts of international trade and finance as well as agricultural policies on food systems, and the growing demand for food sovereignty.

To respond effectively to the dramatic disparities of wealth and resources across the food system, graduates will be well-served by the public health practitioner perspective presented in both previous sections that sees the inextricable links between public health and human rights and the need to manage vulnerabilities through a range of approaches, including the strengthening of resilience of local and regional food systems. The ability for vibrant local and regional food systems to enhance adaptive capacity and reduce food system vulnerability in disparate settings throughout the world draws the engaged intellectual perspective into action. When combined with the Earth system, public health practitioner, and citizen of the world perspectives, the engaged intellectual is alert to the diverse ecological and cultural settings in which agroecology, food entrepreneurship and cuisine, and nutritional health interact; and that alertness begins right in our campus communities that present concrete food systems where these same general interactions are at work. Applying knowledge, values, and skills to ensure that our campus community food systems reflect the same "rooted cosmopolitanism" referred to in the ecosystem discussion calls on students and all members of the university community to draw together meaningfully the Earth system and agroecosystem perspectives with a cultural awareness of place and taste as well as a commitment to public health, human rights, and sustainability all sustained through imaginative, effective action.

Culture and Sustainability

Within the lifetime of today's fifty-year-old, an unprecedented degree of cultural transformation has taken place across the world. Developments in technology, industry and business, demographics, media, religion, government, education, and the family have interacted in manifold ways that have reshaped these basic institutions to such a degree that they now form the foundation of wholly new culture that did not exist fifty years ago; the "global consumer culture."[78] While the consumer culture has deep and varied roots in Western civilization and the late nineteenth and early twentieth century in the United States, the phrase "global consumer culture" is being used here to refer to the unique conditions that have emerged since the end of World War II. Since 1950, world trade has grown twenty-seven fold in volume and world output has grown by nine fold.[79] During this same period, the so-called Asian Tigers of Hong Kong, Singapore, South Korea, and Taiwan and since around 1980 China, were transformed from one of the world's poorest regions to a center of global economic manufacturing, urbanization, and economic growth. One result of that growth has been an explosion of a consumer class that spent more than $20 trillion in just a single year on goods and services at the household level.[80] That household wealth reflects growing income and shrinking extreme poverty rates by more than two hundred million people.[81] However, notwithstanding this astounding rate of growth, the gap between rich and poor is growing within and between countries. The United Nations Development Program observed in its 2007 annual report that the richest 2 percent of the world's adult population now owns more than 50 percent of global household wealth, while the bottom 50 percent own barely 1 percent. In other words, "the gains from global growth are being highly unequally distributed."[82]

The scale of inequality is reflected in a wide variety of statistical indicators but perhaps the most appropriate for sustainability is the 2007 report entitled *Progress for Children*. Published by the United Nations Infant and Children Fund (UNICEF), the report presents statistical trends on key indicators of health and well-being for children. While the statistics show apparent progress in reducing some of the most severe public health trends, the sheer magnitude of the numbers remain staggering: Annual global deaths of children under age five fell below the 10 million mark, to 9.7 million; 1.5 million children die each year from diarrheal disease associated with lack of sanitation and unsafe drinking water; 143 million children aged five and under suffer from undernutrition in the developing world and nearly one-third of them are "stunted" and will be impaired for life;[83] and more than 5 percent of children under the age of five are overweight in twenty developing countries.[84] The report cites progress in capturing the extraordinary health benefits for children under five of exclusive breast feeding for the first six months of life but also reports that each year 500,000 women in the developing world die from complications of childbirth. HIV/AIDS continues to spread, causing nearly 3 million deaths in 2006; more than 10 million adolescents and young adults ages 15 to 24 are living with the infection and globally more than 95 percent of those infected are in the developing world. In addition, while some progress has been noted, the number of children out of primary and secondary school was nearly 100 million in 2006 and continued recruitment and forced participation of children in armed conflict and as victims of human trafficking for cheap labor and sexual exploitation continues globally.[85] The challenge of a global culture of public health, or ensuring what the UNICEF report calls in its subtitle a world fit for children, moves to center stage of cultural responsiveness. Establishing and sustaining such a culture will require sweeping actions and investments from international institutions to the household level in the developed and developing world and clearly runs directly through institutions of higher education.

But as with the climate, ecological, and food systems, the center stage of responsiveness in the cultural system includes many additional challenges that are both equally urgent and interdependent. International development and aid efforts through the United Nations are now being organized around a set of goals that were adopted in September of 2000, known as the Millennium Development Goals (MDGs). The MDGs consist of quantifiable targets to be met by 2015 and focus on social and environmental factors of development.[86] While the goals themselves have not raised controversy, the origins and actual objectives as well as the means of achieving them have: The Millennium Declaration states that "while globalization offers great opportunities, at present its benefits are very unevenly shared while its costs are unevenly distributed." Yet the MDGs and the international process of implementation brings a clear set of assumptions that the means of pursuing these goals will be a continuation and expansion of the free trade and privatization orthodoxy of the International Monetary Fund, the World Bank, and the global economic policy of the United States, Europe and Japan.[87] This concern is deepened by the fact that commitments by wealthy nations to significantly increase Overseas Development Aid (ODA) to provide adequate financing as part of their responsibility to achieving the MDGs have not materialized. In fact, the 2007 MDG progress report from the United Nations found that pledges made in 2005 to double aid to Africa by 2010 have vanished in the face of a *decline* of ODA in real terms of 5.1 percent between 2005 and 2006. The result is that ODA will have to *triple* over the next four years if donors are to deliver on their promises and the goals are to be met. This led the newly elected UN Secretary-General, Ban Ki-moon, to state bluntly that "the world wants no new promises," and instead he called on "all stakeholders to meet, in their entirety, the commitments already made."[88]

The breadth of the MDGs bring us back to the contested nature of sustainable development. The Millennium Declaration called for globalization to be "a positive force for all" and this end was pursued through the World Trade Organization 2001 meeting in Doha, Qatar, where trade negotiations failed to arrive at an agreement on improving the prospects of developing countries; those negotiations, known as the Doha round, ultimately broke down in 2006. Notwithstanding claims of lifting nearly 150 million people out of poverty and broad economic benefits for developing countries through trade liberalization, a World Bank report in 2005 revealed that the most likely trade scenario coming out of the Doha round would in fact only minimally benefit some developing nations.[89] As with sustainable development, contention exists surrounding the authenticity of commitment to the stated values and principles invoked in the Millennium Declaration, including those of human dignity and equality as well as political independence, self-determination, and human rights. The rights and abilities of developing nations to fashion their own development ends and means and to employ public policies, including trade policies with varying degrees of free or restricted trade, to pursue those ends are expressions of cultural independence and cultural development that are fundamental to sustainability.

Throughout this introduction, we have stressed the plural and contested nature of sustainability — a concept like democracy and justice that must be made sense of and worked out on the ground within a diverse array of cultural and ecological settings. We also have emphasized that it cannot mean all things to all people and still have meaning; and that like the closely related concept, quality of life, sustainability has general principles and universal points of reference that provide a grounding for critically appraising and refining localized interpretations. As previously noted, the evolving notion of sustainable development first incorporated culture as a fundamental component, at least in principle, through the work of the World Commission on Culture and Development (the Commission) and its call to bring culture to the center stage of development. The Earth Charter further articulated the foundational role of culture by defining development as "being more, not having more" once basic needs have been met; and this goal of "being more" points to the ethical foundations of sustainability and the central place of culture in determining what "being more" means: The Commission was clear that development and modernization cannot be defined by a uniform, linear path measured by economic growth independent of culture. This same contention and plurality about ends and means is inherent to sustainability, and as a result, sustainability emerges on our campuses as a set of principles and examples, a work in progress that can be advanced only through participation and engagement in bringing those principles into the rhythm of day-to-day life in a way that enables and empowers all members of the community to define and pursue what it means to "be more."

Within the framework of the sustainable learning community, we argue that the central place of culture in interpreting sustainability and working it out on the ground requires that it be incorporated *explicitly* into a shared concept of sustainability, which is why it is one of the four primary initiatives. We also argue that cultural self-understanding is an inescapable requirement of a global sustainability outlook and the key to grasping the cosmopolitan nature of sustainability. As noted earlier, cultural self-understanding is an integral part of the citizen of the world and engaged intellectual perspectives, and without it, it is impossible to understand cultural rights as part of basic human rights, human development, and quality of life; and without that understanding, the ultimate significance of sustaining the bases for defining and pursuing quality of life for all people for generations to come, the big idea of sustainability, is lost. Culture serves as a powerful connective tissue linking climate, biodiversity, and food; it provides a vantage point from which the web of interactions within and across these key systems can be traced to a constellation of environmental and social conditions and trends that are in synch or at odds with sustainability. But it goes beyond that. The Commission noted the critical importance of cultural diversity and experimentation to humanity's creative capacities in the face of a "treasured past and an unpredictable future." And indeed, creativity is on the agenda for higher education in the form of the creative campus movement driven in part by a pragmatic appreciation for imagination and creativity in industry and economic development.[90]

In diverse cultural and ecological settings, then, quality of life and the means of sustaining human flourishing for generations to come will take a multitude of forms that reflect cultural and ecological inheritance and ongoing engagement in the institutional life of the community or society. But as noted in the previous section, the 2002 World Health Organization report observed a globalizing culture of recklessness: "The world is living dangerously," it said, either because of poverty or "because it is making the wrong choices in terms of its consumption and its activities."[91] But what line of reasoning and institutional mechanisms would establish and sustain a uniform culture of recklessness across such a diverse range of cultural and ecological settings? The Commission focused on a concept of development concerned with enhancing the "effective freedom of people involved [in development] to pursue whatever they have reason to value." They argued that "poverty of a life, is caused not only by the lack of essential goods and services, but also a lack of opportunities to choose a fuller, more satisfying, more valuable and valued existence." In other words, culture is the aim of development: the interpretation of cultural and ecological inheritance through engagement in the institutions of the family, education, government, industry, art, religion, and for the majority of the world's communities the media.[92] In sustaining a good life for all, economics is one of the means that enables us to "live the way we value"; but what we value and how we conceive of and sustain a human flourishing is, by definition, a matter of culture.

As we saw in previous sections, scenario exercises have been developed to project trends into the future and to illustrate challenges, opportunities, and a range of collective choices before us. While these scenarios take different forms, three general futures looking out to 2050 and beyond that are presented by the Global Scenarios Group provide a productive framing of the cultural challenges and opportunities that we face.[93] The first is referred to as "policy reforms," in which the status quo continues with some degree of strong, coordinated domestic and international policy reform that improves social equity, ecosystem integrity, and development; this is a conventional world with policy reform that, while clearly different than the status quo, would be recognizable to today's adult population. A second scenario also begins with a continuation of existing values and institutions emphasizing economic growth and trade, but without the policy reform; as a result, problems of climate change, poverty, disease, and political instability overwhelm the adaptive capacity of domestic and international institutions and threaten "unbridled conflict, institutional disintegration, and economic collapse." In response to this threat, a "fortress world" emerges in which wealthy elites exist in protected enclaves and employ and condone authoritarian means to hold on to their wealth and suppress the impoverished majority who inhabit a deteriorating world of repression, environmental destruction, and misery. The third scenario is referred to as the "great transition," in which all of the principles of sustainability are realized through fundamental changes in values and novel institutional arrangements and technologies that reflect the shared commitment to high levels of welfare, equality, and ecological integrity.

Taking these three scenarios as reasonable, stylized representations of the range of choices that face us, it is clear that we face enormous challenges *and* opportunities. The implications of stabilizing the climate system through emissions reductions while meeting growing energy demands and reversing the degradation of ecosystems and food systems as well as empowering billions of people to move from a desperate struggle for survival and subsistence to sustaining a quality of life that affords dignity and meaning are profound. Even the policy reform scenario, while presented as the positive future with the most institutional continuity from our current perspective, assumes *major* policy reforms on the part of governments as well as individual organizations and communities as part of a broad cultural shift away from consumerism and toward the cultivation of quality of life, citizenship, and community. Culturally, a shift from uncritical consumption to the purposeful cultivation of quality of life as a central normative feature of a globalizing culture of sustainability requires active reasoning to be brought to bear on fundamental questions of value within and across the institutional life of our communities and societies. It draws us to questions of quality of life, what it means to "be more."

An analysis by Global Scenarios Group of how a critical focus on *well-being* can support a transition to a global culture of sustainability invokes a 1930 essay by John Maynard Keynes entitled "Economic Possibilities for our Grandchildren." In his essay, Keynes envisioned a world in 2030 where "learning to live well had replaced the struggle for subsistence as the basic problem facing humanity."[94] The Group's analysis takes an optimistic view in which global economic growth from 2001 to 2050 matches the rate of growth for the period 1950 to 2000 thereby creating, at least theoretically, sufficient income for all of world's people to live well. However, this has to be achieved while *reducing* emissions and resource use *and* achieving a relatively equitable distribution of wealth. The way forward focuses on "changing the relationship between well-being and income." In other words, reinterpreting or perhaps recovering a broadly held conception of the good life in which well-being, or quality of life, becomes the goal and income and consumption are among a broader set of means rather than ends.

Conceptually, the relatively straightforward idea is that income improves quality of life up to a certain point, beyond which its contribution to well-being produces diminishing returns. If one is living in poverty, struggling for subsistence on less than $2 per day as half of the world's population is in fact living, then a substantial rise in income will lead to a substantial rise in well-being as food, shelter, clothing, security and access to education are all improved. But once income has reached a level of "comfort," this argument goes, we arrive at a "fork in the road" where we either continue to pursue well-being as a "by-product of gains in income" or we pursue well-being "directly." A simple example of limiting or reducing hours of paid work in order to have time to pursue unpaid activities that directly enhance well-being is cited, what is referred to as "time affluence." Keynes referred to this direct pursuit of well-being as keeping alive and cultivating "the art of life itself," rather than selling ourselves "for the means of life."[95] A global strategy is presented where developing countries could "leapfrog" to the direct pursuit of well-being rather than pursuing income and consumption to the point of unfulfilling and unsustainable extravagance. In the broader context of sustainability, the idea is that the pursuit of time affluence and other direct elements of well-being will reduce consumption and income among the wealthy and temper the growth in consumption and income among the developing world, thereby contributing to equity while increasing well-being and quality of life.

Culturally, conceptions of well-being and quality of life are part of our cultural inheritance and the argument for their direct pursuit thorough means such as time affluence is an interpretation of that inheritance. This call for a critical reappraisal of quality of life is rooted in a recognition that the cultural norm of income growth as a proxy for increasing well-being is a convention that was determined socially and is therefore subject to critical reasoning, and can be changed. As the World Commission on Culture and Development observed, the ability to define our own basic needs is a fundamental freedom and a cultural act. In the current age of globalization, public opinion surveys find that the majority of people want to participate in modernity, "but in terms of their own traditions."[96] The concern is that modernity appears to have become inseparable from globalization of the consumer culture; the consumer culture is embraced by some, but strongly resisted by others due to deep concerns about its serious threats to culture and the environment.[97] From a practical point of view, the Commission pointed to the need for a new global ethics to support the high degree of cooperation required to sustain cultural freedom and diversity through shared commitments, values, and principles centered on peace, democracy, and the human, economic, and political rights that underpin human flourishing. This global ethics, then, stands at the center of a global culture of sustainability and without cultural self-awareness, it cannot be grasped.

The Sustainable Learning Community

With the above scenarios and the Commission's call for a new global ethics in mind, we return to the question of higher education. In each of the preceding sections, we reviewed trends, challenges, and opportunities emerging within and across the climate, ecological, food, and culture systems. We also offered a set of perspectives that, if successfully cultivated in all students, would have the potential to empower them to respond as professionals and as citizens to the profound challenges and opportunities facing the international community. The transition from a global consumer culture to a global culture of sustainability has many implications for higher education. The previous sections have presented a suite of perspectives and capacities to be cultivated as part of a liberal education: the Earth system, citizen of the world, public health practitioner, and engaged intellectual perspectives. As a normative aspiration, the global culture of sustainability is one that should cultivate our humanity, including what Keynes called "the art of living well," as well as a creative citizenship reflective of the global ethics envisioned by the Commission that combines inspiration, creativity, and engagement and that sustains the foundation of democracy through the exercise of cultural freedom and human rights. The educational perspectives presented in this chapter are part of a long-standing dialogue within our own Western culture on the question of what constitutes a good citizen and the kind of education that cultivates and empowers a good citizen. As noted by Martha Nussbaum in her book *Cultivating Humanity*,

> When we ask about the relationship of a liberal education to citizenship, we are asking a question with a long history in the Western philosophical tradition. We are drawing on Socrates' concept of "the examined life," on Aristotle's notions of reflective citizenship, and above all on Greek and Roman Stoic notions of an education that is "liberal" in that it liberates the mind from the bondage of habit and custom, producing people who can function with sensitivity and alertness as citizens of the whole world.[98]

The point is not that habit and custom are inherently bad or good, but that the examined life is conscious, purposeful, and reasoned, so that customs and habits that hold up to reasoned argument are sustained and those that do not give way to what are determined to be better ways of living. In terms of who decides or determines the virtue or vice of cultural norms, we have cast our lot with democracy and liberal education, themselves major inheritances of Western culture. Nussbaum argues that understanding the classical origins of liberal education as a vital part of our cultural inheritance not only helps us to recover powerful and formative arguments that have shaped our contemporary democracy, but it also enables us to recognize that the U.S. system of higher education, built as it is upon a liberal arts foundation, has incorporated these classical ideals "to a degree unparalleled in the world." This recognition is part of the cultural self-awareness that is so fundamental to the sustainable learning community.

The outlook of a global culture of sustainability builds directly upon the classical tradition of liberal education and the perspectives and abilities it cultivates. Nussbaum presents three capacities that are fundamental to liberal education: self-criticism, self-identification as a citizen of the world, and the ability to imagine the world critically from the perspective of others.[99] The capacity for self-criticism entails critical examination of "oneself and one's traditions," the examined life that Socrates implored us to live, a life of reason that cultivates the cultural self-awareness and critical and creative engagement we've referred to previously. This is a capacity and an outlook "that questions all beliefs and accepts only those that survive reason's demand for consistency and for justification." In other words, education is not the passive acculturation or uncritical acceptance of traditional values or familiar habits, be they within disciplines or public policies, but the ability and commitment to critical thinking and reasoning and doing what is deemed best in light of that reasoning. Educationally, then, it is less a matter of memorization and more a matter of *interpretation* or, as the Stoic philosopher Seneca observed, "It is one thing to remember, another to know." Nussbaum makes a compelling argument for the enduring importance of liberal education:

> It is not good for democracy when people vote on the basis of sentiments they have absorbed from talk radio and have never questioned. This failure to think critically produces a democracy in which people talk at one another but never have a genuine dialogue. In such an atmosphere bad arguments pass for good arguments, and prejudice can all too easily masquerade as reason. To unmask prejudice and to secure justice, we need argument, an essential tool of civic freedom.[100]

As noted before, the ability to identify oneself as a citizen of the world extends and strengthens the capacity of all graduates to cultivate a cosmopolitan outlook that recognizes diverse cultural systems and common human concerns. This outlook, as Nussbaum argues, lies at the origin of Socratic questioning and dialogue and ethical reasoning: If our norms and conventions are cultural, as evidenced by the diversity of norms and conventions that exist in the wider world, then critical reflection and examination will either uphold those norms and conventions, or will discover alternatives. The citizen of the world perspective is an identity that transcends more immediate political, religious, and racial identities and nurtures respect; it does not replace or displace one's local commitments and responsibilities or self-identity, but rather enriches their ongoing interpretation. It also facilitates the integration of the Earth system and public health practitioner perspectives and strengthens intellectual independence and the ability to reason with others about our collective choices rather than just trading claims and counterclaims.[101]

Nussbaum's third capacity, the narrative imagination, further enriches critical thinking and interpretation by cultivating the ability "to think what it might be like to be in the shoes of a person different from oneself." This is a creative act that is based on more than factual knowledge; it is a willingness and ability to empathize with a perspective that may be very different from one's own. This is not a suspension of critical thinking or an embracing of moral relativism, but rather part of a robust process of reasoning, for as Nussbaum notes, "the first step of understanding the world from the point of view of the other is essential to any responsible act of judgment." Through the creative act of empathy, one is able to identify with and decipher the meaning and true intention of an action within the context of another's history and social world. Here Nussbaum points to a long-established recognition of the value of the arts, and literature in particular, for citizenship and deliberative democracy through the cultivation of what she refers to as the narrative imagination.[102] It is the cultivated imagination that can see possibilities and alternatives and stir compassion and sympathy for others who may appear very different from ourselves.

As we consider these ancient and contemporary insights, we ask, as we did in the case of climate, biodiversity, and food, what form will our sustainable learning community take to provide the experiences, intellectual grounding, and persuasiveness that the coming generations of our graduates will need to advance sustainability? Not surprisingly, we again emphasize the importance of continuity across the curriculum, operations, research, and engagement functions of the university so that students can appreciate how the knowledge residing in disparate disciplines, professions, and practices can be brought together to improve and sustain community life. The ancient Greek philosophers recognized that "the polis teaches." Whether one thinks of it as socialization, acculturation, or something else, the upshot of this insight is the same: The community teaches, and learning results from the community experience of the learners, not simply what takes place in a classroom. The sum total of our core values and mission and our practices across all aspects of the CORE add up to a powerful cultural and educational force.

So, for example, the case study on Sustaining Democracy described in the Culture and Sustainability section of chapter 5 captures the effort to link a democratic, participatory culture to real problems facing the university community just as the Outreach Scholars program described in that same section and the Carsey Institute described in the Culture and Sustainability section of chapter 4 extend research and scholarship across campus and into local, regional, and national communities through engaged partnerships beyond the campus aimed to supporting communities in their efforts to sustain quality of life. Creativity and collaboration to achieve shared educational goals are seen across numerous case studies that follow, including "Developing a Theatrical Response to Sustainability," described in chapter 2, the "Growing a Green Generation" described in chapter 4, and the development of public art guidelines and commissioning of a figurative sculpture described in "Developing a Sense of Place" in chapter 3. In these and the other programs discussed in the case studies, a genuine sense of place is being cultivated that integrates the ecological concerns of the Earth system, the effort to build a resilient community that supports the goals of the public health practitioner, the cultural self-awareness of the citizen of the world, and the commitment of the engaged intellectual. As students, faculty, and staff become more aware of the active critical and creative interactions of these and many other projects, the full import of the potential and actual impact of the sustainable learning community is apprehended, and learners become aware that they are in the community and it is in them and that the impact is mutual and ongoing.

The global sustainability outlook grows from a cultural perspective in which individuals identify as both citizens of the world and citizens of the Earth even as they engage fully in their immediate communities: what has been called "rooted cosmopolitanism."[103] The Stoic idea of *kosmou polites*, literally citizen of the cosmos, but more generally understood as citizen of the world, describes an integrated identity envisioned as a series of expanding concentric circles that extend from the individual to the family, community, state, nation, world, and ultimately to the greater cosmos. The treatment of the citizen of the world within liberal education is normally explicitly or at least implicitly limited to human-to-human relations, but if we take the Stoic idea of extending our identity to the cosmos and the gods and laws that shape it, then we have a basis for drawing that identity back in toward the individual situated in community, bringing with it not just all human beings and their diverse cultures and shared moral capacity and ability to reason, but the Earth system and the entire community of life. The Earth system perspective makes clear that we are indeed intimately connected to the cosmos: The relationship of the Earth to the Sun and the myriad interactions that give rise to life, including human life, on the third planet from the Sun are now scientifically understood and accessible on a level that would have been almost impossible to imagine fifty years ago, let alone when the Stoic philosophers argued for the virtues of educating the *kosmou polites*.

The Apollo 11 image of the Earth from space has arrived at an iconic status across the globe. And as powerful as it is, our identity as citizens of the cosmos may be even more clearly expressed by what came to be known as the "pale blue dot," the first picture of the Earth taken from deep space (6.4 billion kilometers away) that shows our planet as a tiny, pale blue dot against the enormous backdrop of space. This image captured the Earth in all of its majesty and insignificance. The astronomer Carl Sagan published a book in 1994 based on that image entitled *Pale Blue Dot*; in an often quoted excerpt, Sagan refers to the Earth as "a very small stage in a vast cosmic arena" and articulates what we might call a succinct, popular ethos of the citizen of the cosmos:

> There is perhaps no better demonstration of the folly of human conceits than this distant image of our tiny world. To me, it underscores our responsibility to deal more kindly with one another, and to preserve and cherish the pale blue dot, the only home we've ever known.[104]

The global sustainability outlook that the sustainable learning community endeavors to cultivate in all its members incorporates the Earth system, our human world of diverse cultures and common capacities, the responsibility of respect and compassion that underpins public health and human rights and the inspired imagination and aesthetic sensibilities that reflect a rooted cosmopolitanism, or a global culture of sustainability. Within this culture, we must interpret our cultural and ecological inheritance, with all of its diversity, using what the Stoics recognized as the common human capacity for critical searching and a love of truth. That education is fundamental to this shared human responsibility to interpret our inheritance and bequeath it as a legacy to the next generations is clear. That a truly liberal education can provide a basis for the global dialogue that must transcend a clash of brute interests and impulses to serve a common good is also clear.

Sustainability, it turns out, has pulled us all back from our scattered modernity to face the ancient questions of civilization: What is a good life and how do we sustain a good life for ourselves and future generations on the only pale blue dot that we know of that can sustain life? This is not an abstract question: We have reviewed the profound challenges and choices that we face as an international community. Our ability to argue, listen, understand, and persuade within the context of an entirely new level of cooperation and collaboration is pivotal for the coming generations and our legacy. Sustainability — this big, contested, cosmopolitan, and practical idea that must be worked out on the ground — connects our most pressing problems and engages our creative and moral imagination to "be more" and help to build a world where everyone can do the same. This is a subject and a challenge perfectly suited to a liberal education. We argue here that the global sustainability outlook that can inspire students in all fields builds directly upon the classical tradition of liberal education and the outlook and abilities it cultivates; and that when the perspectives of the Earth system, citizen of the world, public health practitioner, and engaged intellectual are integrated, a concrete body of knowledge, skills, and outlooks emerges that defines the learning foundation of the sustainable learning community. The sustainable learning community model is a modest effort to interpret our inheritance of liberal education in search of a community of reason that is responsive to our world and in so doing, cultivates a responsive individual or a citizen of the cosmos.

Notes

1. Martha C. Nussbaum, *Cultivating Humanity: A Classical Defense of Reform in Liberal Education* (Cambridge, Mass.: Harvard University Press, 1997).
2. W. Steffen et al., *Global Change and the Earth System: A Planet Under Pressure* (Stockholm: IGBP Secretariat Royal Swedish Academy of Sciences, 2004), 5.
3. Kofi A. Annan, *We the Peoples: the Role of the United Nations in the 21st Century* (New York: United Nations, 2000), 5.
4. *Our Common Future, Report of the World Commission on Environment and Development* (Oxford: Oxford University Press, 1987). The WCED is also known as the Brundtland Commission, for Gro Harlem Brundtland, the former Prime Minister of Norway.
5. See Martha C. Nussbaum and Amartya Sen, eds., *The Quality of Life* (New York: Oxford University Press, 1993).
6. The Latin word *integritas* is an abstract noun formed from the Latin adjective *integer*, "whole" or "unblemished." The adjective itself comes from *in* + *tango*, "untouched." The noun could be used for body or soul: integrity of the eyes, for example, meant good eyesight; integrity of the soul meant unblemished. Thanks to R. Scott Smith of the UNH Classics Program for this footnote.
7. Sustainability has much in common with "quality of life," including discussions over universal and relative bases for assessment. For an important discussion of this tension, see Martha Nussbaum, "Non-Relative Virtues: An Aristotelian Approach," in *The Quality of Life*, 242–69.
8. For example, see Timothy Doyle, "Sustainable Development and Agenda 21: The Secular Bible of Global Free Markets and Pluralist Democracy," *Third World Quarterly* 19, no. 4 (December 1, 1998): 771–86. See also Michael Redclift, *Sustainable Development: Exploring the Contradictions* (London: Methuen, 1987); Arturo

Escobar, *Encountering Development: The Making and Unmaking of the Third World, 1945–1992* (Princeton, N.J.: Princeton University Press, 1995); Subhabrata Bobby Banerjee, "Who Sustains Whose Development? Sustainable Development and the Reinvention of Nature," *Organizational Studies* (January 2003).

9. WCED, *Our Common Future*.

10. A concise review and analysis is provided in Robert W. Kates, Thomas M. Parris, and Anthony A. Leiserowitz, "What is Sustainable Development? Goals, Indicators, Values, and Practice," *Environment: Science and Policy for Sustainable Development* 47, no. 3 (2005): 8–21. For Agenda 21, see http://www.un.org/esa/sustdev/documents/agenda21/index.htm.

11. *Our Common Future*, quoted in Kates (2005), 8.

12. Doyle, "Sustainable Development," 774.

13. Banerjee, "Who Sustains Whose Development?" 24.

14. Kates, Parris, and Leiserowitz, "What Is Sustainable Development?" 10. Important conferences that preceded the WCED included the 1972 Stockholm Conference on the Human Environment and the 1980 World Conservation Strategy of the International Union for the Conservation of Nature. In addition, the UN Population Commission was established in 1946 and the first world population conference under the auspices of the United Nations took place in Rome in 1954, followed by the second, which focused on population in Asia, in 1963 in New Delhi, the third in 1974 in Bucharest, the forth in 1984 in Mexico City. Subsequent to *Our Common Future*, the International Conference on Population and Development took place in Cairo. For a summary, see http://www.un.org/popin/icpd/conference/bkg/unpop.html.

15. Banerjee, "Who Sustains Whose Development?" 8.

16. See, for example, United Nations, *Programme for the Further Implementation of Agenda 21* (New York: United Nations, 1997), 7–21. Document available at http://www.un.org/documents/ga/res/spec/aress19-2.htm. See also Earth Summit +5 Portal, http://www.un.org/ecosocdev/geninfo/sustdev/indexsd.htm; and United Nations, *Industry as a Partner for Sustainable Development: 10 Years after Rio: The UNEP Assessment* (London: UNEP, 2002), 8–9.

17. See Joseph Stiglitz, *Globalization and its Discontents* (New York: W. W. Norton, 2002).

18. Doyle, "Sustainable Development," 779.

19. United Nations, Education, Scientific and Cultural Organization, *UNESCO General Conference Twenty-Seventh Session Information Document* (Paris: UNESCO, 1993), 2. Document available at http://unesdoc.unesco.org/images/0009/000957/095724Eo.pdf.

20. United Nations, Education, Scientific and Cultural Organization, *Our Creative Diversity: Report of the World Commission on Culture and Development* (Paris: UNESCO, 1996), 7. Document available at http://unesdoc.unesco.org/images/0010/001055/105586e.pdf.

21. United Nations General Assembly, *International Covenant on Economic, Social and Cultural Rights* (New York: United Nations General Assembly G.A. res. 2200A (XXI), 1976). Document available at http://www1.umn.edu/humanrts/instree/b2esc.htm.

22. See Orin Kirschner, ed., *The Bretton-Woods-GATT System: Retrospect and Prospect after Fifty Years* (Armonk, N.Y.: M.E. Sharpe for the Institute for Agriculture and Trade Policy, 1996).

23. United Nations General Assembly, *United Nations Millennium Declaration* (New York: United Nations General Assembly A/55/L.2, 2000). Document available at http://www.un.org/millennium/declaration/ares552e.pdf.

24. See the Earth Charter Initiative at http://www.earthcharter.org/ (accessed July 2008).

25. All related documents are available on the United Nations website, http://www.un.org/esa/sustdev/documents/agenda21/index.htm (accessed July 2008). The breadth of sustainability is readily visible in the forty chapters of the Earth Summit's Agenda 21 that are organized around four headings: (1) Social and Economic Dimensions; (2) Conservation and Management of Resources for Development; (3) Strengthening the Role of Major Groups; and (4) Means of Implementation. See also http://earthcharterinaction.org/about_charter.html, and Nussbaum and Sen, *The Quality of Life.*

26. Walter V. Reid et al.: *Ecosystems and Human Well-Being: Synthesis, A Report of the Millennium Ecosystem Assessment* (Washington, D.C.: Island Press, 2005), 1. Document available at http://www.millenniumassessment.org/documents/document.356.aspx.pdf.

27. Ibid., 17.

28. The MA defines ecosystem services as the "benefits people obtain from ecosystems," and organize those benefits into the following categories:
    1. *provisioning services* such as food, water, timber, and fiber;
    2. *regulating services* that affect climate, floods, disease, wastes, and water quality;
    3. *cultural services* that provide recreational, aesthetic, and spiritual benefits; and
    4. *supporting services* such as soil formation, photosynthesis, and nutrient cycling.

29. Reid et al., *Ecosystems and Human Well-Being,* 4.

30. See also United Nations Environment Programme, "Climate Change Threat to Pacific Ocean Mangroves," *Environment for Development,* http://www.unep.org/Documents.Multilingual/Default.asp?DocumentID=483&ArticleID=5312&l=en (accessed July 2008).

31. Paula J. Dobriansky, "Renewing the Commitment," in *Our Planet* [Nairobi, United Nations Environment Program] 14, no. 1 (2003). Document available http://www.ourplanet.com/imgversn/141/images/Our%20Planet%2014.1.pdf (accessed July 2008).

32. Reid et al. *Ecosystems and Human Well-Being*, 12.

33. Ibid., 15.

34. Ibid., 1 (emphasis added).

35. Ibid., 92.

36. See the World Bank PovertyNet website, http://web.worldbank.org/WBSITE/EXTERNAL/TOPICS/EXTPOVERTY/EXTPA/0,,contentMDK:20040961~menuPK:435040~pagePK:148956~piPK:216618~theSitePK:430367,00.html (accessed July 2008).

37. Ibid.

38. Adam Wagstaff, "Policy and Practice Theme Papers: Poverty and Health Sector Inequalities," *Bulletin of the World Health Organization* 80, no. 2 Genebra 2002. Document available http://www.scielosp.org/scielo.php?pid=S0042-96862002000200004&script=sci_arttext&tlng= (accessed July 2008).

39. Reid et al. *Ecosystems and Human Well-Being*, 11.

40. Lenny Bernstein, et al., *Climate Change 2007: Synthesis Report, Summary for Policymakers* (New York: United Nations Environment Program, 2007). Document is available at http://www.ipcc.ch/pdf/assessment-report/ar4/syr/ar4_syr_spm.pdf (accessed July 2008). For background and all related documents, see http://www.ipcc.ch/#.

41. P. N. Pearson and M. R. Palmer, "Atmospheric Carbon Dioxide Concentrations over the Past 60 Million Years," *Nature* 406 (2000): 695–99. See also U. Siegenthaler, T. F. Stocker, E. Monnin, D. Lüthi, J. Schwander, B. Stauffer, D. Raynaud, J-M Barnola, H. Fischer, V. Masson-Delmotte, and J. Jouzel, "Stable Carbon Cycle–Climate Relationship During the Late Pleistocene" *Science* 310 (2005): 1313–17. DOI: 10.1126/science.1120130.

42. Bernstein et al., *Climate Change 2007*, 3.

43. Ibid., 12–14.

44. See Eric Klinenberg, *Heat Wave: A Social Autopsy of Disaster in Chicago* (Chicago: University of Chicago Press, 2002). Quotation taken from interview with Klinenberg, July 2008, available at http://www.press.uchicago.edu/Misc/Chicago/443213in.html.

45. Ulisses Confalonieri et al., "Human Health," in *Climate Change 2007: Impacts, Adaptation and Vulnerabilities*, ed. Martin Parry et al. (New York: United Nations Environment Program, 2007). Document is available at http://www.ipcc.ch/pdf/assessment-report/ar4/wg2/ar4-wg2-chapter8.pdf (accessed July 2008).

46. Susan Cutter, "The Geography of Social Vulnerability: Race, Class, and Catastrophe," in *Understanding Katrina: Perspectives from the Social Sciences*, http://understandingkatrina.ssrc.org/Cutter/ (accessed July 2008).

47. Julian Borger, "Climate Change Disaster Is Upon Us, Warns UN," *Guardian Unlimited*, October 5, 2007, http://www.guardian.co.uk/environment/2007/oct/05/climatechange (accessed July 2008).

48. P. Schwartz and D. Randall, "An Abrupt Climate Change Scenario and Its Implications for United States National Security." Global Business Network, Emeryville, Calif., October 2003. Available online through *Grist Magazine* on http://gristmagazine.com/pdf/AbruptClimateChange2003.pdf (accessed June 2008).

49. For example, the AR4 concludes that even if concentrations of all greenhouse gases and aerosols had been kept constant at year 2000 levels, a warming of about 0.1°C per decade would be expected. See Bernstein et al., *Climate Change 2007*, 12.

50. Sir Nicholas Stern, *The Stern Review on the Economics of Climate Change*, http://www.hm-treasury.gov.uk/independent_reviews/stern_review_economics_climate_change/sternreview_index.cfm (accessed July 2008).

51. Ibid., iii

52. Steffen el al., *Global Change*, 14.

53. For a contemporary discussion see http://www.motherjones.com/interview/2006/02/anthony_appiah.html (accessed July 2008).

54. See http://www.un.org/depts/dhl/maplib/flag.html. The official document establishing this emblem is available at http://www.un.org/depts/dhl/maplib/docs/a107.pdf.

55. Dabney P. Evans, "Public Health and Human Rights: Along the Long Arc of Justice," *One World: Global Focus* (Washington, D.C.: American Public Health Association, 2006).

56. "New Film Declares Obesity Epidemic a 'Killer at Large,'" *NewswireToday*, October 25, 2007, http://www.newswiretoday.com/news/25327/ (accessed July 2008).

57. *The Surgeon General's Call to Action to Prevent and Decrease Overweight and Obesity 2001* (Rockville, Md.: U.S. Department of Health and Human Services Public Health Service Office of the Surgeon General, 2001). Document available at http://www.surgeongeneral.gov/topics/obesity/calltoaction/CalltoAction.pdf (accessed July 2008).

58. *Surgeon General's Call*, xiii. The CDC quote is within a press release available at http://www.cdc.gov/od/oc/media/pressrel/r2k1004a.htm (accessed July 2008).

59. *World Health Report 2002* (Geneva: World Health Organization, 2002). Document is available at http://www.who.int/whr/2002/en/ (accessed July 2008). "Burden of disease" is defined as the total significance of disease for society beyond the immediate cost of treatment. It is measured in years of life lost to ill health as the difference between total life expectancy and disability-adjusted life expectancy. See "Disability Adjusted Life Years" at http://www.who.int/healthinfo/bodabout/en/index.html (accessed July 2008).

60. Indoor smoke results from the use of solid fuels including dung, charcoal, wood, and crop residues for cooking and heating. See *Indoor Smoke from Solid Fuels:*

Assessing the Environmental Burden of Disease, Environmental Burden of Disease series no. 4 (Geneva: World Health Organization, 2004). Document is available at http://www.who.int/quantifying_ehimpacts/publications/9241591358/en/ (accessed July 2008).

61. Ibid., 10.

62. *World Health Report 2002*, 10.

63. For the World Food Summit, see *Rome Declaration on World Food Security* (Rome: United Nations Food and Agriculture Organization, 1996). Documents available at http://www.fao.org/wfs/index_en.htm. For the World Bank report, see *World Development Report 2008: Agriculture for Development* (Washington, D.C.: The World Bank, 2008). Document available at http://econ.worldbank .org/WBSITE/EXTERNAL/EXTDEC/EXTRESEARCH/EXTWDRS/ EXTWDR2008/0,,contentMDK:21410054~menuPK:3149676~pagePK :64167689~piPK:64167673~theSitePK:2795143,00.html. For the IAASTD, see Tsedeke Abate et al., *International Assessment of Agricultural Knowledge, Science and Technology for Development (IAASTD) Executive Summary Report* (Washington, D.C.: IAASTD Secretariat, 2008). Document available at http://www .agassessment.org/. (All websites accessed July 2008.)

64. Sophia Murphy and Tilman Santarius, *The World Bank's WDR 2008: Agriculture for Development, Response from a Slow Trade — Sound Farming Perspective, Ecofair Trade Dialogue Discussion* (Washington, D.C.: Heinrich Boll Foundation North America Ecofair Trade Dialogue Implementation Papers, no. 1, October 2007). Document available at http://www.boell.org/docs/WDR2008 _SlowTrade_Critique.pdf (accessed July 2008).

65. Leif E. Christoffersen et al., *Report of the Independent External Evaluation of the Food and Agriculture Organization of the United Nations (FAO)* (Rome: Food and Agriculture Organization of the United Nations, 2007), 3. Document available at ftp://ftp.fao.org/docrep/fao/meeting/012/k0827e02.pdf (accessed July 2008).

66. Christoffersen et al., *Report of the Independent External Evaluation*, 8.

67. Mark Muller et al., *Conference Summary: The Wingspread Conference on Childhood Obesity, Healthy Eating and Agriculture Policy — March 2007* (Minneapolis: Healthy Eating Research, 2007), 9. Document available at http://www .healthobservatory.org/library.cfm?refid=99598 (accessed July 2008).

68. Daryll E. Ray, Daniel G. De La Torre Ugarte, and Kelly J. Tiller," *Rethinking U.S. Agricultural Policy: Changing Course to Secure Farmer Livelihoods Worldwide* (Chattanooga: Agriculture Policy Analysis Center, the University of Tennessee, 2003), Executive Summary, 1.

69. Ben Lilliston, ed., *A Fair Farm Bill for the World* (Minneapolis: Institute for Agriculture and Trade Policy, 2007), 1. Document available at http://www .agobservatory.org/library.cfm?refid=97624 (accessed July 2008).

70. Fred Kirschenmann et al., *Why Worry about the Agriculture of the Middle? A*

White Paper for the Agriculture of the Middle Project, http://www.agofthe middle.org/papers/whitepaper2.pdf (accessed July 2008).

71. See Tsedeke Abate et al., *International Assessment*

72. Anantha Kumar Duraiappah and Shahid Naeem et al., *Millennium Ecosystem Assessment: Ecosystems and Human Well-Being: Biodiversity Synthesis* (Washington, D.C.: World Resources Institute, 2005), 8.

73. See, for example, "Organic Agriculture Can Contribute to Fighting Hunger" (Rome: United Nations Food and Agriculture Organization of the United Nations, FAO Newsroom, December 2007). Document available at http://www.fao.org/newsroom/en/news/2007/1000726/index.html (accessed July 2008).

74. Catherine Badgley et al., "Organic Agriculture and the Global Food Supply," *Renewable Agriculture and Food Systems* 22, no. 2: 86–108.

75. Michael Windfuhr and Jennie Jonsen, *Food Sovereignty: Towards Democracy in Localized Food Systems* (Warwickshire, UK: ITDG Publishing, The Schumacher Centre for Technology and Development, 2005), 1. Document available at http://www.ukabc.org/foodsovereignty_itdg_fian_print.pdf (accessed July 2008).

76. Ibid.

77. See Tsedeke Abate et al. *International Assessment*, 8.

78. The origins and emergence of consumer culture is a complex and contested area of discussion and scholarship. For example, see Kathy L. Peiss, "American Women and the Making of Modern Consumer Culture," *The Journal for Multi Media History* 1, no. 1 (1998). Document available at http://www.albany.edu/jmmh/vol1no1/peiss-text.html (accessed July 2008).

79. *World Trade Report 2007* (Geneva: World Trade Organization Secretariat, 2007). Document available at http://www.wto.org/english/res_e/booksp_e/anrep_e/wtr07-ob_e.pdf (accessed July 2008). According to the report, global trade has grown twenty-seven fold in volume terms since 1950, or three times faster than world output growth, "mainly due to the creation of a multilateral trading system, which has been upheld by the WTO and its predecessor, the Generalized Agreement on Tariffs and Trade (GATT), over the past 60 years."

80. Brian Halweil et al., *State of the World 2004 Special Focus the Consumer Society* (Washington, D.C.: World Watch Institute, 2004).

81. The World Bank, China Country Brief, http://web.worldbank.org/WBSITE/EXTERNAL/COUNTRIES/EASTASIAPACIFICEXT/CHINAEXTN/0 „menuPK:318960~pagePK:141132~piPK:141107~theSitePK:318950,00.html (accessed July 2008).

82. UNDP, *Making Globalization Work for All: United Nations Development Programme Annual Report 2007* (New York: United Nations Development Programme, 2007), 1.

83. Stunting refers to shortness for age and an indicator of chronic malnutrition.

See World Food Programme, "What is Hunger?" http://www.wfp.org/aboutwfp/introduction/hunger_what.asp?section=1&sub_section=1 (accessed July 2008).

84. UNICEF, *Progress For Children: A World Fit for Children* (New York: United Nations Children's Fund Statistical Review Number 6, 2007). Document available at http://www.unicef.org/publications/files/Progress_for_Children_No_6.pdf (accessed July 2008).

85. *Child Soldiers Global Report 2008* (London: Coalition to Stop the Use of Child Soldiers, 2008). See also "Child Protection from Violence, Exploitation and Abuse," *Child Trafficking*, United Nations Children's Fund, at http://www.unicef.org/protection/index_exploitation.html (accessed July 2008).

86. United Nations, General Assembly, *United Nations Millennium Declaration*.

87. Samir Amin, "The Millennium Development Goals: A Critique from the South," *Monthly Review* 57 (March 10, 2006).

88. *The Millennium Development Goals Report 2007* (New York: The United Nations, 2007), 3. The report reveals that only five donor countries have reached or exceeded the long-standing United Nations target of devoting 0.7 percent of their gross national income (GNI) to development aid: Denmark, Luxembourg, the Netherlands, Norway, and Sweden.

89. Timothy A. Wise, "Doha Round's Development Impacts: Shrinking Gains and Real Costs" (Medford, Mass.: Global Development and Environment Institute RIS Policy Brief, No. 19, November 2005).

90. See, for example, the work of Stephen Tepper of Vanderbilt University's Curb Center for Art, Enterprise and Public Policy on the Creative Campus. Document available at http://www.vanderbilt.edu/curbcenter/creativecampus, http://www.vanderbilt.edu/curbcenter/insidearts, http://www.aacu.org/peerreview/pr-sp06/pr-sp06_analysis1.cfm. See also discussion by Deborah Wince-Smith at http://www.aacu.org/peerreview/pr-sp06/pr-sp06_analysis3.cfm; and Ellen McCulloch-Lovell http://findarticles.com/p/articles/mi_qa3895/is_200507/ai_n14800663. In addition, the University of Alabama has a Creative Campus office that is bridging many aspects of campus life in a manner that is very consistent with sustainability. See http://creativecampus.ua.edu/documents/yearend.htm. The Boston Indicators Project is an Innovate project incorporating civic vitality, cultural life, and the arts. See http://www.tbf.org/indicatorsproject/default.aspx. Two relevant Canadian examples include "Making the Case for Culture," at http://www.creativecity.ca/resources/making-the-case/index.html and "Culture as a Key Dimension of Sustainability," at http://www.cultureandcommunities.ca/downloads/WP1-Culture-Sustainability.pdf (all websites accessed July 2008).

91. *World Health Report 2002*, 10.

92. "Overview," International Telecommunication Union, http://www.itu.int/ITU-D/digitaldivide/ (accessed July 2008).

93. The three scenarios outlined above are those of the Global Scenarios Group; see http://www.gsg.org/scenario_descriptions.html (accessed July 2008).

94. John Maynard Keynes, "Economic Possibilities for our Grandchildren," http://www.econ.yale.edu/smith/econ116a/keynes1.pdf (accessed July 2008).

95. Ibid., 5.

96. UNESCO, *Our Creative Diversity*, 28 (see n. 20).

97. "World Publics Welcome Global Trade — But Not Immigration," *Pew Global Attitudes Project*, Pew Research Center, October 4, 2007, http://pewglobal.org/reports/display.php?ReportID=258 (accessed July 2008).

98. Nussbaum, *Cultivating Humanity*, 8 (see n. 1).

99. Ibid., 9.

100. The Seneca quote in Nussbaum continues, "To remember is to safeguard something entrusted to the memory. But to know is to make each thing one's own, not to depend on the text and always to look back to the teacher. 'Zeno said this, Cleanthes said this.' Let there be a space between you and the book." Quoted in ibid., 35.

101. Ibid., 19.

102. Ibid., 85.

103. Kwame Anthony Appiah, "Cosmopolitan Patriots," *Critical Inquiry* 23, no. 3 (Spring 1997): 618.

104. Carl Sagan, *A Pale Blue Dot: A Vision of the Human Future in Space* (New York: Random House, Inc., 1994). Quote from "An Excerpt from *A Pale Blue Dot*," *Space Topics: Voyager*, the Planetary Society, http://www.planetary.org/explore/topics/voyager/pale_blue_dot.html (accessed July 2008).

CHAPTER 2

Teaching and Learning Sustainability

Curriculum and Pedagogy

John Carroll

The University of New Hampshire (UNH) offers its students, both under-graduate and postgraduate, a rich potpourri of courses and programs in the areas of sustainability. Such a variety is extraordinary in its reach toward both diversity and interdisciplinarity, and the great breadth of that diversity is likely unique to UNH.

Innovation toward what we now call sustainability began well before the establishment of the university office that bears that name. UNH scored an early success in environmental interdisciplinarity and sustainability with its establishment in 1970 of INER, the Institute of Natural and Environmental Resources. INER incorporated traditional natural resources education in forestry, wildlife, soil, and water resources, along with agricultural and resource economics and community development, into an exciting new and highly interdisciplinary curriculum called Environmental Conservation. INER, indeed, pioneered the field, bringing recognition to UNH for establishing one of the earliest environmental studies degree programs in the nation. Unfortunately, just as UNH was establishing new centers in the environmental area (for example, the Institute for the Study of Earth, Oceans, and Space, or EOS; see the Climate and Energy section of chapter 4), the university's leadership also decided to disassemble INER. In 1983, program faculty were separated into three departments in two different colleges, largely dividing the faculty into social scientists, physical scientists, and natural resource sci-

PHOTO: In 2006, UNH Provost Bruce Mallory (right) signed on behalf of the university the International Slow Food Agreement of Intentions and Collaborations alongside Carlo Petrini, Slow Food founder. Tom Kelly, UNH Chief Sustainability Officer, is pictured in the background. *Photo courtesy of UNH Photographic Services.*

entists. Twenty-five years later, UNH is rectifying its mistake. In 2008, two of these departments once again were combined into a single department with a new dedication to sustainable living. That department is now also joined to the physical scientists through a new intercollege bachelors program in Environmental Sciences. These programs today reflect the curricular core of sustainability and the interdisciplinarity of not only natural science and social science integration but, given its involvement in the area of ethics and values, of humanities as well.

The very early grassroots sustainability effort at UNH, prior to the establishment of the Office of Sustainability, was led by teaching faculty, assisted by staff and student support, all of whom placed a major emphasis on sustainability in the curriculum. When the endowment grant for sustainability came in, the curricular portion of the effort had an established base. The hiring of leadership in the endowed program additionally brought in an individual committed to the liberal arts (with a background combining music and international environmental policy). With that came a valuable insistence that human culture, and not just natural and social science, has a critical role to play in sustainability.

Culture gives us a chance to ask the most basic values questions pertinent to our way of life. It enables us to see sustainability as a way of putting things together, in contrast to the typical university work of taking things apart. Behaviorally, universities have practiced and championed reductionism, while sustainability education, as it is offered at UNH, is predicated on the opposite. It thus challenges the value system. INER did that in a small way at UNH in the 1970s. The UNH Office of Sustainability does that in a much bigger, campus-wide way today. Focus on culture gives us the big picture. Thus, we recognize that you cannot violate the integrity of the cultural system any more than you can violate the integrity of the ecosystem, the climate system, or the agricultural system if you are to be sustainable. With such recognition did UNH set out on a path unique in the nation, with curriculum a key element alongside research, engagement, and operations.

Curriculum makes a comprehensive statement of the intellectual strengths and interests of the university and its faculty — it is revelatory of the interests and values present in that faculty. We all live in a world where interdisciplinarity is given a great deal of lip service but too rarely is conducted in a serious way. The reward system is still skewed toward the opposite of interdisciplinarity, that is, fragmentation and reductionism. It is obvious that UNH is conquering this problem, for the overlaps among areas discussed below are immense and the boundaries between them are hard to find.

For example, the first set of case studies in this chapter, addressing initiatives in Biodiversity and Ecosystems, draw on offerings by faculty from departments and programs as diverse as Natural Resources and the Environment, Public Health, Environmental Engineering, and a study abroad program in New Zealand. The course on Global Environmental Biology draws on the professor's experience with the Millennium Ecosystem Assessment, satisfies a requirement for the dual major in International Studies, and appeals to a broad set of student interests. The Masters of Public Health (MPH) Program in UNH's College of Health and Human Services addresses globally emerging infectious diseases by exposing the linkages among environmental and public health, biodiversity, ecology, and climate. The Environmental Engineering program, innovative and interdisciplinary in itself, has supported the growth of sustainable engineering, including ties to the Recycled Materials Resource Center and the UNH Stormwater Center. The Department of Natural Resources' exceedingly popular undergraduate program in New Zealand, EcoQuest, provides experience with native New Zealand ecosystems, but also teaches environmental engineering (both water and energy perspectives) and sustainable and organic agriculture as well, and will soon involve itself in sustainable forestry.

In the area of Climate and Energy, cases presented include another general education course that is taught by some of the strongest research scientists at UNH, but goes beyond the usual classroom experience by involving students in deriving solutions to the university's energy requirements. The professor asks whether the "inspirational qualities of research can be brought to the experience of undergraduate learning?" Stepping outside the classroom again, the University's Discovery Program used "Power to the People" as a slogan for a year-long, campus-wide conversation on every facet of the energy challenge, led by the Provost. The third case in this section discusses the pros and cons of campus-wide versus departmentalized approaches to degree programs in the environmental area in terms of inclusiveness versus stability, while the fourth deals with course experience in national and international policy, including the work of the Intergovernmental Panel on Climate Change, the UN Framework Convention on Climate Change, the Kyoto Protocol, and other such documents and arrangements.

In the area of Culture and Sustainability, offerings include an innovative collaboration in education linking a large undergraduate Classics course in Myth with a sophisticated, interactive educational exhibit in the middle of the student union linked to a demonstration solar array. Then, a Theatre professor addresses artistic engagement in this field and connects underground theater and student-initiated theater to a project in support of the annual eco-logical Bioneers Conferences. Campus culture is key to sustaining the university itself, and its inclusive and open focus, and a second University Dialogue, this time on Globalization and Democracy, is described as a cornerstone of cultural sustainability. Finally, the story about the formation of the Sustainability Minor addresses the broader history of the sustainability movement at UNH and the roles of the "Sustainable Living" and "Systems Thinking" courses.

In the area of Food and Society, the first case offered is on the new major in Ecogastronomy, which is the offspring of an unusual collaboration between UNH's College of Life Sciences and Agriculture (nutrition and agriculture), the Whittemore School of Business and Economics (hospitality services), and the Thompson School (Culinary Arts), and has established formal ties with the International Slow Food Movement headed by Carlo Petrini. Also described is a unique program of internships for students seeking to become professional dieticians that stresses in-service training with a wide range of institutions off-campus, as well as University Hospitality Services and the Campus Community Organic Garden. A freshman-level inquiry course entitled "The Real Dirt" provides an orientation to the resources and possibilities of UNH and its campus in the field of sustainable food and agricultural systems, while Project CREAM creates the opportunity for experiential learning through hands-on management and operation of the UNH conventional (Holstein) dairy herd.

This list of sixteen examples supports some of the central ideas presented in the opening of this introduction. Education in sustainability is a diverse and innovative proposition, and contributions can come from just about anywhere on campus. Connections are more important than even infrastructure, for the infrastructure will follow those connections. UNH has put together a seriously diverse, seriously interdisciplinary, and, we believe, seriously sustainable curriculum in sustainability to educate students to the needs of a world and society much in need of true lessons in sustainability!

Curriculum: Biodiversity and Ecosystems

Land grant institutions are charged with developing best practices for land management, and course work in areas of agroecology, forestry, land use, and conservation are expected. UNH is no exception, but our location and unusual farm/forest mix has created both challenges and opportunities that are reflected in the programs and courses that are offered. With over 80 percent of the state's lands in forest, and with tourism and conservation as primary uses, New Hampshire's land grant institution places an emphasis on biodiversity and understanding native ecosystem dynamics. Production agriculture receives less attention here than in farm-belt states, but the need to maintain local food production in a region of high land values has led to an emphasis on emerging markets, such as organic milk and produce (see the section on Food and Society in this chapter).

Courses and programs that relate to biodiversity and ecosystems can be found all across the curriculum. UNH students can approach this subject on campus through courses as diverse as Soil Ecology, with an emphasis on microbial diversity, to advanced seminars on endangered species and their conservation. Some of the more original offerings include a week-long Marine Immersion class exploring coastal and marine systems that occurs during orientation week before the fall semester, a Discovery class (freshman seminar course) on endangered species, and a graduate class on ecological sustainability and values. Through N.H. Cooperative Extension, natural resource volunteers can take classes on being forest stewards. These are just a few of the dozens of classes that touch on these subjects.

The four cases offered in this section also provide unique approaches to interdisciplinary and experiential learning on biodiversity and ecosystems. "Engaging Students in the Science" describes a general education course offered on campus that epitomizes the university's commitment to discovery as an approach to learning and to the integration of several disciplines in addressing a global issue. A course in Disease Ecology takes a similar approach to the interactions among ecological processes and human health, with the goal of educating a new generation of practitioners with an interdisciplinary approach to disease, a strong link to the sustainability initiative on campus. A new initiative in Sustainable Engineering begins to integrate concepts of life-cycle analysis and environmental impacts into the attempt to provide basic quality of life requirements to all societies. EcoQuest provides students with direct experience in conservation and sustainability projects in a living/learning environment in New Zealand, integrated into a semester abroad program.

Case Study: Engaging Students in the Science
GEORGE HURTT

Meeting the many challenges of sustainability requires a rethinking and reengineering of the core functions of society, including the curriculum and pedagogy for teaching and learning science. The challenge for educators is no less than to motivate and empower the next generation to change in fundamental ways, not all of which can be anticipated today. Learning itself must be sustainable, so that the citizens of tomorrow will continue the ongoing process of questioning, research, and discovery needed for solutions ahead.

Global Biological Change, a general education course offered through the Department of Natural Resources and the Environment, was designed in 2002 to provide an introduction to the science of global biological change for students at all levels. Course design began with the identification of specific student learning objectives that span Bloom's Taxonomy of learning:

1. Describe the major ways in which the Earth is changing biologically, and how these changes are known (knowledge);
2. Distinguish the various causes of biological changes over varied temporal and spatial scales (comprehension);
3. Illustrate the ways in which technology has affected the environment, and how it is used for understanding environmental changes (application);
4. Apply understanding of past and current changes to infer and interpret possible future changes (application, analysis);
5. Read and integrate papers from the scientific literature (synthesis);
6. Assess how and how well relevant phenomena are understood, and identify key scientific questions that remain (synthesis, evaluation);
7. Develop peer-to-peer learning skills and the effective communication of scientific information (skills).

All aspects of the course are designed to facilitate student success in meeting these objectives, and to assess the degree to which they have. In part I, the relevant scientific background on the physical and biological history of the planet is provided for perspective. In part II, major contemporary global biological changes are addressed including land cover changes, marine ecosystem changes, freshwater ecosystem changes, biodiversity loss, introduced species, artificial selection, genetic engineering, and human population growth. Part III places these issues in the context of past global biological changes, describes some of the potential causes and consequences of these changes, and provides an outlook to the future. The ways in which technology has affected the environment and how it is used for understanding these changes are central concepts. Emphasis is placed on the scientific basis for these issues, including what is known, how and how well different phenomena are understood, and what scientific questions remain.

Lectures consist of background information, key points from readings, connections to more advanced concepts, and questions. All are inquiry-based. The text consists of an international assessment report summarizing the state of the environment, first published by the United Nations (GEO-3), and subsequently updated to the Millennium Ecosystem Assessment (2005) of which the instructor is a lead author. The course packet consists of a set of primary scientific papers chosen to be accessible and to illustrate key concepts. To promote an active learning environment, students are encouraged to participate in lectures, write and present research papers, develop peer-peer study groups, and attend relevant university seminars. Exams are structured to assess different levels of learning. Student-led research papers introduce them to the challenges of scientific writing and the process of research. Students can earn extra credit by presenting an oral summary of their papers in class.

Selected Recent Student Paper Topics in Global Biological Change

Forest Degradation and Its Devastating Effects: Are We Doing Enough?

Deforestation Effects on Ecosystem Services, and What Can Be Done To Halt the Consequences

Eurasian Milfoil: A Case Study of the Environmental and Economic Repercussions of a Non-native Introduced Species

Impacts of Unsustainable Fishing Practices on Ocean Organisms

Sustaining a Growing Population while Minimizing Land-Use and Related Global Biological Changes

Transgenic Crops and How They Fit in Our Modern World

The Greener Revolution: Arguing for Sustainable Agriculture

Depletion of the Northeast's Fisheries: A Trophic Cascade from Centuries of Overfishing

The Effects of Climate Change on Migratory Birds

Causes and Effects of Desertification

The quality and diversity of the student projects is one of the best aspects of the course and a positive sign of student engagement (see the sidebar). Another measure is enrollment, which in the five years that its been offered has grown from 19 students in 2003 to 122 students in 2007, making it one of the largest NR courses. Perhaps most satisfying are the comments from students who have been most affected. One student recently commented in a letter to the instructor: "The class really should always be available for students because it makes them aware of important issues they never learn about in other classes. The awareness is very valuable for young students like myself because we are trying to decide what we want to do with our careers . . . This class makes students aware of the threats to ecosystems and what can be done to live more sustainably in the future." Another commented "This course did an excellent job of showing that no matter what area of study you go into, everything has an effect on the environment."

Case Study: How Does a Local Master of Public Health Program Address Global Emerging Infectious Disease?
ROSEMARY CARON

Environmental health is perhaps the main determinant of public health, or the health of human populations. The connection between the two is evident in the re-emergence of diseases, such as tuberculosis and malaria, which were once nearly eradicated and today claim millions of lives on an annual basis. Yet, public health and environmental health often are viewed as distinct disciplines and this viewpoint can create a barrier to achieving effective and sustainable disease- and injury-prevention approaches.

Public health is the science of protecting and improving the health of communities through education, promotion of healthy lifestyles, and research into disease and injury prevention. Environmental health encompasses the health consequences of the interaction between human populations and the range of factors in both their social and physical milieu.

To emphasize the link between environmental health and public health in the twenty-first century, the Master of Public Health (MPH) curriculum at UNH offers a course in Disease Ecology that addresses, through an interdisciplinary approach, the importance of biodiversity, the necessary linkages among ecology, climate, and health, and how these ecological interactions influence the public's health via the emergence, re-emergence, and geographical redistribution of disease. To enhance these linkages for students, the course requires that they, as public health professionals, consider their role in how to promote and sustain living in equilibrium with our surrounding ecosystems by inquiring: "At what point does our human impact on natural ecosystems become a disease ecology threat to the public's health? Where did we go wrong?"

The course first establishes a firm foundation in disease ecology concepts (e.g., natural ecosystem services, climate interaction, emerging infectious disease, disease management and prevention, biodiversity, and public health surveillance). Current local examples (e.g., Lyme disease, Eastern equine encephalitis) and international examples (e.g., yellow fever, schistosomiasis) that reflect the above-mentioned didactic concepts are utilized. Through these examples, students gain an appreciation for the special complementary relationship that public health ecology and human health possess, as well as how their interaction influences the public's health and environmental health on both a local and global scale.

The course not only focuses on the loss of biodiversity — that is, the loss of ecosystems, species, populations, and the implications for human health based on these losses — but also seeks solutions to these concerns through public health policy options that consider the issues from a public health and environmental health perspective. For example, the dynamic socioeconomic and ecological patterns of the affected community that result due to modes of transportation, antimicrobial resistance, refugee migration, access to affordable, quality health care, and the like are discussed.

This course is unique in that it is offered by a relatively new program focused on public health, housed in a College of Health and Human Services. The course initially focused on Lyme disease as a disease ecology issue affecting the local communities in New Hampshire. However, due to the absence of an international public health course in the MPH curriculum, the scope of this course has been extended to include global disease issues as well. Whether local or international, the core concepts are the relationship among ecological conditions, climate change, and land-use practices, and how these factors can affect the presence of disease agents, the timing and intensity of disease outbreaks, and the distribution of disease vectors. This course provides a broad foundation for the context of biodiversity, sustainability, and public health in the MPH curriculum.

Both enrollment numbers and student feedback suggest that our Disease Ecology class is of value to our students.

The MPH program recently removed the Public Health Ecology option from its degree offerings, due to resource constraints, while leaving the course offerings in place. Our primary concern was that student enrollment in the Disease Ecology course would diminish due to its historical appeal to students in this option. To our surprise and pleasure, the change actually has increased enrollment as MPH students now have more elective course choices in the curriculum. Today, this course is comprised of students with an interest in public health policy and public health ecology, as compared to earlier years when the students enrolling in this course were primarily interested in the ecological aspect of public health.

A sure sign of success, as interpreted by the MPH program, is the frequency with which we hear from students that it should be a required course for every MPH student. Additional student comments include the following: "Outstanding teaching/learning methods — class discussion, peer-to-peer exercises, team projects, expert guest speakers, depth of knowledge/experience of instructor. Thank you!" and "Excellent course. Good instruction. I'm very glad it is offered in this MPH Program."

Both the Disease Ecology course and the MPH Program have succeeded by emphasizing the complementary fields of public health policy and public health ecology. Both also have benefited from a close relationship with the University Office of Sustainability and its mission to educate students about the relationship among human activities, climate, ecological integrity, and public health. That collegial relationship has led several students associated with the University Office of Sustainability to apply to the MPH program.

Our interdisciplinary Disease Ecology course is unique for an MPH program and we expect the demand for similar ecologically based public health courses in our MPH program to increase based on the rapid rate of environmental change we are experiencing in the world today. The course design and the personal attributes of a small MPH program enable students to engage in the topic and apply the core functions of public health to disease ecology issues affecting communities on a local or global scale. Since the linkage between human activities and ecological health is indisputable, and a balanced relationship is essential for maintaining the health of our human populations and their respective environments, we anticipate that public health ecology courses will become an essential curriculum component of public health programs at both the undergraduate and graduate levels of higher education.

This course also has contributed to the support of the land-grant mission of UNH by fostering research and engaging collaborations across campus, as well as with external partners, such as the New Hampshire Division of Public Health Services. Most recently, these relationships have allowed us to secure funding to address a disease ecological issue, Lyme disease, from a public health prevention standpoint, by predicting when and where Lyme disease is likely to occur in New Hampshire. Furthermore, some of our external partners have offered practical public health experience by serving as guest lecturers in our disease ecology course and other courses in the MPH program.

Finally, this unique, integrated course in disease ecology strives to enable the MPH student to communicate, consider, and value the following by the end of the course:

- to manifest a commitment to identifying the impact that human activities have on our ecosystems and the resultant challenges it creates in determining and preventing the emergence, re-emergence, and distribution of disease;
- to promote the critical role that public health professionals play in securing and sustaining the health of the world's fragile ecosystems for the overall health of human populations at both the local and global levels.

Our ultimate goal is for our MPH students to incorporate these values as they contribute to building a public health infrastructure in New Hampshire and "fulfill society's interest in assuring conditions in which people can be healthy": the mission of public health.

Case Study: Sustainable Science and Engineering
KEVIN GARDNER AND NANCY KINNER

Sustainable science and engineering is an emerging discipline that asks how (and whether) we can meet our present needs for infrastructure, mobility, food, communication, and environmental quality without compromising the ability of future generations to meet their needs. Can we continue the quality and style of life currently enjoyed in today's Western society, and if so, how? Do we expect to help poorer nations to develop such that their citizens can enjoy the comforts and leisure activities of developed countries while maintaining critical life-support functions of the global environment? Sustainable science and engineering address both the UN's Millennium Development Goals of meeting today's basic human requirements of nourishment, education, health care, and environmental sustainability as well as the goal of reducing the environmental footprint of developed nations.

A new course was introduced at UNH in the fall of 2006, Introduction to Sustainable Engineering, that focused on providing students a rigorous approach to analyzing and evaluating alternatives to meeting human requirements for housing, food, energy, water, and mobility while considering the environmental and societal impacts of various choices and alternatives. The course focuses on tools and analysis methods for understanding the relative sustainability of alternatives (e.g., choice of building materials or methods for generating alternative energy) by considering multiple dimensions of sustainability and the various methods by which decisions and tradeoffs can be evaluated.

The fields of Civil and Environmental Engineering are critically linked to human welfare by their focus on supplying society's basic needs, and by their Code of Ethics that puts human safety and welfare above all else. As such, it is essential that individuals being educated in these disciplines have the ability to analyze the ways in which two alternatives (for transportation services, for example) differ along various sustainability metrics and have the capacity to lead municipal officials and public sector entities in an evaluation of alternatives to reach a decision. This course covers a wide range of topics to prepare students for such challenges, including industrial ecology, life-cycle assessment, multicriteria decision analysis, life-cycle and full-cost accounting, evaluation of green building technologies, alternative energy production, and economic valuation of externalities.

In the first offering of this class, it quickly became clear, and was reflected in comments by the students themselves, that sustainable science and engineering need to be integrated throughout the curriculum rather than offered simply as a senior level elective. The science and engineering of sustainability currently is being integrated into the civil and environmental engineering curricula by introducing sustainable science/engineering modules in the first year through our Introduction to Environmental Engineering course and by incorporating life-cycle concepts into the junior year in the Project Engineering course.

Sustainable science and engineering have become a major focus of graduate work in the Department of Civil Engineering at UNH as well. Since 1998, UNH has been home to the Recycled Materials Resource Center, focused on the industrial ecology of highways. The UNH Stormwater Center focuses on low-impact development design and analysis, and represents the foremost expertise in the country on technologies that mitigate development's impact on stream, river, and coastal ocean water quality. A new program in the department provides Ph.D. fellowships in Sustainable Science and Engineering through a competitive process, and aims to achieve a steady-state graduate population of fifteen Ph.D. students in the discipline by 2009. Through integrated education and research, from freshman to Ph.D. students, the department is aiming to develop professionals who are prepared to tackle the complex, multidisciplinary issues of societal sustainability that we face now and in the future.

Case Study: UNH-EcoQuest and Sustainability in New Zealand—
Te Rarangahau Taiao
RIA BREJAART, KIM BABBITT, AND DONNA DOWAL

UNH-EcoQuest empowered me with the skills, knowledge, and confidence to maintain a sustainable life. The program is unique in its ability to bring together students thirsting for an education outside of the classroom and provides an opportunity to live a life that is compatible with their vision of a sustainable future. My time in New Zealand has left a lasting impact on the way I live my life and has also ignited my dedication to creating positive change in the world. —Lauren Thorpe, UNH '07

Here is a sweet story of success, of small is beautiful, and of fostering a drive for sustainability, intellectual curiosity, and the exchange of ideas across the world.

In 1999, the University of New Hampshire forged a partnership with the EcoQuest Education Foundation, a nonprofit organization in New Zealand whose dual focus is education and research in applied ecology and sustainability. At EcoQuest, the values and practices of sustainability are integrated into all aspects of learning. Held firmly is the premise that sustainability can be achieved only by making critical connections between the natural environment and people, including their socioeconomic, political, and cultural realities. The EcoQuest interdisciplinary approach is an integral part of learning about sustainability.

New Zealand is home to a variety of ecosystems, diverse landscapes, and a suite of species that evolved in isolation from mammalian predators and are found nowhere else in the world. This makes for an ideal laboratory setting for applied field studies. The introduction of nonnative species to New Zealand has resulted in extinctions and declines of native species, creating urgency for conservation action. New Zealand is a leader in wildlife management and EcoQuest students work on some very high-profile ecological restoration projects, which also function as learning laboratories. EcoQuest's commitment to service learning enables students to contribute to conservation and resource management initiatives through focused, directed research projects. Some of their results have been published in professional journals.

Sustainability is a process and a way of life. Students not only learn about sustainability while at the EcoQuest field center, they experience it. Most of the water at the field center comes from rainfall, and a variety of filtering systems eliminate the need for chemical treatment before drinking. Students participate in organic gardening, eat foods grown locally and organically whenever possible, investigate solutions to reduce energy use, and will soon contribute to a native tree nursery for restoration projects that are conducted in partnership with the local Maori. Tree planting is also being investigated as a means to approach carbon neutrality for the program.

It takes courage to work toward sustainability. Teachers can open the doors, but it is the student who has to step over the threshold. Our students invariably show the courage to step on through. From small beginnings, and following a path of organic growth in the first eight years, EcoQuest has enrolled over 350 students. Following in the footsteps of their mentors, and with a heightened awareness of the complex nature of sustainability, students are poised to continue their quest for a more sustainable world, and return home with a thirst to continue contributing to society and science. Awaiting students when they return is an on-campus mentor who will present additional opportunities for motivated students. *Te Rarangahau Taiao* means searching for the good world, the natural world. It also means weaving together the strands. We weave the strands of sustainability one student at a time and connect these strands between two countries through this unique partnership.

Curriculum: Climate and Energy

UNH has focused on energy conservation for several decades, including early (1970s) solar energy and garbage-to-energy projects. The development of the Sustainability Program on campus and a strong emphasis on climate-related research on campus (see the Climate and Energy section in chapter 4) resulted in a combination of interest and expertise that allowed some innovative approaches to curriculum on this topic. Energy as a topic reaches into every corner of any institution, and this is reflected in the wide array of offerings.

Beyond traditional classroom offerings, energy is being addressed in some innovative ways through student-driven research and in conjunction with off-campus programs and stakeholders. One is the Chemical Engineering course in which the faculty member helped guide the students through the steps required to have three UNH residences recognized as the first EPA-certified Energy Star dormitories in the nation. Another approach is the use of the "wedge" concept in reducing the carbon footprint of a campus, state, or country. "Wedges" are individual, partial solutions that lower greenhouse gas emissions toward a goal. This approach is used in several classes that involve student interaction with managers and decisionmakers in towns, on campus, and at state agencies.

The four examples included in this section represent the diversity of approaches to integrating and understanding of climate and energy issues across the curriculum and creative ways of achieving this goal. Global Environmental Change is a general education course that uses Discovery techniques and innovative approaches to large-class education to engage eighty students per semester in developing proposals to reduce the university's greenhouse gas emissions. The Energy Dialogue was a year-long, campus-wide activity, an innovation based on the universal book theme, which brought selected writings of faculty to bear on classes across campus and supported a number of speaking and discussion events. A review of the university's current set of academic programs in the environment and sustainability suggests some of the tradeoffs inherent in designing programs that strive for both inclusiveness and administrative support. The Global Climate Change seminar brings the interdisciplinary and discovery-based approach to a class and program based in the social sciences.

Case Study: ESCI 405 — Global Environmental Change
CAMERON WAKE

The formation of the Institute for the Study of Earth, Oceans, and Space (EOS — the section on Climate and Energy in chapter 4) created a new campus focus on efforts to understand the Earth as a system. Research efforts were integrated across spatial scales from molecules to the globe and over time periods from minutes to millennia. Innovative approaches were taken to integrate this systems approach into both research and education. One outcome of these efforts was the development of an undergraduate course, initially inspired by the NASA Earth System Science Education program, titled Global Environmental Change.

In developing this new course, a primary goal, and challenge, was to bring the inspirational qualities of research to the undergraduate learning experience. Lectures included stories about leading scientists and their discoveries (to provide insights into the scientific method), an exploration of stocks and flows of water and major biogeochemical cycles (to expose students to systems thinking), and case studies that illustrated the role of science in informing environmental policy. Carefully selected and integrated visual imagery captured the attention of even the most restless students.

Another key component of the class was role-playing in simulations and negotiations. Gaming and simulations offer interesting and fun ways to experience the power of collaborative problem solving, to learn and practice critical thinking and negotiation skills, and to appreciate and anticipate the underlying complexities of working in groups. As one example, early classes included the role-playing game *Fishbanks*, developed by UNH Professor Dennis Meadows (co-author of *Limits to Growth*). In this two-hour activity, students working in small teams experienced the "tragedy of the commons" phenomena and the benefits of collaborative problem solving in ways that were both memorable and fun.

So began an effort that continues today to step outside of the standard formula expected of an introductory, general education class in the sciences. The class has now been taught 23 times since 1992, with an average enrollment of 80 during the academic year, and 15 during the summer session. Continuity for teaching the academic-year version of the class has been provided by research faculty from EOS and staff from the University Office of Sustainability.

The current version of the class has benefited greatly from collaboration with the University Office of Sustainability and courses taken in college teaching given by the UNH Teaching Excellence Program. The course, while seeking to retain the inspirational qualities for which it was originally designed, is now arranged around six student learning objectives. Students must be able to:

1. Describe key components, interactions, and concepts that characterize the Earth system;
2. Describe and evaluate the relative importance of various natural processes and anthropogenic (i.e., human) activities that shape the modern Earth and lead to global environmental change;
3. Analyze greenhouse gas emissions at UNH and evaluate methods to reduce them;
4. Develop an appreciation for the scientific method;
5. Read, discuss, and summarize the main points discussed in scientific papers relating to global environmental change;
6. Learn data analysis tools, peer-to-peer learning, and effective communication for working in groups.

The first two-thirds of the class follows a relative standard format for many large general education offering, but with a few twists. Even with a large class, considerable effort has been made to ensure an active learning environment and class participation during every lecture. This is accomplished by encouraging discussions with students beginning with the first lecture, and is nurtured throughout the semester by allocating time for interaction. For example, each lecture starts with a review of the previous lecture and asks specific questions of the students. Lectures lasting 30 to 40 minutes are often followed by a range of classroom assessment techniques, including one-minute papers and think-pair-share (where students pair up and discuss a question posed by the professor and then report on their answers). However, the most unusual aspect is the final third of this course, which is focused on the search for sustainability, where students take what they have learned about global environmental change and apply their knowledge to reducing greenhouse gas emissions from UNH.

One of the questions we asked ourselves is, "How do we engage students in the search for solutions to global environmental change?" Our answer was twofold. First, make the solutions connect with student's daily lives. Second, develop an inquiry game-based learning activity that was grounded in reality and provided key input to curriculum, operations, and engagement on campus. While the main learning objectives of the mock negotiation is for students to improve their research, critical thinking, and oral presentation skills, one of the additional outcomes is the development and analysis of a varied set of strategies for reducing greenhouse gas emissions at UNH. Research for the negotiation begins early in the semester. The students are split into eight to ten groups of six to eight students. Each of these groups is assigned a role model in the greenhouse gas reduction negotiation that reflects a real representative on campus who plays an important role in campus decisionmaking. These role models include the UNH president, provost, vice-president of finance, vice-president of research (also chair of the Energy Task Force), energy manager, campus planner, campus transportation planner, and housing representative. Student research includes gathering a set of specific facts about their role model and meeting with the role model for 30 to 60 minutes to ask a series of prepared questions, both of which help the students better define their respective role model's negotiating position. The groups then write, and hand in for review, a briefing paper that articulates the basic background facts and negotiating position for their role model. In addition to the students who represent UNH role models, a group of six to eight students are selected to serve as facilitators and are tutored by staff from the University Office of Sustainability.

The briefing paper then becomes the grounding reference for the mock negotiation. Six to eight negotiations occur simultaneously (over three ninety-minute periods); each negotiating table consists of one member from each of the role-model student groups and is lead by one facilitator. Each negotiating table must develop an agreement to reduce greenhouse gas emissions from the university by an assigned amount (usually something like 3 percent per year reductions below current emissions). This negotiation relies heavily on the UNH Greenhouse Gas Emissions Inventory (see the Climate and Energy section in chapter 3), which forms a central component of the university's Climate Education Initiative and tracks UNH efforts to reduce greenhouse gas emissions. All of the negotiations are constrained by two factors: carbon emissions and cost. Every strategy proposed and negotiated by the students requires analysis to estimate the carbon reductions as well as the cost (or savings) to implement.

Once the negotiations are completed and each negotiation table has reached an agreement, the main strategies from each agreement are presented to the entire class on the last day of classes. However, the agreements do not languish. After the class is completed, the facilitators are then asked to synthesize the results from all of the agreements and present the findings to the Energy Task Force (see chapter 3). In this way, the student work is not theoretical. It informs actions on a variety of levels in the university and provides a strong student perspective in a discussion that might otherwise exclude them.

Case Study: The Energy Waste Watch Challenge and Student Energy Captains
MICHELE HOLT-SHANNON AND SARA CLEAVES

The University Dialogue (see the section on Culture and Society in this chapter) is an ongoing effort to engage the UNH community in a series of discussions and activities that explore a common theme. Conceived as an alternative to the now-traditional selection of a single book to be read and discussed by all new students, the Dialogue unfolds during the fall and spring semesters in classrooms, at film showings, in residence halls, and in conjunction with other activities both on and off campus. A major component of the Dialogue is a series of papers written by faculty (that year's Discovery Authors) on the chosen theme and discussed in classes and at special events throughout the year. Co-curricular programs are an important part of each Dialogue.

In the second year of this initiative, "Power to the People: A University Dialogue on Energy" was the theme, and students were asked "What can I do to watch my waste?" The UNH Energy Waste Watch Challenge was one answer to that challenge and has become a sustained innovation of the Dialogue process.

The Waste Watch Challenge is led by Energy Captains, undergraduate students living in the halls and apartments on campus. The Energy Captains volunteer to work closely with the UNH Energy Task Force and staff from the University Office of Sustainability, Residential Life, Housing, and the Energy Office to develop educational and promotional displays, serve as role models, and share with students many concrete steps they can take to reduce consumption and waste.

The presence of Energy Captains in each apartment building and residence hall fosters an increased acceptance of sustainable behaviors. Peer-to-peer education has been identified as the most powerful tool to effectively increase awareness of energy and water usage and facilitate the adoption of behaviors that reduce consumption and waste. Energy Captains are not expected to work alone, but can recruit other Captains or "deputies" to help them carry out their projects and help their building's residents reduce waste. Tools developed to help explain the contest and offer tips for success include a list of steps each student can take to reduce energy and water use (see sidebar).

During the first year of the Challenge (2006–2007), Energy Captains in one hall hosted a lights-off dance. In another, they commandeered the hall lobby for a demonstration of how much water it takes for a five- versus ten-minute shower. And in most halls, Energy Captains made use of pledge cards

Steps Recommended to Students in the Energy Waste Watch program

Beginner
- Open your shades for natural light when you are indoors (particularly in your room);
- Unless you are handicapped, do not use automatic handicap doors;
- Activate your computer's power management options;
- Set your computer monitor to sleep after ten minutes of inactivity. Screen savers do not save energy, but sleep settings do!
- Turn off the water while brushing your teeth;
- Do not use toilets as a trash can;
- Rinse your razor in a little bit of water (in the tub or sink) rather than running water constantly.

Intermediate
- Study outside, in the library, or other public spaces;
- Don't use halogen lamps. One halogen lamp stand draws more power than the average computer!
- Unplug appliances that are not being used or turn off the power strip or surge protector. Most appliances (e.g., TVs, VCRs, cordless phones, microwaves, cell phone chargers) consume energy even when switched off. As much as 10 percent of energy use for appliances is consumed in these "vampire" energy charges when appliances are off or after it has been fully charged;
- Share a fridge with your roommate or friends and unplug yours;
- If possible, use ink-jet printers since they consume 95 percent less energy than laser printers;
- When you can, use laptops, since they use 90 percent less energy than desktop computers.

Advanced
- Keep the lights off in your room constantly and study or hang out outside during the day, in the hall where the lights must stay on, or in public spaces;
- Don't turn on the TV;
- Share a clock with your roommate;
- Combine laundry loads with friends so that you only do full loads;
- Air dry your laundry using a drying rack in your room. Use the dorm fridge and unplug those in your room;
- Laptops use 90 percent less energy than desktops — if you don't have access to one, borrow a friend's;

(Continued on next page)

(Continued from previous page)

- Don't flush the toilet after just peeing;
- Turn off the water when soaping up in a shower and run the water only when rinsing;
- Collect greywater for plant watering;
- Put a container in the shower with you to collect water that would otherwise go down the drain.

that were then posted on hall doors. One need only walk down the hall to see who was choosing to buy EnergyStar appliances and electronics, take shorter showers, or wash their clothes in cold water.

In 2007, the Energy Captains not only applied for and won grant money to give away reusable bags to students to help them lower their waste, but also combined forces to establish a new student organization on campus called the Ecological Advocates. Along with running the Challenge, this new student group expanded its peer-to-peer educational programming beyond the Challenge to include new Earth Day events, tabling near student dining halls, editorials in the student newspaper, and rallies on campus around issues like recycling, consumption, biodiversity, climate change, and more.

The Challenge is judged by reductions in the per capita energy and water consumption of each building compared with its own average use from the past three years. The three buildings that achieve the greatest reductions in use receive cash prizes deposited into their hall accounts. Many winners have gone on to use these cash prizes to help make their buildings even more sustainable, such as buying an EnergyStar microwave for a common kitchen area or compact fluorescent light bulbs for all students in the building. The overall winner also receives the Challenge Trophy — a handmade creation by past Energy Captains — to be displayed in their building until the end of the next competition.

Since 2006, three rounds of the Challenge have been held, and each year the savings continue to improve. During the four-week Fall 2006 Challenge, halls and apartments saved a combined 125,203 kilowatt hours and 286,802 gallons of water. These savings translate into nearly $18,000 less in energy and water costs and emissions the equivalent of 92 barrels of oil or not driving eight passenger cars for one year. During the four-week Fall 2007 Challenge, halls and apartments saved a combined 227,600 kilowatt hours and 1,669,000 gallons of water. These savings translate into $45,000 less in energy and water costs and emissions the equivalent of 272 barrels of oil or not driving twenty-five passenger cars for one year. The Fall 2008 Challenge should be the best yet: The students have agreed to expand the now-annual fall event from four to eight weeks.

The energy and emissions savings from the Challenge are significant. But more than that, the Challenge is inspiring student learning around sustainability outside of the classroom, fostering knowledge, values, and behavior changes that they can take with them when they leave UNH.

Case Study: Organizing a Curriculum on the Environment: Inclusiveness or Security?
JOHN ABER

Teaching, learning, and discovery at the University of New Hampshire are guided by an Academic Master Plan enacted as a five-year, rolling, living document. One of the goals of that plan is to improve the alignment of academic programs and areas of intellectual and research strength.

The Research chapter (chapter 4) of this book describes the dominant role that environmentally and sustainability-related research plays in the university's research and scholarship activities. Following the goals of the academic plan, graduate and undergraduate degree programs should be available that build on this research strength.

But how to organize a topic as diverse and extensive as the study of the environment into structured programs that fit within colleges and departments? This is a challenge faced by many institutions. Existing examples suggest four ways of integrating faculty and students across campus. These include:

- Virtual or web-based — relevant courses and research projects are listed without offering degrees or departments;
- Second major — requirements of both a primary major in a traditional field and the second major must be met;
- Interdisciplinary major — degrees are offered jointly by two or more departments with courses given in each or all;
- Interdisciplinary department with majors — the most completely integrated structure, melding the permanence and focus of a department with interdisciplinary degrees offered by that department.

The final two options provide coherence and a clear degree path. The interdisciplinary major can extend beyond departmental and college boundaries to include the largest number of faculty and students, but may lack the focus and administrative attention and support offered by a structured department. Establishing a new major also may present fewer administrative problems than forming a new department. However, being part of a single, established department provides permanence, continuity, and administrative muscle that may help to ensure longevity and support. On the other hand, no one academic unit can encompass all of the disciplines that touch on the environment or on sustainability, so attempting to focus all teaching and scholarship in a single unit may discourage participation by faculty from outside that unit. This is the classic academic dynamic between permanence and inclusiveness.

Through a number of separate actions over time, UNH has chosen a combination of interdisciplinary majors and departments. For example, there is a single, integrated Ph.D. Program in Natural Resources and Earth System Science, founded purely on faculty enthusiasm, that reports directly to the Dean of the Graduate School. Founded in 1989, this program operated without budget and with a volunteer chair for its first fourteen years. Despite this lack of a traditional home or permanent budget, the program grew to be the largest Ph.D. program on campus, and currently has about eighty students. The program spans the entire spectrum of topics, from ethics to policy to science, and everything either in between or tangential, all in one program. Students in the program are supported primarily through research assistantships provided by external grants, with additional support by research programs and teaching assistantships provided by other units.

Two undergraduate degree programs have been formulated recently in Environmental Sciences and Environmental Engineering, which complement a long-standing program in Environmental Conservation, and others in traditional areas of natural resources and ecology. The Environmental Sciences program spans two departments in two different colleges, while the Environmental Engineering and Environmental Conservation programs reside within existing departments, but in different colleges. A number of other programs on campus relate to environmental concerns as well.

Up to this point, UNH has not tried to bring all of these related programs together in a single unit. It may well be that the range of topics that contribute to environmental and sustainability research and education is so broad that any attempt to unite them would by necessity limit the scope of faculty and student participation. However, without that unity and permanence, the future of such programs might always be in question.

*Case Study: Science, Politics, and Policy from Global to Local
in an Undergraduate Seminar*
STACY VANDEVEER

"Global climate change" may seem too large, too distant, and too technical to address in an undergraduate setting. Nevertheless, our students have a sense of its importance and an interest in learning more about it from different personal and intellectual perspectives. At UNH, one approach to answering this need is a seminar, entitled Science, Society and Politics: Exploring Climate Change from Global to Local.

The goal of this class, developed with support from the campus-wide Discovery Program, is not simply to teach students political science and atmospheric chemistry, but also to inspire their interest in multiple disciplines and in interdisciplinary thinking. The course combines materials from a number of scientific and social science fields and explores:

- The process of constructing scientific consensus;
- the nexus between scientific information and policymaking;
- the interactions between American and international politics and debates;
- public understanding of scientific and technical information;
- media representations of environmental politics and of scientific information;
- political activities of "stakeholders";
- the concrete connection between complex issues and state and local policies.

Climate change is only one of many important issues that engage students with sustainability. Others include pollution, poverty, or the role of visual or theatrical arts in human development (for example, see the Culture and Sustainability section in this chapter). For this seminar, climate change is the organizing theme or "hook" around which we explore, examine, and debate the connections and contradictions among some of the ways of knowing and learning common in natural science, social science, and the humanities.

The seminar includes a combination of lecture and discussion, and begins with an introduction to Science and Technology Studies, an interdisciplinary field that examines the societal context in which science is conducted and the relationships among science, social debate, and politics. Then the seminar turns to potential policy options related to climate change and to discussions of major actor groups or categories related to climate-change politics. Broad types of policies are introduced and a host of options for public sector policymaking are reviewed.

The final third of the course focuses on social debate and policymaking at various levels of governance, from global to local levels. Students read and discuss the Intergovernmental Panel on Climate Change and international agreements such as the United Nations Framework Convention on Climate Change and the Kyoto Protocol. National- and continental-level materials compare climate policies in the United States, Canada, and the European Union, while regional, state, and local politics are presented via materials on the many policy measures undertaken by U.S. states, cities, and universities across New England.

The final written assignment takes the form of a research-based policy recommendation memo. Students are asked to incorporate the semester's materials and discussions and their own research and values into a paper that outlines a set of policy recommendations they would make to their state government, local government, or university administrators (they choose which of these to advise). This assignment is designed as a vehicle to improve students' research skills and methods, offering them opportunities to combine their views with empirical research and course materials and to bring climate-change politics and policy issues down from the large and off-putting scale of global politics and institutions to levels of governance that often seem more accessible to them.

Finally, both this concluding assignment and the course as a whole seek to encourage students to look for connections between their education and their roles as citizens — to ask how Biology 101 connects to their English and Politics courses, and to the life beyond the campus.

Curriculum: Food and Society

The technical and social aspects of food production and delivery are natural areas of expertise at a land grant institution. New Hampshire's relatively marginal standing as an agricultural state, and a sophisticated interest in alternative methods of production and the value of agriculture in preserving open space and local food supplies, has combined with the energy of the Sustainability Program to create a unique perspective toward food and society on campus. Some of these approaches are co-curricular and involve students with practitioners.

For example, UNH hosted the first of four regional Soul of Agriculture conferences in the Northeast in 2001. The Soul of Agriculture is an international initiative to reconnect communities and their food supply, and with the conferences held during the fall term, student participation can be maximized. On campus, courses such as Food and Society, offered through the Animal Science Department, consider the cultural significance of food from historical, psychological, social, political, and economic perspectives.

Four very different aspects of teaching and learning about food and society are presented in this section. EcoGastronomy is a new dual major at UNH that is linked closely to the Slow Food Movement established in Italy. Students pair their courses in this area with a traditional major, enriched by language and cultural experiences and a semester abroad. The Dietetic Internship fully integrates sustainability concepts into the working/learning experience by engaging students with several community partners in different parts of the food security and health system. "The Real Dirt" is an experiential course that provides background information through lectures, discussions, and films, then takes students out to farms, markets, and community events related to sustainable food systems. UNH CREAM is a capstone class for students in dairy sciences, but also much more, providing seniors from across campus with real-time experience in animal management, but also with business, personnel, and technology challenges.

Case Study: Dual Major in EcoGastronomy
JOANNE CURRAN-CELENTANO

"Eat food. Not too much. Mostly plants." This simple mantra starts the narrative of Michael Pollan's 2008 book titled *In Defense of Food: An Eater's*

Manifesto that describes with alarming detail changes in our food supply impacting global food security. Pollan's book supports the warnings of physicians, nutritionists, economists, and policymakers about the recent increases in obesity and diabetes that are creating extraordinary public health challenges. According to a recent report from the Institute of Medicine, "the great advances of genetics and biomedical discoveries could be more than offset by the burden of illness, disability and death caused by too many people eating too much and moving too little over their lifetime."

The UNH campus is already deep in discussion on local and regional food and related health issues. Alongside teaching and research in agriculture, public health, nutrition, and hospitality management, a series of stakeholder meetings were held between 2000 and 2006, including four regional conferences titled "The Soul of Agriculture," a citizens' panel on the future of food in New England, a symposium on "Eating as a Moral Act," and a year-long statewide strategic planning process for the New Hampshire Center for a Food Secure Future. This sustained dialogue with state and regional food producers and policymakers, as well as researchers and educators, spurred interest in building a curriculum around sustainable food systems, from farm to fork to nutrition and health.

We realized we had the opportunity to coordinate and integrate interest in food across campus and arouse passion about and opportunities to affect the food we produce and eat. To do this, we planned to integrate three broad fields of study and practice that are of growing interest and concern for public health, employers, and graduates: sustainable agriculture, hospitality focused on sustainable practices and regional cuisine, and nutrition. Our goal was to provide a unique and systemic educational experience to prepare students to become actively involved in the complex and holistic nature of our food community from growing food, to food preparation, to understanding the health consequences of our selected cuisine. We wanted to embrace "gastronomy," which is defined as "the art and appreciation of preparing and eating good food," as it is paired with social, economic, political, and ethical issues associated with food production and eating. "EcoGastronomy," then, represents a highly interdisciplinary, complementary, and innovative approach to curriculum. Because of this, we realized that EcoGastronomy would best be considered a dual major. At UNH, a dual major represents a course of study that is linked to a primary degree granting major. The dual major is noted on the transcript and diploma. Given its highly interdisciplinary nature, offering a dual major in EcoGastronomy rather than an independent major allows not only greater flexibility across departments and colleges but also enables students to complement and enhance their primary major. In addition, the students within the dual major will represent many disciplines, areas of study, and points of view that will enhance the interdisciplinary experience of the EcoGastronomy dual major.

While planning the dual major in EcoGastronomy, the committee successfully nominated Carlo Petrini, founder of Slow Food International, for a prestigious honorary degree. We were able to host Carlo Petrini and a group of his colleagues from the University of Gastronomic Sciences (UNISG) in May 2006, at which time the University of New Hampshire became the first university in the United States to sign on to the Slow Food Principles. We thus became part of a worldwide network of universities and research institutions linked with Slow Food International agreeing to work to protect agricultural biodiversity, the environment, and natural resources, and to support training and education about local and sustainable food practices and the right of people to self-determination with regard to food. In our meeting, we were able to initiate an academic relationship with UNISG in Pollenzo, Italy. In addition, we began to design a plan to establish an exchange between the two institutions. In October 2006, UNH sent a ten-person delegation to Terra Madre in Turin, Italy. Terra Madre is a network of food communities committed to producing quality food in a sustainable way. The meeting is designed to network the food communities of farmers, cooks, and academics, allowing for the sharing of specialized knowledge within the global food world to make good, clean, and fair food possible.

While in Italy, the UNH delegation met with the faculty and staff of UNISG to continue the shared curriculum development and to tour the facilities as we began to imagine how best to engage the U.S. students in this unique gastronomic experience. We left convinced that we had all the pieces ready to create a valuable experience for our students and to develop educated leaders with an understanding of the food systems needed by our contemporary society.

The dual major in EcoGastronomy unites diverse strengths at UNH from many programs across several colleges. It will provide students from various backgrounds and academic homes an integrated experience linking food production with cuisine and health outcomes. It will enhance the sustainable food community across the university's curriculum and operations. For example, the dual major will provide an avenue for the hospitality major to engage with the green movement in lodging and food service, and give the nutrition student experience with sustainable food systems, sustainable diets, and food security. All students will be working in the field growing food, in the kitchen preparing food, in the laboratory examining food and health, and in the public arena understanding how food policy is established, and the consequences of such decisions.

As a land grant institution with over a century of agricultural tradition, teaching, research, and extension, UNH is situated perfectly to offer the dual major and in addition offer a rich exchange program for gastronomy students from UNISG. Critical agricultural infrastructure to support experiential learning is in place. Over 1,100 acres of farmland and woodland support a number of working farms, two research dairy operations including the organic research dairy, kitchen facilities, and research laboratories. A cross-disciplinary team, supported by the substantial and diverse pool of expertise across campus, developed the curriculum for the dual major and the design of the international experience and student exchange.

The dual major in EcoGastronomy consists of 24 credits of course work at UNH, including a senior synthesis project and a language proficiency that prepares the student to engage fully in the required semester abroad. The courses include an Introduction to EcoGastronomy, Sustainable Food Production, Food and Beverage Management, and Food and Society. The program includes a 15-credit semester at UNISG that is commonly planned for the spring of the junior year.

The dual major in EcoGastronomy is one additional component to a broad set of collaborations that are organized around the needs and opportunities of the State of New Hampshire and the New England region's farmers, students, families, businesses, and communities with the goal of adding informed citizens with varied academic interest to the continued deliberations on food, agriculture, and nutrition. This sustained dialogue with state and regional producers, chefs and restaurateurs, nutrition and dietetics professionals, and food and agriculture policymakers, as well as researchers and educators, identified the need for greater integration of disciplines to support a food-system or food-community perspective in all students, consistent with the land grant mission and aimed at fulfilling the professional need for an emphasis on the connections among sustainable agriculture, food, and nutrition. The proposal for the dual major in EcoGastronomy will educate and train competent and confident professionals ready to engage in and advance these connections.

Case Study: Integrating Sustainability into the Professional Development of Dietetic Interns

JOANNE BURKE

Eaters, that is, must understand that eating takes place inescapably in the world, that it is inescapably an agricultural act, and that how we eat determines, to a considerable extent, how the world is used. This is a simple way of describing a relationship that is inexpressibly complex. —Wendell Berry, The Pleasures of Eating, in *What Are People For?* (New York: North Point Press, 1990).

Sustainable food systems include wholesome agricultural production, environmental stewardship, fairly priced and culturally acceptable foods, and the promotion of good health and nutrition. Traditional dietetics education includes both theory and practice in community care and planning, food service, nutrition research, and applied nutrition care. Relatively little attention is given to agricultural practices, environmental impact, or food system analysis. Those presently engaged in the teaching and training of agriculture, food, nutrition, and hospitality professionals are uniquely positioned, and indeed have a mandate, to frame sustainability principles as an integral component of their educational programs for students and community audiences alike.

The University of New Hampshire's Dietetic Internship incorporates sustainability principles using a combination of graduate level course work and practicum affiliations. Placements focus on developing expertise in food service management, community, research, and clinical nutrition care as specified by the American Dietetic Association (ADA). The ultimate goal of the dietetic internship is to promote the development of knowledgeable, reflective, and activist dietetic professionals who meet or exceed national accreditation standards. They will have the knowledge, skills, and ideally the passion, to provide leadership and expertise for the advancement of sustainable food system practices in personal, professional, and political arenas.

Historically, our internship explored concepts of food security and sustainability as independent concepts. However, extensive scientific research, government and environmental reports, and books in the popular press stress the value of a comprehensive, systems approach that integrates sustainability into all areas of application. We have achieved this integration by partnering with campus programs, developing mentoring opportunities, conducting targeted research projects, and revising dietetic course content. We include both practical experience and theoretical concepts from farm, to fork, to nutrition and health outcomes. Examples of each strategy are provided here to highlight selected experiences, rotations, and educational resources that we have found instructive.

The University Office of Sustainability (UOS) provides leadership and promotes engagement on campus, statewide, nationally, and internationally. Faculty and staff from across campus are an integral part of the UOS initiatives and partnerships. Staff from the UOS meet with our interns, who have been invited to critique materials and participate in a UOS-coordinated, statewide planning process for an emerging center dedicated to promoting food sustainability and security from farm, to fork, to nutrition and health outcomes. The students witness firsthand both the challenges and the richness of focus group work.

Rotations with University Hospitality Service serve to meet food service competency requirements. Interns have participated in the UNH Annual Local Harvest Dinner since its inception in 2005. This campus and community event features local food and showcases local producers. Tasks include marketing, cooking, serving, educating, and conducting customer satisfaction surveys of the patrons. Interns also develop a purchasing guide for Hospitality Services that identifies local food vendors and their available products. Other activities include a marketing campaign to minimizing plate waste, including the "Save it for Seconds" campaign. "Portion distortion" concepts have been presented to diners, to highlight the link between portion sizes and caloric content.

The Organic Garden Club is another valuable campus resource. When interns arrive in the summer, the garden is up and running. Interns plan an organic lunch, incorporating many of the garden crops into the menu. The luncheon project includes menu planning, costing, eating seasonally and locally, recipe nutrient analysis, marketing, and quantity food production. Interns tour the garden, meet the staff, and pick the selected vegetables. Staff and campus mentors are invited to attend. Some interns have led cooking demos or provided recipes with nutrient analysis for the crops sold at the weekly Organic Garden Club campus farmers' market. Others have opted to spend additional time at the garden on days off or at the end of their rotation days. Interns learn sustainable gardening skills while securing extra food for themselves or their families. The farm benefits from the extra help. This represents a true win-win situation.

Our Cooperative Extension Educators are community-connected mentors who immerse the interns in many of the food security and sustainability issues. Placements include a regional food bank, University Health Services, Women and Infant (WIC) clinics, local health clinics, and schools that serve low-income families. Students experience the health, education, and food inequities and insecurities faced by the working and nonworking poor and their children, and often feel frustrated when faced with these conditions. They are encouraged to identify short- and long-term solutions designed to address hunger and food insecurity. In 2006, interns wrote to legislators regarding the reformulation of WIC allocations after critically reviewing the proposed legislation.

Research projects provide interns with discovery experiences while simultaneously generating important data for our food security and health outcomes research. For the last two years, interns analyzed the cost of eating according to the USDA sample MyPyramid menu, which incorporates the newest dietary guidelines into a sample week meal plan. The project required literature research skills, food costing using "as purchased" and "edible portion" calculations, menu nutrient analysis, data entry, and management skills. The cost of the menu as purchased was then compared to food-stamp reimbursement rates. Estimated food costs were considered in the context of local costs for rent, heat, and electricity. Minimum wage salaries were calculated, and government defined "poverty levels" and livable wages were considered. The food struggles of the working poor become strikingly evident when calculations are conducted using real-time data. Research results were presented by interns and staff at yearly dietetics meetings, at Cooperative Extension professional in-service meetings, discussed on our state public radio station, and shared with our Washington, D.C., representatives through our state affiliate dietetic delegation.

Using a focus group approach, interns also have assisted Cooperative Extension in conducting research on debit card use at farmers' markets. In 2005, interns determined and described campus vending-machine products. Results were shared with our Hospitality Services and presented at a regional dietetics meeting. This project served to highlight the potential impact of the "food environment" on food selection practices at our university.

More recently, interns have been working with faculty from the Department of Animal and Nutritional Sciences Department as part of the Young Adult Health Risk Screening Initiative (YAHRSI). The health status of UNH college students is being assessed based on biological, anthropometric, clinical, dietary, and wellness survey results. The results will be shared on campus through our UNH Community Food and Nutrition Profile as well as via national science meetings.

Our graduates will be joining the ranks of the professionals working on the front lines to advance food and nutrition health care as policymakers, hospital purchasing department heads, community health center workers, researchers, educators, food bank administrators, and dietitians. It is our goal that professionals from the UNH Dietetic Internship will enter the profession with an understanding, commitment, and vision for advancing secure and sustainable food systems.

Case Study: "The Real Dirt"
JOHN E. CARROLL

The Real Dirt is an Inquiry course for first-year students just out of high school and arriving on the UNH campus for the first time. The course serves additionally as an orientation to the university farms and woodlands (College Woods Natural Area, Woodman Farm including the biodiesel facility, Campus Community Organic Farm, UNH Organic Dairy at Burley-Demerritt Farm, Kingman Farm and its U-DOO composting operations, and Fairchild Dairy Research Center); to the town (Durham Farmers' Market, Durham Marketplace); to the public transit system usable to get to the university farms (Campus Connector, Wildcat Transit); and to programs such as the Food and Society Initiative of the University Office of Sustainability, the New Hampshire Farm to School Program, and others.

Through field labs, class discussions, films, class guests, and readings, all focused on sustainable food and agriculture, students get an in-depth taste of the broader questions of ecological sustainability, especially surrounding food, with an intense focus on local and regional issues and circumstances. Real Dirt students, young and impressionable, are open at this stage to these experiences and ideas. They then have four years of residency (including as many as three thousand meals taken on campus and in Durham!), to put this course knowledge to use, and thereby to affect life and sustainability at UNH.

Academically grounded in six books, a dozen films, and class lectures and discussions, including the film, "The Real Dirt on Farmer John," for which the course is named, the students find themselves:

- Roaming the pastures with the Jersey cows, and comparing this experience to the conventional confinement herd of Holsteins in the dairy barns;
- Touring Durham Marketplace with its irrepressibly enthusiastic and successful owner, Chuck Cressy, whose business acumen and obvious commitment is not lost on the students;
- Visiting the farmer-vendors at the local farmers' market;
- Learning about the wonders of compost and its production, from

the dining halls to processing at the university's Kingman Farm to its
return to campus for many uses;

- Meeting student peers who run the Campus Community Organic
  Farm and the Organic Gardening Club, and learning how they can
  become a part of this enterprise;
- Touring College Woods Natural Area with a forester who has nearly
  half a century of experience with the nurturance and protection of this
  highly accessible, on-campus, old-growth forest and natural area;
- Recording their reactions to the annual UNH Fall Harvest Dinner and
  the many tastes to be experienced there, in addition to meeting the
  farmers who provide this gala meal;
- Learning about Project CREAM at the Fairchild Dairy Research Center from the faculty and students who are involved in that program;
- Learning about biodiesel and a host of horticultural experiments
  toward sustainability at Woodman Farm from Farm Manager John
  McLean.

And, perhaps more than anything else, Real Dirt students find themselves
constantly writing, and writing some more, about their many and wide-ranging experiences across the UNH Campus, and linking these experiences to
books, films, and class discussion in this very writing-intensive General Education Inquiry course. By semester's end, the students enrolled have a real
sense for "The Real Dirt."

Case Study: UNH CREAM
DREW CONROY AND PETER ERICKSON

Dr. Tom Fairchild, returning to teaching after years in UNH administration,
wanted to develop something new in education at the UNH Dairy Teaching
and Research Facility. He believed that one way to increase the number of
students involved in agriculture and the dairy farm on campus was to create
a program open to students in any major who wanted to gain experience in
animal care and management, provided they were willing the make the time
commitment required. The result was a course called CREAM (Cooperative
Real Education in Agriculture Management) that put students on the front
line for both management and operations of this on-campus facility.

The course has been very successful and has attracted students from
across campus. Some students enroll in CREAM to acquire the large-animal

experience necessary for veterinary school admission. Others, such as those from the business school, have come to gain experience in business and personnel management. Dairy students often enter the course thinking they already have all of the tools they need to be successful in managing a dairy farm. However, for dairy students, the management of student schedules, finances, and group dynamics are the critical skills they acquire.

CREAM is about bringing people together and working as a team. Early in the fall semester, students without dairy experience often feel overwhelmed by skills they must learn and the amount of information they are given in a short period of time in this course. Some students say the course feels like "boot camp" during the first few weeks, with feeding and milking shifts starting at 3:45 A.M. and then again at 3:00 P.M. In some ways, it is more like a job experience than a class. The experiential nature of CREAM forces students to incorporate what they learn daily, and by the semester's end, most are surprised at how much they have learned.

Challenges arise regularly for students working with the CREAM cows. The live-animal model forces students to engage with the course, as animals depend on them daily. Cow care and student accountability are critical. Students soon realize the importance of delegating tasks and communicating effectively with peers. These skills are emphasized in committee meetings and business meetings that occur weekly in the course. In addition there are weekly one- to two-hour education sessions, where students learn skills critical to the care and management of their herd.

At the end of the first semester, students are ready to go beyond chores and work together as a group to make changes and see successes of their own making. For example, in 2006, we started the year with a high somatic cell count (too many cows with mastitis). A student committee was formed, tasks were assigned (by the students), preliminary findings were reported, and the entire group then used this information in a business meeting to making decisions. Changes were made in the management of the cows, with positive results seen right away. Students used what they learned in courses such as anatomy and physiology, dairy cattle diseases, microbiology, management courses, statistics, and skills of persuasion to solve this problem. This is the epitome of CREAM. It is a capstone course that takes what students learn at UNH and puts them in a real-world situation. Students are not asked to regurgitate information. CREAM demands that students work as a group to face challenges and sometimes make difficult decisions. In this course, some of those decisions were life-and-death decisions (for a cow), which might have to be made at 4:00 A.M., before a full day of classes and other activities.

Peer grading is a critical part of this course, as the instructors cannot be at the farm to supervise every student over the course of the school year, in their seven-day-a-week job of feeding and caring for dairy cattle. Students grade each other in numerous areas, such as chores, committee meetings, business meetings, initiative, timeliness, and effort. Faculty advisors meet with each student to discuss peer grades and suggest ways to improve performance. However, student comments mean more than anything the faculty member could say.

For example, one classmate said this in her final evaluation of a peer: "I cannot begin to say how important she was to the class. She was clearly at the heart and soul of the class. She never complained, and was a hard worker." Another student summarized her performance like this: "Your drive and inquisitive nature are refreshing and added a lot to the CREAM classroom experience."

At the beginning of each year, students do not believe it when we tell them this course is more about managing people and learning business skills than it is about cows. By the end of the year, most agree that we were right. CREAM is about using a live-animal model to learn critical skills that could be applied anywhere in life.

Curriculum: Culture and Sustainability

In chapter 1, Tom Kelly rewords the question "What is sustainability" to "What sustains us." The emphasis on culture in the sustainability programs at UNH, as a fourth co-equal initiative, is a key part of the answer to that question. This focus broadens participation in the endeavor and engages a very diverse set of disciplines and programs. Community is key to sustainability, and so a wide range of activities and classes that build community contribute to sustainability at UNH.

The four cases presented in this section draw on a wide range of UNH experiences and demonstrate the diversity of initiatives that coalesce around the theme of sustainability. "The Promise of the Sun" was an interactive exhibit in the Student Union building that brought the potential and basic properties of solar energy and the cultural relationship of the Earth to the Sun into a well-frequented space. The confluence of sustainability and theater in the second case study emphasizes the power of writing and acting as tools for understanding human connections and motivations on questions of the environment, as well as the value of theater as a teaching tool. The University Dialogues are an important and innovative part of a sustainable university community. With a different focus each year, the Dialogue process emphasizes civil discourse and community consensus as a way forward in a complex and diverse organization. An academic program, the Minor in Sustainable Living, unifies the experience of the lifestyle with coursework that questions how we live and develops a "sustainability mindset."

Case Study: The Promise of the Sun
TOM KELLY

The Promise of the Sun was a public education exhibit on the potential of solar energy installed in the campus student union (Memorial Union Building or MUB) from 2000 to 2005. But it was much more than that. While undertaken and designed with educational goals clearly in mind, the exhibit was also a collective act of making public art, and so a linking of curriculum and culture.

The Promise of the Sun originated in a series of discussions in 1999 between the University Office of Sustainability, the Arts and Society Program, the Classics Program, and an Art History professor. Professors and students from

UOS and these academic programs were exploring collaborative possibilities for strengthening the cultural dimensions of sustainability on campus, and formed a small learning community to begin open-ended discussions on the nature of that collaboration.

Chapter 1 offers a reframing of the focus of the UNH sustainability program from "what is sustainability" to "what sustains us." That reframing brings the fine and performing arts to the forefront of the effort. As part of its Culture and Sustainability initiative, since 1999 the UOS has co-sponsored a broad range of cultural excursions and events, and developed other projects including the Ed and Mary Scheier film and exhibition (See the Culture and Sustainability section in chapter 5).

The collaboration with the Classics was also rooted in the questions of "what sustains us" and an interpretation of cultural inheritance. The classics program articulates this well on its website:

> To study the classics is to come into direct contact with the sources of Western civilization and culture, both pagan and Christian. An intimate knowledge of our Greco-Roman heritage furnishes students with historical, political, and aesthetic perspectives on the contemporary world and is part of a sound liberal arts education.

Just prior to these discussions, UOS had coordinated a successful grant application to the New Hampshire Governor's Office of Energy and Community Services to place a 1 kilowatt photovoltaic array on the roof of the MUB and to develop an educational exhibit associated with the array. This very quickly became the focus of our collaborative discussions, as it provided a concrete project with a need and opportunity for creative thinking and design. While the grant didn't require anywhere near the elaborate and complex exhibit that resulted, it provided an ideal vehicle for creative collaboration and an unusual and productive linkage among the arts, engineering, and campus operations.

The grant for the photovoltaic array included plans for the link between the array and the exhibit. The Campus Energy Office and a professor from Electrical Engineering designed a system with panel-tracking hardware to compare efficiency of fixed panels to a system that tracks the position of the Sun. Data were to be downloaded automatically to a hard drive and a graphic interface to display plots for live and archived data was designed in consultation with the Research Computing Center in the Institute for the Study of Earth, Oceans, and Space.

The question for sustainability and the liberal arts was how this array and the data would be framed and presented to achieve broader educational goals. A series of planning sessions and consultations throughout late 1999 and early 2000 produced a shared vision of a multimedia exhibit that would explore the relationship of the Earth and the Sun both physically and culturally. The group envisioned a museum-quality installation that would integrate images, text, surveys, and written materials; images would include the Sun in physical and mythical form; the exhibit would be organized around four areas:

- The solar context: exploring the relationship of the Earth and the Sun;
- The energy context: an exploration of our past and present energy decisions;
- Choices: exploring the individual and collective energy choices before us;
- Action: what we can and should do individually and collectively for sustainability and how those decisions will be made.

Ideally, the exhibit would engage visitors in a kind of Socratic dialogue within and across the four areas and connect ideas, data, and reasoning to action.

The decision was made to title the exhibit *The Promise of the Sun* and to incorporate the myth of Phaeton as one focal point of the exhibit. From the perspective of the Classics, the Phaeton myth offered not only a direct connection to the Sun (Phaeton's father was Apollo the Sun-god), but also presented the problem of irrevocable commitments; the absolute inability to alter a course of events even as it becomes clear that they are headed for tragedy. In the myth, Apollo promises to grant his son, born of a mortal mother, one wish of his heart's desire in order to prove to him that he, Apollo, is in fact Phaeton's father. Phaeton leaps at the chance and immediately asks to drive his father's chariot, the chariot that pulls the Sun across the sky from east to west. Notwithstanding Apollo's entreaties for his son to wish for something far less dangerous and more pleasurable, Phaeton refuses to change his mind, and the die is cast. Apollo is in an inescapable bind; by promising to grant *any* wish his son makes, he has made an unbreakable oath that even he, a god, could not revoke. When he grants Phaeton his wish, it ends in his son's tragic death.

The myth provides an opportunity to reflect on hubris, impulse, choices, and consequences. But *The Promise of the Sun* also communicated the great potential of harnessing the great energy of the Sun to meet our energy needs without making our own irrevocable oath, in the form of greenhouse gas concentrations, that ends in the tragedy of climate disruption and instability on a global scale.

The exhibit used enlarged images set on a black background under each of the four headings. The famous painting by Rubens depicting the fall of Phaeton along with a satellite photograph of the Sun were juxtaposed under the solar context. Under the energy context was a striking aerial photograph of the Seabrook Nuclear power plant, located some 20 miles from the UNH campus, surrounded by coastal wetlands. For choices, there was an image of the photovoltaic array on top of the MUB. For actions, it was a student riding a bicycle on campus.

Computer stations provided web-based explorations that were limited to the links built into the web portion of the design. Links were selected to provide publicly accessible background in each of the areas. For example, the climate context included links to the UNH Climate Change Research Center, continuous weather data from a campus-based weather station, and real-time incoming solar radiation from the roof of the MUB. The culture section provided links on the myth of Phaeton and the UNH Classics Department. Each section also included a link to a course offering that was particularly relevant including, for example, a team-taught course on an introduction to cosmology. The website also had a survey with questions spanning issues of the Earth and the Sun, climate, energy, myth, art, action, and activism. A number of large general education courses on myth also used the exhibit as part of the course and required all students to visit the MUB and take an online quiz that included questions dealing specifically with aspects of the exhibit. Also included were two coffeetable-size books on the Sun mounted on swivel bookstands.

It is difficult to assess the impact of the exhibit. It transformed a blank and aesthetically sterile wall into a panoramic display of the Sun, the Earth, the arts and sciences, and our sense of place. All were interwoven in a form that could be experienced visually and tactilely and that asked questions of the visitors, even those standing in line waiting for coffee who happened to glance over. The project succeeded in bringing together faculty, staff, and students from across colleges, departments, and disciplines in a single effort to manifest our commitment to education and sustainability in a very public way in a shared space. It also spawned an additional exhibit on climate and air quality in the lobby of the main campus library. The project created a very strong foundation for collaboration between the Classics and the University Office of Sustainability that continues to grow. It also allowed us to experience the virtue of humility so valued by the ancient Greeks. None of us had ever attempted to conceive, design, and sustain a public exhibit. It turns out to be a very complex undertaking that takes a sustained commitment of many kinds of resources.

*Case Study: Artistic Engagement — Discovering and Developing
a Theatrical Response to Sustainability*
DAVID KAYE

Theatre art at the University of New Hampshire often has been utilized by various departments and programs as an effective teaching and engagement tool. The Theatre Department's productions have served as a useful center point for symposiums, panel discussions, and lectures on topics related to politics, society, psychology, religion, and history.

A relationship between the Department of Theatre and Dance and the University Office of Sustainability (UOS) began when the UOS was approached to explore a sustainability connection to a symposium on U.S./Latin American relations, which itself had been catalyzed by a production of *De Donde?* by Mary Gallagher. The result was a lecture by Columbian scientist and environmental activist Guillermo Rodriguez on the urgent need to bring the world's attention to the rapid destruction of the Sierra Nevada region of Colombia, South America. Rodriguez served on a postperformance panel discussion linking the play's central immigration themes with the precarious state of the environment in Latin America. This effort was the beginning of a continuous exploration into the ways in which theater could be utilized to address more directly issues related to sustainability.

That exploration quickly revealed that virtually no appropriate plays have been published on sustainability issues. To deal with sustainability through theater, we were going to have to create our own scripts. At the time, an innovative professional theater company, The Underground Railway, based in Arlington, Massachusetts, was touring an original "eco-cabaret" to high schools and civic groups throughout the region. Founded in 1976 in Oberlin, Ohio, the company created new works to bring attention to the impact the ever-worsening environment would have on the social, political, and economic well-being of all the Earth's inhabitants. The company recognized that even the most serous topics, when brought to a group of people utilizing theater art, would be most effective if they took advantage of the art form's capacity to inform and provoke thought, while also being entertaining. In most cases, this meant infusing their work with as much humor as possible. To borrow a quote from the late great director Harold Clurman, "the truth is like castor oil. First you get them laughing, and when their mouths are open, you pour it in."

Excited by the quality of the company's work, the UOS suggested bringing in Wes Saunders, one of the group's co-founders and a passionate environmental activist, to conduct a workshop with UNH Theatre students. The goal would be to develop our own, UNH-specific "eco-cabaret." In 1999, twelve students took part in the one-week intensive workshop. Although everyone in the group had a strong interest in the overall goal of social justice, virtually none had any substantial knowledge of environmental issues and their effects on politics and society. Saunders needed to begin by creating a knowledge base within the group that would provide both factual information and artistic inspiration.

To this end, he based the workshop around Anita Gordon and David Suzuki's book *It's a Matter of Survival*. By describing what the world may look like in the year 2040, this text provided a working understanding of the fundamental material, while stimulating the artistic imagination through its story-telling format. In addition to discussions and theatrical explorations of the ideas revealed in the book, Saunders also guided the group through various exercises geared to give a more visceral understanding of the crucial issues at hand. These included such drills as requiring each individual in the group to carry a trash bag at all times in order to collect and examine the amount of garbage generated during the week.

What created the greatest impact, though, were theater exercises where the group explored the reality of human existence in an America transformed by environmental catastrophe. These were improvisational exercises where the students made connections among issues related to the environment and sustainability and the world of human behavior. This offered the opportunity to move beyond talking about these issues to actually experiencing them. By the end of the week, the group had generated a collection of monologues, sketches, and songs in the eco-cabaret style. These pieces, all related to sustainability issues, directly connected to the life of a UNH student. Some of this work found its way into a play performed yearly as part of freshman orientation. The most notable outcome of the week-long intensive, however, was the deep impact it had on the workshop participants. By going through the theater-based exercise related to these powerful issues, every member of the group was profoundly changed. We had become passionate standard bearers for a sustainable future because we had actually *lived* a possible outcome to our future.

Over time, the original student workshop transformed into "WildActs," a student Social Justice Theatre Troupe. While continuing to work in the traditional theatrical model, the group experimented with methods and techniques to stimulate dialogue and action through interactive experience. Starting with "forum theater," where the audience works with the actors to confront problems, we also incorporated psychodramatic techniques. Here, the audience was given the opportunity to delve actively into the motivated behavior of the characters in a scenario. The major obstacle that continually presented itself was how to utilize this evolving process specifically for use in addressing issues of sustainability and possibly to stimulate environmental activism. Our techniques, as we discovered, relied on clearly defined human relationships. Members of the audience were able to participate in the action on the stage because they could identify with the roles being played and the relationships that arose as they entered into conflict. Everything worked well when applied to social issues like intolerance toward difference or gender bias. Here, it was easy to identify the various roles (oppressor and oppressed) and to isolate the basic conflict (confronting gender bias in a department meeting, for example). But who is the "oppressor" when dealing with sustainability issues? If an honest exploration of relationships is where the technique is most effective, who are the players in this relationship?

In 2002, UNH hosted the first Northeast Bioneers Conference. This was a golden opportunity to apply our exploratory work if we could solve the one remaining obstacle: How can we translate these environmental issues into the world of human relationships? We finally struck upon three basic structures: the Environmental Hypocrite (two characters in conflict within the same person, causing self-oppression); the helpless or incapacitated environmental activist (oppressed by the inability to effect change within his or her immediate circle of relationships); and activists in conflict (the relationship between a group striving for change and the oppressive role of a more powerful, entrenched group resisting change). For all the structures, the WildAct student troupe created short plays, devised to establish the roles, relationships, and issues to be explored with the audience. For the Bioneers Conference, we chose to investigate the "helpless activist" because of the "coalition-building" theme. The playlet featured a simple scenario: a UNH student trying to convince her roommates to leave their cars at home and use the university's free public transportation system. The playlet was structured so that the protagonist eventually is dominated by the "antisustainability" forces and eventually surrenders. At several points during the scenario, characters would stop the action of the play and speak their inner thoughts to the audience. This allowed all the characters to express their frustrations, confusion, and overall reaction to what was occurring. After the playlet concluded, the workshop participants were able to ask the characters questions and eventually the scene was replayed with audience members making suggestions or actually taking the place of the actors and playing the roles themselves. The end result was a dynamic experiential event that gave all the participants a chance to rehearse for the future of coalition building within their immediate circle of friends and family.

Exploration and expansion of this work has continued, including a presentation at the Association for Theatre in Higher Education (ATHE) national conference in 2004. This work has also led to the development of full-length plays. Although these have not dealt directly with issues of sustainability, they have always connected indirectly. For example, a play we created in 2006 delved into the Palestinian/Israeli conflict. The initial interactive theatrical explorations focused on how water may be the key to what either brings these peoples together or what completely destroys them. WildActs continues to develop these techniques as applied to environmental and other issues and now actively seeks opportunities to train other groups and individuals in this process.

Case Study: The University Dialogue and a Sense of Place
JOANNE CURRAN-CELENTANO

"What is the impact of agricultural subsidies on the global distribution of food?"

"Am I supposed to want to buy a more expensive t-shirt?"

"How can we participate in creating and sustaining a democracy when the information we get from the media is so confusing and inaccurate?"

These are just some of the questions posed by students as a part of the University Dialogue, one component of the Discovery Program at the University of New Hampshire. This annual program commenced in 2005 to engage the entire campus community in a big question or issue of importance. With particular attention to our newest members of the scholarly community, our first-year students, we position the question in a way that will encourage serious consideration across all aspects of campus life. Globalization, energy, democracy, and poverty are topics that have thus far come to life.

The University Dialogue is designed to increase the deliberative capacity of our campus community, to teach, learn, and generate knowledge about the arts, skills, and habits of democracy. Ultimately, our Dialogue becomes a venue for education in democratic principles of justice, equity, and freedom and in democratic practices of inclusive dialogue, public reasoning, shared governance, conflict transformation, and collaborative policymaking and action.

Faculty members across disciplines are selected to share their understanding on the chosen theme in a position paper. Selected papers are produced into a monograph that serves as a common text for a variety of conversations in and out of class. Surrounding programming connects students with the authors for movie discussions, simulations, book groups, and forums. Each year's dialogue culminates with a simulation of a New England–style town hall meeting where the authors and students explore the challenges posed to our community and the lessons learned throughout the year. This year, the Honors Student Advisory Board requested that student essays be added to the monograph and they will play a primary role in the culminating events.

The centrality of sustainability on our campus is observed clearly in the University Dialogue. Each year's theme resonates with our campus identity and affords linkage across campus — issues of sustainability on and off campus are naturally included. For example, the inaugural year featured the theme, "Where in the World is UNH: A University Dialogue on Globalization." Our Chief Sustainability Officer was a featured dialogue author and organizer of programming throughout the year on the impact of globalization on human rights, ecological security, and infectious disease, to name a few. Events included a forum on sexually transmitted disease in global perspective, as well as a play entitled "The Palestinian," in which we confront our own beliefs, prejudices, sympathies, and fears with the realities of Palestinian life. This play was written collaboratively by the student actors and the director, David Kaye, Professor of Theatre at UNH.

In the 2007–2008 academic year, the Dialogue was "We Hold These Truths: A University Dialogue on Democracy." With presidential primary season in full force, it was a great time to be at UNH.

In a short time, the University Dialogue has become a part of the UNH culture, spurring programming around democracy, sustainability, and responsibility for our choices. The Dialogue is introduced at the Academic Convocation and is highlighted by a special display at the University Museum. Themes are coordinated with activities at the students' Memorial Union and with other campus centers and speaker series on campus. The University Writing Center and First-Year Composition Committee use the Dialogue theme for student writing and are organizing a student award based on their engagement and writing. Co-sponsoring events with the many opportunities for students, faculty, and staff helps to create a University Dialogue that illuminates issues and questions important to our sustainable community.

Case Study: How the Sustainable Living Minor Came to Be
ROBERT ECKERT AND BERT COHEN

In the late spring of 1993, a group of twenty dedicated faculty, staff, and administrators including Bill Mautz, dean of the College of Life Sciences and Agriculture, and a few people from other communities met in a classroom to discuss the idea of sustainability and what it might mean for UNH. The first author had called the meeting, and interest and enthusiasm was so great that we were all energized to move forward. Several other meetings followed and workshops gave birth to a strong grassroots effort to make sustainability happen on campus. Donella Meadows came to UNH and delivered a talk. Later she e-mailed the organizer:

Community is the essence of sustainability. We ARE in the same community. It was exciting and inspiring to me to see what you all are putting together at UNH. I could feel the potential and the power in the room. Dana

He printed this message and mounted it on his office wall, and will always treasure it, especially since she is no longer with us.

There was, and continues to be, dialogue and debate about how best to teach sustainability at a university. While infusing sustainability across the curriculum is one of the most effective solutions for reaching the most people, the faculty in the Department of Natural Resources felt that benefits would come in establishing a minor that contained courses that would foster dialogue about what we mean by sustainability, provide experiential opportunities, and offer methods and tools for measuring sustainability. Furthermore, it seemed imperative that a systematic method for thinking holistically about the world become a critical component of the minor in sustainable living.

To this end, we developed two courses: Sustainable Living and Systems Thinking for Sustainable Living. Both courses begin by building a strong functional learning community. Through them, students are urged to acquire a "sustainability mindset," components of which include the ability to use systems thinking, while being academically grounded and ethically motivated. We work to achieve the sustainability mindset in our students using multiple techniques for teaching, including mini-lectures, base-group and whole-group dialogue and discussion, an author's night where students interact with the authors of the texts we use, and field trips to homes and institutions pursuing sustainable living.

In the Sustainable Living class, students examine their own ecological footprint by collecting data on their use of resources, explore the power of money in their lives by examining the real costs and real income generated by their means of support, and study their relationship to nature by various techniques used by professional naturalists to blend in with nature. The Systems Thinking for Sustainable Living course focuses on system dynamics as a method for holistic thinking. Students diagram increasingly complex situations using causal loop diagrams while searching for leverage points for change. By seeing and making connections using this approach, students learn a systems language that enhances their ability to understand complex interactions and to convey this information to others. Our approach uses several systems games, including the *FishBanks* game mentioned in the Climate and Energy section of this chapter.

We know that both immediate and long-term feedback provides us with information from which we can learn. In addition to in-class feedback and evaluation practices, we also have instituted annual Sustainability Course Alumni gatherings each spring. Students from any year may attend and we always have a session where students provide feedback on their lives and activities and how the courses influenced their lives. Some of the stories are amazing. We are gratified that many alums use the principles we teach to make life choices, including decisions to buy smaller homes, live close to work, or have fewer children. Those who are teaching use many of the topics and some of the methods we demonstrated in class in their own classrooms.

These two sustainability courses supply 8 of the 23 credits required for the minor. Other courses support the following categories of focus in the minor: general ecological knowledge, current issues, student interest/competency, and an internship experience in sustainability. By taking the minor in Sustainable Living, students gain a solid basis for understanding and evaluating sustainability issues and other kinds of complex problems. They gain practical experience, and, we hope, develop a sustainability mindset.

CHAPTER 3

Practicing Sustainability

Campus Operations

Douglas Bencks

A university campus is an ideal context for practicing sustainability. It is a city that must deal with all of the day-to-day complexities of urban activities in a setting that places a high value on the landscape and ecology of its place. It provides the stimulating energy of a city with the calming harmony of verdant open space. And it is all under the control of a single property owner. Because the university is a massive employer as well as housing and meal provider, we have the opportunity and responsibility to demonstrate best operational practices at a scale that has regional significance. When done well, these sustainable practices yield both educational lessons and environmental benefits for the greater community as well as internal economic savings.

Most of the challenges of achieving truly sustainable practices stem from the risks of change, a tendency to cling to the familiarity of day-to-day routines, and the fear that the new will be more costly to operate then the status quo. For the University of New Hampshire, these challenges are tempered by a long-standing culture of frugality and doing more with less that lends itself quite well to being sustainable. Sustainability fits the New England tradition of pragmatic, principled use of the resources available, focusing on the local community to enrich the lives of all. By identifying the opportunities that best fit our circumstances, the university has taken best advantage of its limited financial capacity through successful public-private collaborations, aggressive solicitation of public agency support, and strong state-community interaction in peer and intergovernmental groups.

PHOTO: The EcoLine connects methane gas produced from a local landfill with the university's co-generation plant. When completed, most of the university's heat and electricity will be provided by this renewable energy resource. *Photo courtesy of UNH Photographic Services.*

Concomitantly, we must keep in mind the future generations of students and faculty, as well as those who are here today. The physical campus is an important legacy that has been handed down to us to nurture and in turn we must serve as careful stewards, ensuring a robust and efficient set of systems for future operations. This requires a very holistic approach to planning, design, and operations of all aspects of the campus environment.

As we have developed and refined our own sustainable practices, we have come to understand that in many ways being a sustainable campus means remembering the approaches that were embedded in the means and methods that first formed this campus and guided its development up until World War II. Using local materials, using the most advanced and energy-efficient process, making things that endure and are simple to maintain, and forming a campus with visual meaning are the principles that they applied and that are so relevant today. Over the past twenty years, we have gradually reintroduced these principles with new practices in campus energy, transportation, food, building design, water management, and land planning so that we are on a solid course in our long-term stewardship of the campus.

One aspect of this broad array illustrates the challenge and the approach to sustainability that we use at the University of New Hampshire.

Colleges and universities see themselves as part of a very long lineage of great thinkers, experimenters, and scholars and they expect to sustain this tradition indefinitely. This implies that a campus should project visually this continuity of past to future. The strategic plan needs to include the visual identity of the school, and this is certainly true of any campus, like ours, that grew up in the early twentieth century. Like it or not, the image of the campus is a significant aspect of how the public, our peers, and our potential faculty and students perceive the school. And so the design of the campus and individual buildings should reflect the institution and its locale.

Architecture is the most public, social, and in the wrong hands, most dangerous of the arts. The fact that it has to be useful and be part of a community means that it can't simply be a personal artistic statement about a moment in time. It needs to be enduring, adaptable, high performance in the way it functions, efficient, and engaging. We should embrace the past by respecting the traditional building, and we have to find the best ways to have the new ones fit into this context while not imitating the old, but rather looking forward. Architecture critic Robert Campbell refers to the challenge this way:

> There is no energy in architecture if it is only a memory of the past. There is no energy if it is only an invention. I find that the connection between memory and

invention has been severed in our culture. Either people hate modernism and love everything old — and that's by far the majority — or they think it's boring to imitate the past and everything should be new and daring . . . My own definition of architecture is the art of making places for human habitation. To truly appreciate architecture you must inhabit it and experience it as a place. But it is critical to understand that architecture provides us with reassurance of stability, and we ask that it not change too quickly because it is a language of conventions. It is only through the meaning of a conventional language that architecture can reinforce a sense of place and time.

For our campus to have meaning, our construction projects must respect the architectural conventions of what exists, but allow room for fresh and careful inventiveness that feels like it belongs. This same thinking is how the University of New Hampshire has to approach all aspects of campus sustainability. It is essential to understand and respect tradition and culture, while designing a campus that works well. As this is done, the university moves into using new systems and fresh approaches that fit within the existing culture and framework.

This chapter explores some of the most exciting new endeavors that the University of New Hampshire has undertaken in the areas of campus energy and transportation, and it looks at the sustainability principles, structure, and processes we have established across all aspects of campus operations — engaging students in energy efficiency, using locally produced foods in our dining halls, managing our landscape, formulating a public art program, making land-use decisions, designing buildings, and measuring our impacts and our progress. This has happened gradually, but we now have a solid footing for further opportunities, as we learn from our successes and our mistakes along the way.

Our efforts reach into almost every facet of university life, as we are continually reminded how intertwined is our puzzle of sustainability. Sometimes we are inclined to move cautiously, others times more boldly, always striving to have long-term stewardship of the campus be our guide.

Operations: Biodiversity and Ecosystems

The landscape of the University of New Hampshire is an essential and attractive part of the campus environment. At the same time, our campus is a thriving small city, with eighteen thousand students, faculty, staff, and visitors on the grounds every day. We provide the infrastructure, residences, and services that support the diverse activities that constitute any city, with the important difference that this is a city with a single property owner that determines the physical and social conditions within its boundaries. Managing this city in the landscape means constantly weighing the operational needs of its people against the vitality of the landscape that makes it such a special place. In this way, our campus is a small-scale representation of the land-use pressures that now occur regionally and nationally. We serve as an example, good or bad, for addressing the issues of land use and landscape development.

We have in place a comprehensive Campus Master Plan that guides our land-use priorities and decisions and a Landscape Master Plan that is a road map to how we care for and develop our land. The university has undertaken several focused sustainable-landscape improvement projects with mixed results, and we have come to appreciate how critical perceptions and expectations are to the success of such projects.

For example, when we built our new Environmental Technology Building in 1999, the project included the creation of a large area of new successional woodlands adjacent to the building. This shaggy-looking area was perceived as unsightly for the first five years and so it was necessary to have interpretive signs explaining that it wasn't a case of neglect. The same was true for the meadow grasses between the building and the existing wetlands, which are an appropriate sustainable landscape for this location, rather than the typical manicured lawn. Today, these landscapes have been accepted, but we still have to be cautious in how we adopt these approaches in other parts of campus.

We also find it important to put our current circumstances into a historical perspective. Through the mid-1800s, forests in southern New England were being converted to croplands, pastures, and orchards, until only 25 percent remained wooded. With agricultural abandonment, the forests have returned to cover nearly 75 percent of the land area.

Our campus has seen a similar progression. In the 1890s, the land willed by Ben Thompson for the formation of the New Hampshire College of Agriculture and Mechanical Arts (the predecessor of the University of New

Hampshire) was stripped of almost all of its trees. Through periods of rapid expansion and quiescence, characterizing university growth across the country, the campus landscape has matured into an attractive park-like form in which a tight, walkable core-campus environment is combined with a wonderful mix of the collegiate and native landscapes throughout.

This section will focus on some of our biggest successes, including our structure and process for dealing with land-use decisions and our landscape master plan that lays a solid path for nurturing and enhancing our campus environment. But we also recognize that we have had our share of setbacks as well, as the story of the MUB meadow shows.

Case Study: Landscape Master Plan
DOUGLAS BENCKS

Planning, designing, and managing a sustainable campus landscape requires blending goals for biodiversity and aesthetics with the working needs of the university community. As with buildings, a landscape design is sustainable only when it addresses environmental issues as well as the long-term functional and aesthetic expectations of the campus community. At UNH, the goal of preserving the traditional character of the grounds is balanced with the need to develop and maintain the campus landscape in an ecologically sound manner — a complex undertaking!

The university has developed a Landscape Master Plan that provides a holistic frame of reference for the design and management of the campus landscape by establishing design guidelines and landscape standards that foster sustainable design and management practices. To ensure continuity, the Landscape Master Plan is founded upon the same planning principles that guided the development of the overall Campus Master Plan. These principles are all based on tenets of sustainable design and management. These principles are described in the following paragraphs.

Express the academic vision of the university. Landscape design and open-space planning strive to improve the appearance and general condition of the university grounds to facilitate the recruitment and retention of an exceptional and diverse faculty, staff, and student body. We recognize the landscape as an important educational resource and teaching tool fundamental to the successful fulfillment of the university's land grant mission. Open-space planning recognizes the crucial role that the campus grounds serve in sustaining a healthy and biodiverse community.

Support the daily life of the university. Campus open space needs to be designed to foster social interaction. Accommodations shall be made for a variety of uses ranging from large gathering spaces to small niches that facilitate casual encounters and quiet contemplation. Outdoor recreation areas shall be designed to accommodate multiple uses. Outdoor areas shall be designed to accommodate active, scheduled recreation as well as spontaneous activities. The campus landscape shall be enriched by the placement of appropriately scaled sculpture and public artwork.

Preserve the New England character of the built and natural campus. Landscape design strives to reinforce the unique and authentic character of the regional landscape, incorporating the use of local building materials and native plant species whenever feasible. Open-space planning and design strives to strengthen the campus's unique sense of place by reinforcing the image of a small New England liberal arts college, preserving campus woodlands and groves, and reconnecting fragmented habitats and restoring degraded ecosystems. Open-space planning and landscape design shall foster the development of a "walking campus" by reinforcing existing circulation patterns and strengthening pedestrian connections that are poorly defined.

Strengthen the relationship with our communities. Landscape design shall enhance the quality and character of campus edges. Landscaping, signage, lighting, and other site amenities shall be used to enrich the interface between campus and community and minimize adverse impacts on adjacent neighborhoods. Campus gateways shall be defined clearly and enhanced with landscape treatments that are inviting and announce arrival. Open-space planning shall strive for the development of outdoor spaces, such as hiking trails, which serve all members of the Durham community, residents and students alike.

Regional influences and the character of the landscape define a sustainable strategy. The campus is a microcosm of the larger region incorporating the towering white pines and the rugged outcrops that recall the mountains; the pastures, corn fields, barns, and orchards reflecting images common to the river valleys; and the marshes and wetlands reminiscent of coastal inlets and waterways. When assimilated, these images collectively define the unique character of the campus landscape. These are great teaching tools as well as images that define the campus.

Woodlands, meadows and farm fields constitute a major portion of the campus open-space system. These open spaces serve an important environmental, social, and recreational role on campus. They are also valuable educational resources and are highly valued as formal teaching laboratories and outdoor classrooms. It is important that they are protected from undue encroachment.

Gateways, streetscapes, roads and walkways, and bike facilities are the essential components of access and mobility that must be handled carefully and sensitively in the framework of the walking campus concept. The Campus Master Plan calls for the eventual displacement of many parking lots in the core campus, but solutions must maintain a balance between parking demands and open-space considerations.

Campus quadrangles are well-defined areas enclosed on three or more sides by academic or residential buildings. They represent one of the basic building blocks for defining campus open space, especially in the dense academic core. The well-defined character of a quadrangle strengthens its perception as an outdoor room. Consequently, quadrangles are expected to accommodate a multitude of active and passive uses, including social functions such as weekly barbecues and annual alumni receptions.

Campus courtyards are important campus open spaces. They serve as social hubs and "urban stages" upon which the drama of university life is played out. They are areas where social gathering and interaction occur. They should be spatially well-defined and flexible in design to accommodate a variety of events ranging in scale from political rallies and protests to solitary retreats. Courtyards should be designed and detailed to a pedestrian scale and are most successful when the automobile is excluded.

Campus lawns serve a multitude of aesthetic, cultural, and environmental roles. Flowing freely around buildings and through open spaces, lawns create a sense of balance and harmony among diverse campus spaces. Cultivating large expanses of turf is expensive and can entail runoff of fertilizers and pesticides that may contaminate surface and groundwater. On the other hand, lawns, like trees and other plants, help minimize soil erosion, trap dust particles, filter and purify water, and moderate surface temperature and humidity.

Campus gardens are developed with restraint and require a long-term maintenance plan that ensures their vitality. Gardens offer opportunities to reinforce the region's unique sense of place by creating pockets of natural habitat that enhance biodiversity on campus. Generally preference is given to the use of native plants and a maintenance regimen that fosters natural succession.

Landscape Design Guidelines establish a framework for a sustainable strategy. These guidelines build upon the campus's rich design heritage by emphasizing simplicity, balance, and ecological sensitivity. The Landscape Design Guidelines are principle-based, founded on the tenets of sustainability and the belief that landscapes should be managed, not simply maintained. They are flexible and allow for contemporary expression. Long-term management considerations must be weighted equally with issues of aesthetics and sustainability. These guidelines are divided into three parts:

- **Landscape Preservation.** A set of specific policies are delineated in the Landscape Master Plan to protect the campus landscape before, during, and after construction. Construction envelopes contain the construction activity, minimize utility impacts, preserve topsoil, and restore soil that is compacted during construction, and provide tree and root protection.
- **Landscape Restoration.** The university takes a proactive position with respect to the restoration of degraded landscapes, streams, and wildlife habitats. Reconnecting the fragmented landscape, stream restoration, habitat restoration, and tree and plant management are all important elements of the restoration.
- **Landscape Enhancement.** These enhancements are meant to inform the general planning and standard site-design policies and procedures. Adherence to the guidelines will ensure the development of an attractive and cohesive campus incorporating accessibility, safety, seating, stairs, walls, fences, grading, drainage.

While this comprehensive plan has given us a road map for a sustainable landscape, it has been very challenging to put in place the design, construction, and operational practices that execute this plan. When doing an individual building project with a limited area of landscaping, there is still a strong tendency to think within the boundaries of the construction, rather than holistically. Operationally, old habits die hard, and the people who are responsible for the day-to-day maintenance and care of the landscape often feel these ideas are imposed upon them and that more resources, equipment, and staffing are necessary to keep up with these sustainable approaches. Finding the right balance, the training, and above all the commitment to a truly sustainable approach to the landscape are key to the progress we have made so far, and hope to make in the future.

Case Study: Land Use Committee
TOM LEE

The University of New Hampshire owns and manages more than three thousand acres of agricultural and undeveloped land, much of it donated by friends and supporters and by owners hoping for long-term conservation of lands they value. How should UNH inventory, manage and, occasionally, dispose of these holdings in ways that support the campus commitment to sustainability?

Management

For the first century of the institution's existence in Durham, agricultural and undeveloped properties were managed by the appropriate academic units. By the late 1970s, the university's farmland was managed by the College of Life Sciences and Agriculture (COLSA), in consultation with the COLSA departments that used these lands for research, teaching, and outreach.

Forested lands, or those in early stages of forest succession and not used for agriculture, also were managed by COLSA. For the first half of the twentieth century, these lands were used for teaching and research, but were also harvested for wood products, providing a source of revenue to COLSA and for certain scholarship funds. By the 1970s, all UNH forest lands were managed day-to-day by two Woodlands Managers, graduate students who received a half-time stipend for their efforts, and who were advised by a Woodlands Committee, composed of knowledgeable faculty and staff, mainly from the natural resource fields. Timber management was conducted on a sustained-yield basis using methods that would not reduce land capability. However, a full inventory of resources was never completed, and sustainability of nontimber resources, particularly nongame biodiversity, was not evaluated routinely.

In addition to the focus on timber and selected wildlife, some of the university's undeveloped forest lands were perceived as having unique biological or geological value for education, research, and outreach, and these were set aside as natural areas. In the early 1960s, a group of faculty made a compelling argument for the permanent protection of a roughly 60-acre portion of the College Woods, adjacent to the core campus area, which harbored eastern white pine and eastern hemlock trees that were very large and quite old (greater than 250 years). In 1962, the College Woods Natural Area was established and human disturbance was prohibited. Three other natural areas, similarly restricted, have been established since 1962. These areas exist only by decision of the USNH Board of Trustees and thus their protected status could be changed at any time.

In the late 1970s, a Natural Areas Committee was established to advise the Woodlands Office on policy for the four natural areas. In the 1990s, the Natural Areas Committee was merged with the Woodlands Committee, to produce the Committee on Woodlands and Natural Areas. The Woodlands Office became the Office of Woodlands and Natural Areas.

As the four UNH natural areas made up less than 10 percent of the university's forested lands, the vast majority of these lands continued to be managed by COLSA's Office of Woodlands and Natural Areas for wood products and wildlife, as well as education, research, and recreation. Faculty, staff, and students were encouraged to use these UNH properties for courses and research projects, and simply were asked to fill out a use form and have the request approved by the Woodlands Office before proceeding. These lands were used by dozens of UNH courses, and research conducted on them generated numerous graduate theses, undergraduate papers, and scholarly publications. Between 1950 and 2000, each of the fifteen forested parcels located within a half-hour's drive of Durham was used for research, coursework, or both, and each experienced at least one major timber harvest. The more remote parcels were used less intensively, but between 1950 and 2000, timber harvesting occurred on nearly all them.

Inventory: A Mandate to Review Undeveloped Lands

By the mid-1990s, COLSA's Woodlands Office was managing twenty-eight properties containing over three thousand acres of forested land. While the Woodlands Managers and COLSA administrators, as well as many COLSA faculty and staff, were cognizant of the day-to-day uses of these tracts, others in the UNH community including the USNH Board of Trustees were less aware of these activities. In the late 1990s, the USNH Board wondered if some outlying properties might serve the university better if they were sold. (Concern about UNH lands was heightened when an abutter informed the university that it owned a 140-acre tract in the Ossipee Mountains; the university had not been aware of this parcel.) The trustees asked the university to review its undeveloped lands, and the UNH administration responded by making a list of all UNH-owned lands, with each parcel ranked by its apparent value to the university. In 1999, the Society for the Protection of New Hampshire Forests was asked to review the land list, assess the conservation value of each parcel, and make recommendations about disposition, should UNH elect to divest itself of some of these properties.

UNH also created a three-tiered system of committees to assess and review land holdings. The Committee on Woodlands and Natural Areas (CWNA) advises the Woodland Managers on day-to-day management of forested lands. The Advisory Committee on Land and Property Use (ACLPU), populated by knowledgeable faculty and staff, interacts with the Woodlands Committee about land-use issues and informs the university administration through its interaction with a new group, the Committee on Real Property Acquisition and Disposal (CRPAD). This last committee, chaired by the Vice President of Finance and Administration, has the final say on land use and disposition, and includes administrators and faculty with expertise and interest in land issues.

In 2001, the university initiated a natural-resource assessment of its undeveloped forested land, beginning with those farthest from campus. The ACLPU recognized that a comprehensive field evaluation would be prohibitively expensive and time consuming. Instead, working with UNH Cooperative Extension and friends of the university, this group adopted the Biological Timber Inventory (BioTimber Inventory, or BTI) as the primary instrument of natural-resource assessment.

Developed by the Society for the Protection of New Hampshire Forests, BTI uses a field survey to obtain information about forest structure, wildlife, disturbance history, plant biodiversity, invasive plants, and historical and cultural features (such as cellar holes and old cemeteries) and then uses a GIS (geographical information system) to combine these data with information obtained from the state's GRANIT database. The latter information included bedrock geology, watersheds, soil types, and groundwater resources. For each property, field data were used to define "land types" and "management units," and these units as well as data on each of the individual resources (soil, wildlife sign, etc.) were mapped using GIS. Finally, a stewardship plan was written for each property. Stewardship plans interpret the data generated from field BTI and GIS, but include information obtained from other sources. Deed information, history of previous ownership, and the history of land use prior to UNH were obtained from historical records at town offices and from the UNH Office of Woodlands and Natural Areas. The history of use by UNH for research, teaching, and resource extraction (mainly logging) was obtained from the Office of Woodlands and Natural Areas and individual faculty and staff. Stewardship plans also included extensive recommendations for forest and wildlife management written by UNH Cooperative Extension staff. These contributors reviewed the BTI data on forest composition structure and wildlife and in many cases actually visited the sites to make additional observations.

The result of this natural-resource assessment process is a set of fifteen stewardship plans for managing forests and wildlife. While the incomplete nature of the biological inventories and lack of detailed information on aquatic ecosystems were real limitations of these documents, the stewardship plans provided an excellent starting point for decisions about land disposition as well as future stewardship and management by UNH or subsequent owners. The Office of Woodlands and Natural Areas uses the plans routinely in making management decisions. Faculty and students have made use of the plans for developing research projects and class exercises.

Disposal: Evaluation of Properties

Based on these stewardship plans, the university groups ranked eight of the outlying properties relative to the university's mission, as well as its value for conservation or other uses. An evaluation matrix was developed that graded each property based on deed restrictions; accessibility from UNH; actual and potential value for teaching, research, outreach, and recreation; conservation value; human history and cultural features; potential economic value; threats from adjacent lands; approximate market value; and potential buyers.

Based on the matrix analysis, the University recommended that five properties be retained by UNH and that three be sold. Given the high conservation value ascribed to these three parcels, it was recommended that an effort be made to convey these parcels to conservation organizations.

The Future

While considerable progress has been made in using an ecosystem approach to evaluate and manage UNH forest lands, much more still needs to be done. A number of properties have not yet been inventoried. Wetland and aquatic communities are particularly poorly known, but even forested and open lands lack complete animal, plant, and microbe inventories. Lack of funding is the major impediment to completing this work. The university can only be sure that it is managing its undeveloped properties sustainably if the biological diversity on these lands is well documented and monitored.

Case Study: The MUB Meadow
JOHN L. HART

Meadow Found Guilty in Wildflower Trial
— must serve ten to fifteen years as lawn —

The campus landscape has always served as classroom and laboratory for numerous courses in a variety of departments and colleges, including art, biology, botany, environmental conservation, forestry, horticulture, and water resources. The landscape is also the fundamental environment within which the buildings, infrastructure, and human community exist and interact on a daily basis. As such, the campus landscape has great potential as an all-encompassing living tool to demonstrate and educate in such areas as natural systems, bioregional concepts, and sustainable design and practice. This is one of the founding principles of campus botanical gardens and arboreta.

In 1995 at UNH, this took form as the New England Ecological Garden, conceived by a group of interested educators as a campus botanic garden based on plant communities and plant/environment/human interrelationships and interactions. The idea was to strengthen the role of the campus landscape in university education, research, and outreach, and also to help move the management and maintenance of the landscape to more sustainable practices. With a generous establishing grant from the UNH Parents' Association, the seed germinated and struggled to life.

With the advent of the Office of Sustainability Programs in 1997, the concept of landscape as teaching laboratory grew rapidly and blossomed in a number of landscape projects. Tom Kelly, the first Director of the Office of Sustainability Programs, envisioned an efficient and sustainable campus community where "everything is curriculum, and everyone is an educator." Buildings became classrooms for energy efficiency, water conservation, recycling, display of art; transportation on campus began to demonstrate visibly the values of mass transit, car-pooling, biking, and reduction of automobiles in the core campus; likewise, an energetic effort was made to move campus grounds management to more sustainable practice and to utilize the landscape more broadly as an educational tool.

One of the first in-the-ground landscape projects attempted was the restoration of a one-acre terraced slope — essentially a construction zone — adjacent to a recent expansion of the Memorial Union Building (the MUB), the student center on campus. Installation of standard lawn on the site by landscape contractors had failed twice in as many seasons with as many contractors and as many lawsuits.

The original design for the slope called for an amphitheater, with a series of retaining walls and grass walkways falling away from the building. When retaining walls were felled by the cost axe, they were replaced on the fly by an alternating series of level areas and 45-degree slopes, all to be seeded to lawn. However, there was no money for topsoil, and a 45-degree slope of lawn is far beyond recommended specifications for maintenance, erosion, stability, and runoff. Two contractors had failed to establish an acceptable lawn. The slopes were eroding, compacted, sparsely vegetated, bare in many places, and dominated by crabgrass.

This was an opportunity to educate about the effort and expense of turfgrass lawns, and the cost effectiveness, ecological function, and aesthetic interest of alternative solutions, especially on a difficult site such as this. The design team proposed a trial to evaluate different levels of site preparation, species mixes, and maintenance regimes. Campus Planning, Design/Construction, Facilities Services, Grounds and Roads — all signed on with varying levels of enthusiasm but with an apparent willingness to try something different, and at a very reduced price.

The final design called for a number of different treatments (site prep, species, and maintenance) from the bottom of the slope to the top:

1. At the bottom of the slope and on the best soil, the standard turfgrass mix would be planted (Kentucky bluegrass, creeping fescue, and perennial rye), requiring fertilization, liming, irrigation if possible, mowing on a weekly basis, and pest control as needed.
2. Next, a mix of dwarf turfgrasses recently introduced to the market, needing fertilization, irrigation, pest control, but much-reduced mowing.
3. Above that, a mix of more rugged grasses, primarily tall fescues (6"), needing no fertilization, no irrigation, no pest control, and much-reduced mowing.
4. Next, little bluestem, a taller native grass at 12" to 18", with no maintenance needs beyond an annual mowing to keep trees and shrubs down.
5. And at the top of the slope, near the building, a native mixed herbaceous meadow, needing no maintenance at all, save an annual or biennial mowing.

The overarching concepts were to derive a financial comparison of the relative costs (time, energy, labor, chemicals, water, equipment, etc.) of lawns when compared to a number of native and lower-maintenance alternatives, and to provide a strong visual demonstration of the diversity and beauty of a more natural groundcover (meadow, native grasses) when compared to the common lawn. To support these concepts, there were discussions with Grounds and Roads on maintenance regimes, articles in the staff and student newspapers on the project, meetings with building staff and with the student Board of Governors of the MUB, student involvement in terms of planting and maintenance, an interpretive poster at the building entrance, free bookmarks explaining the project in bullets and graphics.

For two years, the wildflower trial was a relative success. The native herbaceous meadow took hold in the nonsoil (gravel) and flourished. Erosion ceased, a large variety of colors and textures and heights of plants prevailed, birds and insects in generous diversity were frequent visitors, and no maintenance was required (no irrigation, fertilization, mowing, liming, insect and disease control, etc.). Below the wildflower meadow, in the areas of native grasses and lawn grasses, results were not so pronounced, mainly because all plots were maintained identically, including mowing to 2 to 3 inches. This low and frequent mowing regime does not work well with 6- to 18-inch-tall native grasses and herbaceous perennials.

About two years into the "MUB Meadow Trial," the entire site was summarily mowed back to nubbins and replaced with . . . sparse lawn, crabgrass, and erosion.

How did this happen? To a fair degree the campus landscape — like a public park — is everyone's backyard, and most everyone has an opinion about what makes a good backyard. At a university, there are many individuals, many constituencies, and many opinions. And (surprise) the university is not immune to politics. A number of events conspired to find the meadow "guilty":

- Some in the administration and in facilities at the time, from grounds crew and supervisors to highest-level administrators, never fully accepted the concept of alternatives to lawn, and in some cases, actively worked against the project.
- The different maintenance regimes for the different trial areas never were implemented on the ground — it was too much trouble and unclear to the workers.
- A very supportive MUB director left the university, replaced on an interim basis by an actively negative staffer.
- The Admissions Office had trouble interpreting this "weedy" site to prospective students and their parents.
- Classes never became involved in sampling and inventorying the site, and no real data on economy and ecology were developed and analyzed.

In large part, the termination of the wildflower trial was due to a failure of education in the above areas. The grounds crew, top down and bottom up, didn't really get it. Some administrators on campus and some staff in the building didn't get it. The site never became a part of any course or lab work. In spite of a fair amount of publicity, too many people on campus were not aware of the point of the trial, why this area looked different, why it was "unkempt" and "messy." And, in hindsight, the area was probably too close to a building and too central to the relatively manicured campus, at least to serve as a first test case.

On a more positive note (and mining deeply here), some of the underlying concepts made their way into the campus landscape master plan. Lawn areas have been prioritized into three levels of maintenance, from a high level in the core campus to much lower levels in outlying areas, thus reducing inputs overall. And in particular, the campus landscape is now seen in part as a collection of fragmented native plant communities that need to be identified, valued, strengthened, knitted back together, and utilized in university-wide education, both formally in courses and informally in daily life. The campus landscape, after all, is the local model of ecosystem Earth.

Operations: Climate and Energy

The operational needs of a contemporary college campus can be summarized as: (1) how we move around (and park); (2) how we control the temperature of space; and (3) how we provide electrical power. These fundamental needs determine how much energy we use and our impact on climate change. We have roughly 18,000 people on campus everyday, 6,500 parking spaces for their cars, our own bus system, our own telecommunications infrastructure, central heating, cooling, and power plants, campus-wide energy controls, the array of complex equipment required for research, teaching, and student life.

UNH has invested heavily in infrastructure upgrades to increase energy efficiencies. We continually look for ways to renovate buildings to make them more energy efficient, and to reduce the number of trips to campus. We have put in place effective ways to measure our progress in reducing greenhouse gas emissions, and developed an organizational structure that brings together around one table the diverse interests of students, faculty, staff, and administration relative to energy and climate issues.

Indeed, a major part of the university's success in reducing our climate-change footprint has been an inclusive, considerate, and questioning response to internal constituent pressures.

This section focuses on the most significant ways in which UNH is confronting the climate-change challenge. The campus energy system has been completely redesigned to include a co-generation facility and, soon, access to methane generated at a local landfill. The transportation system has moved to a holistic approach to access and mobility (and parking) based on Transportation Demand Management and the acquisition of alternative-fuel vehicles. UNH was among the first to develop a methodology for determining greenhouse gas emissions for a university campus; an approach that has been adopted on hundreds of campuses nationwide and that allows us to measure the impact of all of the steps taken to reduce our carbon footprint. An Energy Task Force, reporting through the VP for Research to the President's cabinet, has helped understand and plan the energy system and to enact the changes needed.

Fundamental change, either physical or cultural, does not come easily on college campuses, and entails many significant risks. UNH has always been a resource-limited institution, which has fostered a practical attitude and an ability to develop creative strategies and partnerships. The campus has embraced the sustainable energy effort at all levels. Students, staff, faculty, administration and, perhaps most significantly, the Board of Trustees, have all proposed and supported creative solutions and accepted the shared risks. One of the most significant results of this integrated effort is the realization that saving energy, even when significant investments are required up front, also saves money. As the in-state business magazine once proclaimed, UNH is both "Lean and Green."

In the end, we believe the decisions that have been made have resulted in a unique identity and set of sustainable practices that will stand the test of time and position the institution for balanced and smart growth over the long term.

Case Study: It's Risky Business Doing the Right Thing — The Co-Gen Plant and EcoLine
PAUL CHAMBERLIN AND MATT O'KEEFE

Finding the right energy solutions for our small-city-sized campus is not easy. With increasing enrollments and expanding research portfolio, the university has a growing appetite for energy, and that means we have to challenge ourselves to find a truly sustainable approach to our energy system.

Real-life energy decisions are all about evaluating the risks and the rewards of the opportunities and alternatives. At UNH, we constantly strive to find cost-effective solutions for sustainable energy consumption. However, the biggest potential gains are often those that involve new processes and technologies. The unfamiliar can be daunting and for the unprepared can lead to failure, unforeseen operating costs, and disillusionment.

Considering that we are a cautious institution with limited resources, we recently have taken some large and extraordinary steps toward sustainable energy solutions to powering, heating, and cooling our campus. These steps were not something that came easily or quickly. The process started with relatively safe, incremental, low-risk steps and built to where we are now taking some large risks with very large rewards — if we can execute our plans.

The First Effective Steps

The energy crisis in the late 1970s led to the establishment of the first campus-wide Energy Office at UNH. This office was charged with reducing energy costs through conservation and efficiency. Energy efficiency first was addressed in small, incremental projects: new light fixtures and motors, thermal upgrades, variable frequency drives, occupancy sensors, and the development of a centralized building-automation system to control demand.

Our energy office also has worked with design and construction teams to minimize the energy consumed in newly constructed and renovated buildings. Using more stringent requirements than required by the state code, our buildings function far more efficiently than the average for the region. In response, UNH was awarded the first Energy Star labels for residence halls in the country and has been listed in the top 5 percent of energy-efficient research universities by the U.S. Department of Energy. We have outlawed incandescent lighting and established a purchasing standard that requires Energy Star office equipment and appliances, motor-replacement policies, and other policy initiatives. All have contributed to the University of New Hampshire saving more than $4 million annually in energy costs compared to peer institutions.

All of these steps were relatively low risk because they used known technology, the main challenges being to find the right ways to best fit this campus and then educate the staff and building users in how to utilize the central controls to their best advantage. This means giving people a limited level of personal control to allow them to come in and turn on the heat or air conditioning in their office or lab on the weekends or at night when the building systems typically are turned back. It means installing sensors to remind researchers not to leave fume hoods in the open position when people aren't working at them. It means educating people that they shouldn't expect 75 degrees in their office in the winter and 68 degrees in the summer.

Next Step Focuses on the Central Plant

With efficient building-operation systems in place, the next area for energy improvement, the central heating plant, involved much greater risks and potentially greater rewards.

The university has had a central, steam-based heating plant since 1893. In 2005, when the existing 1930s-vintage plant was due for serious renovations, the university chose to invest in a combined heat and power (CHP) or cogeneration plant. The concept capitalizes on the waste heat generated during electric production to heat steam for use in the existing steam- and hot water–distribution systems. The efficiency of energy capture from fuels can be increased from about 34 percent to over 80 percent through this technology.

This is not new technology and has proven successful in many locations, but by making our central plant the primary electrical generator on campus, we also incur greater risk. What happens when the system goes down? Can we operate and maintain a type of utility with which we had no experience? Could we be sure that this new generator would be as reliable as our trusty old heating plant? And, including a central chiller plant component, the CHP was a $28 million investment. Will the savings recoup that investment in a reasonable amount of time?

To address down-time and total capacity, the system was sized based on thermal load, and the existing power plant and connections to the regional electric grid were maintained. The 7.9-megawatt combustion turbine generator produces 95,000 pounds of steam per hour, which can supply 95 percent of the campus peak-heating requirements. The electricity generated at full load is equal to 70 percent of the maximum campus load, and about 85 percent of all the campus electricity can be generated onsite. By retaining the existing heating plant as back-up for heat and the existing electrical grid as back-up for power, we are able to limit our operating risks. Allowing for the additional costs of maintaining this diverse set of energy resources, our economic models still show that we will save enough to make this plant pay for itself within a decade.

Co-generation also reduces our campus carbon footprint (total greenhouse gas emissions) by 20 percent (see figure 3.1). As the old plant used heavy #6 oil, and required the purchase of electricity from the grid, operation of the

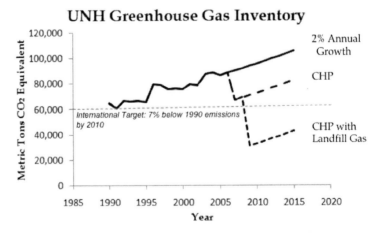

FIGURE 3.1. Greenhouse gas emission reductions resulting from the installation of the combined heat and power plant (CHP — also known as the co-generation plant), and anticipated from the completion of the gas processing plant and pipeline that will deliver landfill gas to campus.

CHP also yields a reduction in emissions of more than 600 tons of sulfur dioxide (SO_2) and 100 tons of nitrous oxide (N_2O). The CHP is a dual-fuel turbine that can run on natural gas or #2 heating oil, adding fuel-switching as a means for minimizing fuel costs and mitigating disruptions in supply.

A Creative Leap Forward

As the new combined heat and power plant was under construction in 2005, the most active hurricane season on record occurred in the United States, including two of the worst ever, Katrina and Rita. In addition to the death and general destruction that devastated the Gulf Coast, the disruptions to natural gas supplies and oil production caused wild price spikes. Concerns about availability made us nervous about our own future here in New Hampshire. How could we get our own source of energy and limit our exposure to the volatility of the energy markets?

Coincidently, one of the largest New England landfills, operated by Waste Management, Inc., and located just 12½ miles from campus, was trying to deal with the increasing quantity of methane gas being produced from the million tons of trash deposited there every year. The landfill is required to collect and destroy gases generated in the landfill and has more than 300 wells scattered through the property for this purpose. Landfill gas is about 50 percent methane, and so requires special combustion equipment to generate electricity, but Waste Management generates about 12 megawatts of power today for local use. Although more landfill gas is available to generate electricity, the power grid serving the landfill has no capacity to handle additional generation, and Waste Management's emissions permits cap their ability to process more of the gas for use. With no other option, Waste Management was forced to send the excess landfill gas to a low NO_x candle flare. This optimized NO_x emissions for the gas, but a huge energy opportunity was being lost.

The university has long contracted with Waste Management to handle its trash, and Waste Management has been a strong supporter of UNH athletics. So frequent and wide-ranging communications occur between the two organizations. During an informal conversation, an idea first formed to build a pipeline from the landfill to the campus so that the university could use the excess landfill gas as fuel for the new combined heat and power plant. It would solve issues for both entities and provide huge environmental benefits. The gas could be the primary energy source for the university for at least the next twenty years and likely for much longer, depending upon the growth of the landfill.

Since UNH had just invested in a 7.9-megawatt turbine that can run on natural gas or oil, a process needed to be put in place to clean the raw landfill gas to bring the composition of the fuel closer to commercial natural gas. A processing plant will be located at the Rochester landfill to separate the methane from the nitrogen, oxygen, CO_2, and contaminants, yielding a much higher methane content that is acceptable for the current turbine. Getting the processed landfill gas (PLG) to campus required an additional investment. A 12.7-mile pipeline has been built, mostly along state highways and railroad tracks, and across university land.

When the CHP converts its main fuel source to PLG, the environmental benefits will be substantial. Since landfill gas is a byproduct of the conventional decomposition process, it is considered by the U.S. Environmental Protection Agency as a carbon-neutral fuel source. This makes it a renewable, carbon-neutral energy source with zero carbon emissions, in contrast with natural gas, the fuel source that it is supplanting. This reduction in CO_2 emissions will drop UNH's greenhouse gas emissions by 67 percent compared to 2005, or 57 percent compared to 1990 (see figure 3.1).

Based on the energy content of the PLG and expected flow rates, the amount of PLG available will exceed the energy requirements for the existing 7.9-megawatt turbine. With the additional gas available, UNH has opted to add a second turbine with a capacity of 4.6 megawatts. Initially, the electricity generated by this turbine will be exported to the New England power grid. Over time, if the campus winter steam demand increases, the ability to add a heat recovery boiler to the 4.6-megawatt turbine can be considered.

The detailed actions required to make this happen are staggering in number and complexity, and the administration and Board of Trustees required double and triple checking of all aspects before agreeing to the project. Would the new CHP turbine that was designed for commercial-grade natural gas be warranted for landfill gas? Would the processing plant at the landfill be able to clean contaminants and unwanted chemical components from the gas stream and achieve the quality of fuel required? The financial, environmental, and security gains all depend on the successful functioning of all the complex parts of the entire system, and each step and process involves risk.

The total project cost to the university, for both the CHP and EcoLine, is $45 million and should have a payback period of ten years (at 2008 energy prices). It also makes UNH a national leader in campus sustainability, energy efficiency, and reductions in greenhouse gas emissions.

Case Study: Transportation and Land Use
STEVE PESCI

Transportation is a perennial and often contentious thread tying the campus experience with the outside world. Whether it be commuter-related traffic impacts on a host community, parking (the big P), intra-campus mobility, accommodation of resident car storage, or simply visitor and delivery access, a university faces challenges beyond that of most large employers, including a number of assertive and engaged constituent voices. Over the past twenty-five years, the UNH response to transportation and campus growth has transitioned from suburban-style accommodation to a holistic demand management approach. This case study will look at the characteristics of that transition and focus on current strategies that balance core university values with need, addressing mobility with a balanced, intermodal system.

Transportation policy affects both campus land-use practices and the university's bottom line. When the co-gen–landfill-gas system previously described is operational, transportation will be the next arena in which to find energy and emission reductions.

Transportation impacts include both commute trips and core business fleet operations. In addition, as major housing providers, universities face the additional responsibility of accommodating and managing resident recreational and off-campus work trips as well as vehicle storage (long-term or remote parking).

Car ownership can be a major cost for university students. Creating a living and learning environment that offers resident and commuter students transportation choices — both for accessing campus and for moving around the region — results in reduced financial strain for the student, reduced land-use demand for vehicle storage, reduced traffic impacts on the host community, and reduced energy use and greenhouse gas emissions.

On the university plant side, the capital and operational cost of fleet (transit and nontransit) is a significant figure. UNH-owned fleet fuel costs represent the fourth-largest energy cost for the campus — approximately $250,000 in FY 2007. In addition, the capital depreciation, maintenance, and replacement cost of the fleet represents a significant university expense.

The Changing Nature of Transportation at the University of New Hampshire

The university's transportation policy has changed significantly over the last three decades. Through the early 1980s, surface parking was added to meet (or nearly meet) demand. Land was available, asphalt prices were low, and private vehicle operations were cheap. There was no meaningful discussion of alternatives.

In the mid-1980s, fuel price spikes and a housing shortage that required the university to rent off-campus facilities led to the initiation of the UNH transit system, an alliance with the nascent public transit agency of the region. Transit service and use grew until the early 1990s, when budget cuts resulted in a 50 percent reduction in route service and a downward spiral of ridership as service frequency fell below critical mass. In place of transit, the university focused on the construction of several major surface parking lots, adding over two thousand spaces in a ten-year period.

The transportation policy paradigm — for both campus access and fleet — began to shift in 2000. It was clear that several new trends were pointing to a need for a more balanced approach. The campus had run out of proximate, cheaply paved surface land for parking. A campus transit system was now required simply to shuttle attendees from new surface lots. Suddenly, transit was *necessary* again. In addition, it had become clear that perception of parking problems was becoming an increasing irritant to all members of the campus community — the status quo simply was not working. In a climate of frustration, leadership of the Transportation Policy Committee was assumed by the Vice President for Finance and within two years a report was adopted that charted a new course.

The 2003 Transportation Policy approved by then-President Ann Weaver Hart began with a clear statement of reality: "The current status of parking and transportation at UNH is structurally irrational and unacceptable and must change." After much debate, the university adopted a demand management-based policy that shifted the focus from accommodation of parking and commuter convenience to a plan that "emphasizes health, safety, efficiency, cost-effectiveness, and fairness" consistent with Academic and Master Plan principles. The proposals included increased costs and eligibility requirements for parking, the expansion of a free transit system, the development of transportation alternatives and infrastructure beyond parking, the introduction of transportation planning staff, and an increased dialogue with the host community on traffic impacts. A directed effort was underway to define the "parking problem" as an "accessibility and mobility" problem that could only be rectified through increased investment in a balanced and holistic transportation system that demonstrated best practices.

By 2004, the time of the update of the Campus Master Plan, these principles had become enshrined in numerous levels of operation, policy, and discussion. It became apparent that the university's vision of itself as a small New England Liberal Arts College was being undermined by suburban-style parking-lot expansion and traffic generation — practice that was at odds with both policy and vision. The university's Academic Plan, in stressing a living-learning community, pointed the way for practice to represent goals.

The Master Plan included, for the first time, a focus on transportation and land use beyond simply a "traffic and parking" perspective. It called for a significant long-term increase in on-campus housing — with a result of reduced commute trips to campus — even through a twenty-year projected period of moderate growth. In addition, the images used in the Master Plan reflected balanced streetscapes with accommodation for a growing transit system, a walkable campus, and streets that were safe and accommodating to cyclists.

At the same time, the university devoted significant new staff effort to pursue outside funding sources to assist with the transition to a more balanced system. Federal legislation, such as the Intermodal Surface Transportation Efficiency Act (ISTEA) and the Transportation Equity Act (TEA-21) provided opportunities. UNH's progressive proposals and willingness to use its transit fleet to highlight alternative-fuel systems resulted in successful receipt of over $6 million in federal transportation funds. With support from the New Hampshire Department of Transportation, Durham became a demonstration site for other communities in the state. Projects ranged from quality transit shelters to a new alternative-fuel fleet, as well as multimillion-dollar renovations of Main Street and the historic rail station to expand transit capacity and improve pedestrian and bicycle friendliness. Given the timeline of application through receipt of funds, many of the projects envisioned in 2001 are just now being implemented.

As a means to position itself for these federal investments, and in line with its adopted climate education principles, UNH has moved aggressively to switch its fleet to cleaner fuels. A developing set of clean-fleet standards will exceed state and federal requirements for fuel efficiency and emissions for newly purchased university vehicles. Under the auspices of the Energy Task Force, the university hopes to formally adopt a comprehensive screening program for all fleet purchases that begins with right-sizing and need demonstration and follows through to purchasing/procurement requirements.

Alternative-fuel and high-efficiency vehicles are identified with an Eco-Cat logo to highlight and educate the community. UNH now has a fleet of small transit vehicles powered exclusively by compressed natural gas (CNG) and unveiled them with an exterior bus education campaign. As of press time, UNH is expanding its CNG fueling facility and fleet and as markets permit, moving toward the introduction of hybrids and electric vehicles into its fleet.

In addition to these internal efforts, the university benefited from several fortuitous changes and new partnerships that reinforced its transportation efforts. The most significant was the return of intercity rail service between Boston and Portland, Maine, with daily stops on campus. The Amtrak Downeaster service has grown from its initial ridership of five thousand in 2002 to a projected sixty thousand riders in 2007. Many students now ride the train to and from campus.

UNH also has:

- positioned itself as the lead in a state effort to introduce B20 (a blend of 20 percent biodiesel and 80 percent petroleum diesel) into the state-run fueling station, and has moved the majority of its diesel fleet to use of low-sulfur B20;
- expanded bike and pedestrian infrastructure as well as a focus on increased downtown development, in concert with the host Durham community;
- supported new technologies that have created web-based ride matching, carpooling, and transit-management systems; and
- participated in and presented at peer conferences in traditional academic, transportation planning, and trade circles. We also have been active partners with programs such as EPA Commuter Choice and USDOE Clean Cities.

Demonstration of Success:
Metrics and Community Attitude Shift, 2000–2007

From 2005 to 2007, UNH assessed the success of its transportation initiatives by analyzing metrics and surveying community opinion. A five-year status report was published in late 2005 documenting quantifiable changes and trends that were in line with the original Transportation Demand Management (TDM) policy goals. In 2007, the university repeated a 2000 community survey that it had used to measure baseline attitudes and opinions regarding the transportation and parking systems and to gauge willingness to pay for improvements via permit prices. Both surveys yielded positive trend and attitude information, including dramatic increases in student housing choices near transit routes and willingness to pay for transit services. This was supported by transit ridership that nearly doubled during the same period

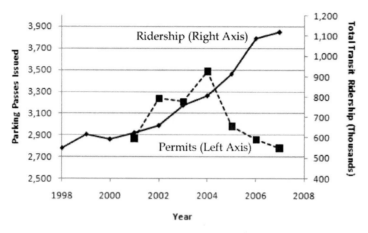

FIGURE 3.2. Recent changes in sales of student commuter-parking permits and in total ridership on the UNH transit system.

and a significant decline in student commuter-parking permit sales since 2004 (figure 3.2). UNH student-body support for the transportation system has increased proportionally, with self-imposed student fees in support of transportation increasing by as much as 50 percent in a single year. These investments in turn have boosted ridership year after year, making UNH the largest transit provider in the state of New Hampshire.

New Challenges and Opportunities

The quantifiable success of UNH's transportation initiatives has brought new challenges. Fuel-cost increases on the transit side and deferred lot-reconstruction costs on the parking side have created a revenue challenge that must be faced. UNH, like many academic institutions, faces the additional challenge of redesigning a parking-permit rate structure that is constrained by union contracts as well as general equity and ability-to-pay issues. The rapid growth in ridership has created a strain on the existing fleet. UNH is in the enviable position of having many buses full at or beyond capacity on regional routes. Accommodating this demand results in additional operating and capital expenses, and fleet replacement is a long timeline and big ticket investment. Maintaining the current level of service and meeting increased expectations will require a significant revenue increase.

The community has stated its willingness to pay a reasonable increase in permit fees to accommodate existing services and some expansion in regional transit. Current proposals include a salary-scaled, zone-based system that provides choices from free access via regional transit to core-access parking that would average $250 per year for faculty and staff. Student parking prices (especially resident student) would also increase.

A university community's attitude toward transportation and parking remains a key indicator of its commitment to sustainability.

Case Study: UNH Greenhouse Gas Inventory
BRETT PASINELLA

In the winter of 2000, the University of New Hampshire's University Office of Sustainability (UOS) developed a partnership with the Portsmouth-based nonprofit Clean Air-Cool Planet (CA-CP) to produce a greenhouse gas (GHG) inventory tool that adapted national and international inventory methodologies to the unique scale and character of a university community. Combining financial and intellectual resources, the partners hired a UNH graduate student to develop the tool and gather data, with support from UNH faculty and staff. Using the inventory tool, UNH's greenhouse gas emissions were documented beginning in 1990 and the first version of the inventory was published in the spring of 2001.

The partners continued to work together to package the inventory methodology into a generic tool that could be used by other campuses. By the fall of 2001, the "Clean Air-Cool Planet Campus Carbon Calculator" became available, and over the next eighteen months, was employed by about ten other Northeast campuses. UOS and CA-CP then hosted a series of technical meetings to continue to refine and simplify the calculator, leading to the development of a revised calculator. As the calculator was adopted by more and more campuses, the revisions continued. Today, the calculator is in its fifth version and another version is planned for 2008. It has been adopted by more than five hundred campuses and that number continues to grow due to its acceptance by the American College & University Presidents Climate Commitment (ACUPCC) as the recommended tool for campuses not already participating in another GHG inventorying program.

UNH has continued to use the latest version of the calculator to update its own greenhouse gas inventory, and since 2001 has published two more updates to its inventory, in summer of 2004 and again in the fall of 2006. Both updates were conducted primarily by UNH graduate students working under the direction of UOS with support from UNH faculty and staff.

With the expanded role of the UNH Energy Task Force (see the next case study) and the signing of the ACUPCC, it is becoming increasingly important to maintain and update the inventory more frequently. In the summer of 2007, a group of UNH staff members who have been providing the data for past inventories met to discuss plans for future updates. At that meeting, it was decided to form a new subcommittee of the Energy Task Force to maintain the inventory on an annual basis. Each member of the new subcommittee would report the necessary data to UOS at the end of each fiscal year, and the new inventory results would be published biannually. Longer, more detailed reports, similar to the first three versions of the UNH inventory, will continue to be published, but on a less frequent (mostly likely five-year) schedule. Currently, the data for the 2006–2007 financial years are being submitted and the first biannual report is in progress. It is expected to be completed, along with a comprehensive review of all historical data, by the summer of 2008.

Case Study: The Energy Task Force — A Cross-Campus Collaboration to Address Climate Change
SARA CLEAVES

It's not often that you sit in a meeting and see attendees talking excitedly about new initiatives and ideas, eager to take on more. But the enthusiasm of the UNH Energy Task Force (ETF) is contagious, and the cross-campus faculty, staff, and student members are up for the challenge of engaging the entire university in reducing energy use, associated costs, and greenhouse gas emissions.

Chaired by the UNH Vice President for Research and coordinated by the UNH University Office of Sustainability (UOS) and the UNH Energy Office, the ETF is the formal working group behind UNH's broad Climate Education Initiative (CEI). Initially developed in 2005 by then-UNH President Ann Weaver Hart to develop new ways to reduce energy consumption in response to fast-rising energy prices, the mission of the ETF soon broadened to serve in an advisory capacity to the UNH president and make recommendations on the full range of issues that relate to climate change and energy. These issues include everything from energy generation, demand management, efficiency, and conservation, to greenhouse gas mitigation policy and action, participation in energy and carbon markets, and curriculum, research, and outreach opportunities related to climate and energy. The overarching goal is to guide the university toward a systemic and integrated energy policy that emphasizes

health and integrity, climate protection, efficiency, cost-effectiveness and stability, fairness for all university constituents, and consistency with priorities
set by the UNH Academic Plan and UNH Campus Master Plan.

The ETF's role in advising the campus administration on climate and
energy issues took on even greater prominence when UNH became the first
land-grant university in New England to sign the American College & University Presidents Climate Commitment (ACUPCC) in February 2007. A
member of the leadership circle of ACUPCC signers, UNH pledges to take
immediate actions to reduce greenhouse gas emissions and to develop a plan
to move the university toward carbon neutrality. The ETF is charged with
taking the actions necessary to implement the ACUPCC, including:

- developing timelines, targets, and action items under a UNH Climate
  Action Plan (called "WildCAP") to help move UNH toward carbon
  neutrality;
- developing immediate and future actions to reduce energy costs, lower
  greenhouse gas emissions, and improve energy conservation through
  technological improvements, increases in efficiency, reductions in
  waste, and selection of fuels;
- inventorying and promoting curricular, research, and engagement programs intended to increase awareness of and behaviors around energy
  use, efficiency, greenhouse gas emissions, and climate change.

The ETF has been successful in meeting its charge for a number of interconnected reasons:

- **Cross-campus membership.** Administrators, faculty, staff, and undergraduate and graduate students sit on the ETF. Such a wide range of
  members allows the ETF to develop interdisciplinary, collaborative,
  and innovative projects that integrate curricula, operations, research,
  and engagement around climate and energy. It also ensures that all
  stakeholder groups at UNH have a voice.
- **Leadership at the top.** The ETF is chaired formally by the Vice President for Research, and was chartered in 2007 by UNH President Mark
  W. Huddleston. This gives the ETF formal credibility. Members know
  that their ideas and work are being heard and taken seriously by the
  campus administration and that good ideas are finding their way "up
  the ladder" to supportive administrators. What's more, this leadership
  at the top helps those policies and practices the ETF develops and the
  administration endorses have "teeth" and staying power.

- **Ownership at all levels.** Although chaired by a vice-president, the day-to-day work and dynamics of the ETF are purposefully collaborative. Every member of the ETF, from the vice-president to the undergraduate student representatives, has a voice.
- **Vision that unites.** Behind everything the ETF does, from educational campaigns aimed at saving energy in offices and dorm rooms to recommending changes in UNH building standards or purchasing guidelines, lies a motivation to act now in addressing climate change. Members are united in the common goal of continuing to make UNH a sustainable learning community that not only reduces its emissions but also educates the next generation of citizen-professionals to advance climate protection in their lives when they leave campus. It's a mission that inspires and — no pun intended — fuels the enthusiastic work of the ETF.

Operations: Food and Society

University Hospitality Services (UHS), UNH's self-operated hospitality services, employs over three hundred people and includes UNH Dining, which operates three dining halls and eight retail operations across campus; University Conferences & Catering, which provides catering services for meetings and events; and the New England Center, a hotel, conference center, and restaurant located on the UNH campus. Serving almost seventy thousand meals per week in the dining halls alone (during the academic year), UHS is an important social, economic, and health driver at the university.

In recognition of the significant contributions and impacts of a college or university dining services, UHS and the University Office of Sustainability (UOS) began collaborations soon after UOS was established in 1997. In 1998, a pilot program was conducted to study the feasibility of composting food waste produced by UNH Dining. The program took the form of collecting pre- and postconsumer food waste from a single dining hall. From that small step grew a robust Compost Program that collects and composts food waste from all campus dining halls. Additional efforts to increase UHS's sustainability were happening at the same time, including an increase in food procured from local and regional sources, collaboration with the UNH Organic Garden Club and campus research farms to provide produce for the dining program, the establishment of an annual Local Harvest Dinner, and targeted efforts to reduce energy and water usage. These efforts culminated in the Local Harvest Initiative at UNH, officially established in 2005 to "raise awareness and educate students, staff, and community members about our local agricultural landscape and its role in sustaining our physical and economic health and well-being, now and in the future" by procuring food grown and produced locally and regionally whenever possible, offering more sustainable and fair-trade options.

This section presents three related case studies. The first examines the development of the UNH Compost Program. The second looks at the evolution of the UNH Local Harvest Initiative, the umbrella initiative that now includes the Compost Program as well as other sustainable efforts administered by UNH Dining. The third describes how an innovative approach to scheduling dining hall services reduced plate waste. These examples reveal how applying a systemic, food-systems perspective to university dining can bring about innovative, sustainable changes in operations, which in turn can have positive social, economic, and environmental impacts.

Case Study: The UNH Compost Program — From Waste to Compost
ELISABETH FARRELL AND RICK MACDONALD

The UNH Compost Program was started in the 1990s as a research site for faculty at the UNH College of Life Sciences and Agriculture's (COLSA) Kingman Farm, and included waste such as animal manure and leaves. In 1998, a report submitted to the New Hampshire Office of State Planning by UOS and UNH faculty researcher George Estes, *A Review of Food Waste Composting Literature and Experimental Protocol for Proposed Composting Activities at the University of New Hampshire*, detailed an experimental protocol to pilot the integration of food waste material into the existing compost program (quotations included here are drawn from this source). Prior to the study, food waste at UNH was going to the Durham Wastewater Treatment Facility and, as noted in the report, "the heavy load of organic material into the facility contributes to nutrient enrichment of the surrounding river and estuary and reduces the life of the wastewater treatment facility." The University Office of Sustainability (UOS) and UNH Dining collaborated with COLSA to collect food waste from a single dining hall. Due to the success of the integration, the program was established formally and, over the course of several years, expanded to include all three UNH dining halls, as well as community restaurants and retail outlets.

The Pilot Study

The Compost Program pilot study at UNH took place between July and November of 1998, with the ultimate goal to "increase the sustainability of the current waste management strategy." Additionally, researchers hoped the "pilot study could serve as a model for other communities considering composting."

The pilot study collected food waste from one dining hall twice weekly and integrated the waste into the existing compost windrows at Kingman Farm. Initial investments included an onsite storage facility for the finished product, toting containers for the waste material, and a pickup truck with a hydraulic tailgate (essential given the weight of food waste), which was purchased with funds from UOS, UHS, and the COLSA Dean's Office. UOS hired two student interns to collect the waste and drive it to the farm, located approximately two miles from the main campus. UNH Dining installed a Somat food-waste pulper in one dining hall dish room. The pulper chops up food waste, extracts liquid, and leaves the waste. This process reduces odor

and speeds up the windrow composting process and requires the cooperation of UNH Dining to ensure the proper sorting of waste, UOS to oversee
the intern labor, and COLSA farm staff to manage the windrows.

Beyond the basic infrastructure needed to conduct the study, strong partnerships and commitment to the goals of the study and the ultimate goal
of "implement[ing] an institutional-wide program of food waste composting at UNH" were necessary. This meant that the process had to work within
existing routines to the greatest extent possible, particularly in the kitchen.
As noted in the literature review and experimental protocol, "it is mandatory
that sanitation in the dish room not be compromised in any manner" and
"that food waste collection occur in a timely fashion." Consistent communication among the various partners was also vital to sorting through challenges and fostering cooperation.

Program Expansion

Following the successful completion of the study, UNH Dining saw the value
not only of continuing the program, but also of expanding it to incorporate
other dining facilities. COLSA and UOS also were committed to continuing, and a Compost Program was established. The collection of preconsumer
waste began at other dining facilities and, within a number of years, food-
waste pulpers were installed in each of the dining halls to enable the collection of postconsumer waste. In addition, as UNH Dining was designing a
new dining facility, they planned with composting in mind. The new dining
hall, which eventually was named Holloway Commons, was equipped with a
Somat food-waste pulper as well as a walk-in refrigerator built specifically to
hold food waste awaiting collection. This refrigerator serves to reduce odor
and pest issues.

As the quantity of food waste increased, UOS hired additional interns to
collect the waste. The enthusiasm of the student interns was such that the
program expanded to include educational outreach efforts in the dining halls
and around campus. The intent was to inform the community about the project and encourage dining hall guests to "take what you want, but eat what you
take," in order to help reduce waste. In an effort to connect with the broader
Durham community, preconsumer waste collection also expanded to several
downtown businesses and local schools. COLSA began bagging the finished
compost, marketed as "U-DOO," for sale through one of the businesses from
which waste was collected, The Durham Marketplace, as well as at a local
hardware store.

In 2006, budget constraints and a hiring freeze in COLSA forced UOS to a decision point. How long should the office subsidize the Compost Program considering the delayed possibilities of establishing academic and research programs or securing grants? Before a difficult decision was made, UNH Dining stepped forward and offered to fund the cost and to manage the function of collecting and delivering the waste. UNH Dining now hires its own staff to collect the pulped food waste and transport it to Kingman Farm, where COLSA staff maintain the windrows and prepare and sell the finished compost. UOS continues to support the program through its communications and overarching Food and Society Initiative.

Successes and Challenges

The Compost Program at UNH has demonstrated a viable method of diverting waste from the wastewater stream and, at the same time, producing a valuable product. It is a concrete way of revealing the "food loop" to students and the campus community, and because of this, has experienced a good deal of publicity and general buy-in. The fact that the value of the product goes back to the community and campus through sales to the general public and use on UNH farms makes it a tangible, beneficial campus-community partnership.

These benefits, however, do come with some challenges. Most pressing is the overall cost of a compost program of this scale. Investments in equipment at the farm (including a tractor and windrow turner and sifter for the finished product) and the dining facilities (including food-waste pulpers and waste containers), truck maintenance, fuel, insurance, labor (at the farm, in the dining halls, and for waste collection), and other miscellaneous expenses makes the program quite expensive to maintain. While revenue from the finished product helps offset these costs, significant ongoing investments must continue to be made by all partners.

A parallel challenge to this financial cost is the difficulty in calculating the cost savings of this program. UNH and the town of Durham have an arrangement whereby the university provides drinking-water treatment and the town provides wastewater treatment. As a result, the incremental costs are not transparent or calculated. UHS is charged an across-the-board fee for its water use. Since the majority of food waste formerly was being handled through the wastewater system, it has been very difficult to project the savings that the Compost Program provides to the University.

A further challenge to the program is that COLSA has limited faculty hiring, due to severe financial constraints. The ability to develop academic tie-ins to the program have been nearly impossible. Currently, no research efforts and few teaching activities link with the Compost Program. The risk is that the program will be simply an operational activity, rather than evolving into a comprehensive effort embodying the sustainable learning community notion of integrated, place-based, on-the-ground operations, research, and education. This issue is one of ongoing discussion to determine how these links can be made in the future.

Case Study: Acting Locally — The UNH Local Harvest Initiative
ELISABETH FARRELL AND RICK MACDONALD

As the Compost Program grew (see the previous case study), so too did an interest in demonstrating other food system–related sustainability practices at UNH. In 2001, the University Office of Sustainability (UOS) established its campus-wide Food & Society Initiative (FAS), with the overarching goal of developing UNH as a "sustainable food community" in the state and region. A working group consisting of faculty, staff, and community members was formed to flesh out the objectives and activities of the FAS initiative. Through these discussions, it became clear that one way of demonstrating the commitment of UNH and University Hospitality Service (UHS) to being a sustainable food community was to increase efforts to purchase foods grown, produced, and manufactured locally and regionally. Given the climate and generally small scale of food production in New Hampshire and New England, not to mention the sheer quantity of demand (nearly seventy thousand meals currently are served in UNH dining halls every week during the academic year), this was no easy task. Using the same strategy as the Compost Program — starting slowly, building relationships, and testing various approaches to see what works — local procurement is a growing force at UNH.

Meeting the Demand for Local Food Procurement

Support for local and regional businesses has always been an important aspect of UHS's approach to making purchasing decisions. As the focus turned to increasing local and regional food procurement, UHS was able to begin looking a bit differently at its purchasing decisions. Products already were being purchased from numerous local and regional companies, including Stony-field yogurt, Cabot cheeses, a local meat processor, a local farmer from whom Dining purchased butternut squash and other products, Barber chicken, local bagels, and more. UHS also had an ongoing relationship with UNH's own

Woodman Horticulture Research Farm, from which they purchased fresh apples every fall. Many of these products were served in the dining halls, and additional local products were introduced for special events through UHS Conferences & Catering.

In order to reach out to more students and the broader campus community, UHS determined that having one large meal featuring local foods could highlight ongoing sustainability efforts as well as have a real impact on raising guest awareness about local food and agriculture. Named the Local Harvest Dinner, this now-annual event built on relationships established with farmers through the earlier local purchasing efforts and also brought in new farms and products. UHS and UOS began working in the spring of 2005, planning the logistics of the event, contacting farmers, securing product, and placing orders early (this was especially important for purchasing meat products). In order to enhance the informal educational opportunities that the dining hall offers, organizers planned a display area under a tent adjacent to the dining hall in which to have farmer and organization exhibits. This has continued each year, with many of the featured farmers presenting information about their farms, side by side with campus groups like the Student Nutrition Association and off-campus organizations such as NH Made and Slow Food Seacoast.

The first annual dinner was held at Philbrook Dining Hall as a "test site." The dinner attracted over sixteen hundred diners — about six hundred more than Philbrook Hall served on a typical night — and included many faculty, staff, and community members. Feedback from guests was extremely positive and enthusiastic. The following year saw the dinner move to Stillings and brought in approximately nineteen hundred guests. Year three saw the dinner move to the largest dining hall on campus — Holloway Commons — and attracted over thirty-seven hundred guests. The dinner has become a campus tradition, one that is both celebratory and educational. It also won the 2007 Loyal E. Horton Large School Bronze Medal in the Theme Dinner category from the National Association of College & University Food Services. Based on the success of the first dinner, UHS and UOS decided to establish the Local Harvest Initiative as an umbrella program continuing the Local Harvest Dinner and ongoing local and regional food procurement efforts, the Compost Program, and other food-related operational and programmatic efforts made by UHS.

Challenges and Opportunities

While procuring local food for a single event is not easy, sorting out how to integrate local and regional products on a regular, ongoing basis is even more difficult. Trying to do so presents a number of challenges. Most obvious, given the location of UNH, is the issue of seasonality. While some products, such as dairy and meat, can be found year-round, most of the fresh produce grown in the state and region is gone by the early fall — the start of the fall semester. Another major issue is the scale of the university versus the size of local and regional farms. As noted earlier, UNH Dining serves approximately seventy thousand meals per week during the academic year in its dining halls alone. Add to this the additional obstacles that institutions face when attempting to procure local food, including shrinking agricultural infrastructure, and you have a difficult effort indeed.

However, with creative and strategic thinking, UNH and similar large universities can find ways to incorporate local and regional products in an ongoing way. Finding the "right fit" for products is an important way to achieve this. For instance, UHS determined that it could purchase all its shell-on eggs from a cage-free, humane-certified New Hampshire farm (the first college or university in the country to do so) by offsetting the increased costs of this purchase elsewhere in their budget. The farm was large enough to meet the university's demand. This move brought UHS positive recognition for its efforts, and provided a product that is available year-round and that can be managed financially with a bit of flexibility. UHS also has been able to integrate more local and regional products by working with its distributors to identify items that are or could be offered from local and regional sources and by seeking out local farmers for contract growing.

In addition, UNH is unusual in that it is a land-grant university with several active research farms. Working with these farms to purchase products is another way in which UHS is able to introduce more locally grown foods while also demonstrating the rich agricultural holdings of UNH. UHS has purchased apples from Woodman Research Farm and squash from Kingman Research Farm. UHS was also a founding supporter of the UNH Organic Garden Club, serving on the club's advisory committee, providing a startup financial investment to the club, and offering ongoing revenue to the club for the purchase of produce for the dining halls and New England Center. These efforts help make clear to the campus community the value of UNH operations, land holdings, research, and engagement.

Conclusions

Over the course of nearly ten years, UNH has been working actively to integrate the principles of sustainability into its dining operations. From building a large-scale Compost Program to increasing local and regional food procurement to hosting an annual Local Harvest Dinner, much has been accomplished. In addition to these food-related efforts, UHS has made many other sustainable operational changes, including recycling and waste reduction, replacing traditional urinals with waterless urinals in Holloway Commons, installing Energy Star and other efficient equipment and lighting, incorporating methods of "green cleaning," and purchasing alternate sustainable packaging.

Of course, many areas remain to expand upon. Most importantly, we are keenly aware that operational efforts, no matter how positive, are most effective when done in concert with curriculum, research, and engagement efforts. To demonstrate operationally what is taught in formal curriculum, to research what is carried out operationally, and to engage the campus community in its efforts creates a cohesiveness that is necessary to fostering a sustainable learning community. With ongoing education and outreach to, and collaboration with, faculty, staff, students, and the community, the integration of operations across curriculum, research, and engagement will be realized.

Case Study: Innovative Dining Hall Hours and Plate Waste
RICK MACDONALD

They said it couldn't be done. You couldn't successfully operate a dining program with continuous operating hours combined with meal plans that offered unlimited access to dining halls whenever they were open. Food costs would skyrocket! Waste would be rampant! Students would find ways to share plans so that one plan could feed several. In other words, the sky would fall.

UNH Dining moved forward anyway, even with some doubters among its own management team. The ultimate goal was to increase guest satisfaction by removing one of the biggest sources of dissatisfaction in college and university dining programs — meals that disappeared after a week or semester or academic year and left students feeling ripped off. A thoughtfully designed combination of meal plan choices and technology has helped UNH Dining to author a tremendous success story.

All residential students are required to purchase an unlimited meal plan. Plan holders can enter any dining hall whenever it is open and eat as much as they choose to eat. UNH Dining restricted the use of the plan to only the plan holder by investing in biometric technology. Students enter the dining halls through a turnstile that is opened by a hand geometry reader. A plan holder enters his or her ID number in the reader and places a hand on a platform in the reader. The software matches the live reading of the hand to the stored template (captured during an enrollment process) and releases the turnstile if they match. This eliminates another major issue for guests — the displeasure that is created when a student forgets his or her ID and is denied entrance into the facility.

UNH Dining hoped to create the feeling that students could use the dining program as their own kitchen. It worked. It seems that when the number of available meals is limited in any fashion (day, week, semester, or year), there is a pressure to eat all one can eat. If the plan allows three meals a day — breakfast, lunch, and dinner — during each meal you know that the next opportunity to eat is several hours away. The reaction is to overestimate your food needs and create waste or simply to overeat. The result of offering unlimited plans actually reduced plate waste and overestimating food needs. The conclusion by UNH Dining is that creating unlimited opportunities to eat relieved pressure to stock up in one visit. It is the same as being at home. When you know that you have plenty of food in the kitchen, there is no need to eat it all at once, since you can always come back for more.

Since launching this meal plan package, UNH Dining has seen a steady rise in the sale of meal plans. Students who move from campus housing and are not required to purchase a plan tend to buy a plan voluntarily. Customer satisfaction is up as well; students, faculty, staff, and parents all sing the praises of UNH Dining. They proved it could be done.

Operations: Culture and Sustainability

Yankee frugality is in our roots. As New Hampshire's land-grant college, the school first came into existence in 1866 by sharing facilities with Dartmouth College and building only one facility for itself during its seventeen years in Hanover. With a will written in 1863, but kept secret until his death in 1890, Benjamin Thompson, a Durham farmer, gave his entire estate and land to the State of New Hampshire to establish a state agricultural school at the site of his farm. Having never married, Ben's lifetime of Yankee thrift (some would say parsimoniousness) and shrewd investments became a catalyst for the school to move to Durham.

Over the next forty years, the growth of the New Hampshire School of Agriculture and Mechanical Arts, with no more than a hundred students, into the University of New Hampshire, with almost two thousand, was a testament to the individuals who wore many hats and took direct responsibility to make things happen. Charles Pettee, Dean of the Faculty, also oversaw the construction of Main Street and the development of the water system that served the school and the town. Professor Eric Huddleston, Chairman of the Department of Architecture, was also the supervising architect for designing and overseeing construction of all campus buildings from 1915 to 1946. These are just a couple of examples of the direct involvement that established a culture of accomplishing the most effective physical-needs solutions of the campus within the very limited resources available. A concerted effort was made to provide solutions that would be enduring, easy to maintain, and, just as importantly, create a setting that would have meaning to its graduates for a lifetime — a truly sustainable way of thinking. This culture formed an environment that is not flashy or ostentatious, but provides the means for distinguished achievements in learning, research, and campus life.

This tradition is fundamental to our thinking today. In many ways, it is a guide, a reference for how we need to think sustainably for what we do now to the campus.

This section will focus on two aspects of creating a meaningful environment: public art and sustainable building design. Both are grounded in the traditions of frugality and getting the greatest value from the limited resources available, which is the only way we can sustain this campus.

Two of the cases relate to designing and preserving public art. The Committee for Campus Aesthetics has developed guidelines for selecting and placing works of art on campus and managed a first major project. In the renovation of the campus Engineering building, an important investment was made in preserving, moving, and restoring a wall-sized mural painted by a UNH Professor of Art in the 1950s.

Sustainable building design requires careful attention to the efficiency of the structure and the materials used to construct it, and also to how the building sits within the campus landscape and reinforces the sense of meaning and place. The case study for Sustainable Building Design describes the university's holistic approach and the tools and processes that have been established. The last case study offers a simple but effective way to illustrate the importance of sustainable design and construction strategies to everyone.

Case Study: Developing Our Sense of Place —
The Role of the Committee for Campus Aesthetics
VICKI C. WRIGHT

We hear it so often from visitors to the University: "Oh, what a beautiful campus!" Indeed, the University of New Hampshire is marked by its attractive campus, situated in a lovely historic town (Durham) in a very "livable" part of our state (the Seacoast region). But for many of us who live and work on this campus, something was clearly missing — a sense of purpose about the physical details of our campus landscape. Certainly, we had a campus master plan that guided the development of our buildings and infrastructure, but over the years, not much attention had been paid to the smaller details that contribute to the way a campus looks. Benches in a variety of styles and materials dotted the landscape; memorial trees of numerous species (including some not native to our region) were being planted with minimal thought given to placement and maintenance; directional and building signs did not consistently follow the approved graphic identity guidelines; and there were no provisions for caring for the few works of art that existed in public places on campus.

Creation of the Committee for Campus Aesthetics

In the fall of 1997, at the request of then-President Joan Leitzel, Provost Walter Eggers called for the creation of the UNH Committee for Campus Aesthetics. Its members were drawn from the breadth of the campus community, including faculty, staff, administration, and students. Although a number of pending issues demanded our immediate attention, during the first months we focused on defining our mission, articulating our concern for the physical elements that affect our cultural landscape. The formation of the committee coincided with the founding of the UNH Office of Sustainability, and its director was an early and important member. His involvement and enthusiasm were instrumental to our understanding of the central role that our cultural landscape plays in sustaining the university as a community. Indeed, as the committee's work evolved, we began to share a vision that, through the thoughtful development of our physical landscape, we could have a meaningful impact on the community's sense of place and appreciation for its cultural heritage.

Initially, the committee was asked to consider and make recommendations to the university president on a number of specific projects and issues. It soon became apparent that, rather than addressing a profusion of individual requests, the committee should review existing policies and recommend revision or formulation of new guidelines, thereby providing frameworks for appropriate individual units on campus to respond to specific requests.

Thus, we formed three subcommittees to address important physical and aesthetic components of our campus: Campus Signage and Graphic Identity, Physical Memorials and Tributes, and Public Art. During the first few years of the committee's existence, while we continued to address specific issues that arose, the subcommittees set to work on refining existing policies and defining guidelines in these areas. Each of these committees established guidelines and procedures for proposing, accepting, siting, maintaining, and possible eventual disposal of signs, memorials, and public art.

Guidelines for Public Art

A crucial example of this process was the public art subcommittee's charge to develop guidelines for the acquisition, placement, and maintenance of public art on our campus.

What we developed is a comprehensive document that combines the structure necessary to carry out a public art program with a clearly stated philosophical rationale. Based on successful public art programs at other universities and those administered by state and federal agencies, the guidelines for a public art program at the University of New Hampshire are designed to provide a framework for the acquisition, management and care, and educational promotion of public works of art on campus. They are procedural in nature, outlining the following key areas of a public art program:

- A rationale for a public art program at New Hampshire's state university;
- the role of committees concerned with public art projects, including

the Committee for Campus Aesthetics and individually appointed Art Program Committees to facilitate each public art project;

- the procedure(s) for selecting artists and works of art;
- educational opportunities and promotional efforts throughout the process of commissioning, installing, and displaying works of public art;
- the funding and management of the public art program, including possible sources of funds, contract and schedule requirements, and professional collection management requirements.

We completed the draft of our public art guidelines in the spring of 2002, which turned out to be an eventful year at UNH. President Joan Leitzel retired and a new President, Anne Weaver Hart, was inaugurated; the university embarked upon a major and comprehensive revision of its campus master plan; and a proposal emerged for the commissioning of a sculpture to celebrate the university's athletic program mascot, the wildcat.

Testing the Guidelines for Public Art: A New Sculpture Commission

Shortly after President Leitzel approved the UNH Guidelines for Public Art, the Committee for Campus Aesthetics was approached by the executive director of the UNH Alumni Association and the university's athletic director, who proposed commissioning a larger-than-life-sized sculpture of the university's mascot, the wildcat. Although a mascot sculpture may not have been the first choice for a work of art for some of the committee members, its broad appeal to students, alumni, and local residents made it an ideal project to gauge the level of community support for public art and to "test" our newly approved guidelines.

The process was extensive, but inclusive of many voices. Our guidelines called for the formation of a selection committee, or Art Program Committee, that included representatives from the alumni association, athletics, the art faculty, the student body, the aesthetics committee, and arts professionals from outside the UNH community. A description of the project was drafted and a request for proposals was distributed nationally, through art publications, organization newsletters, and state arts councils. After reviewing proposals from over forty artists, the committee invited four finalists to visit the campus and give public presentations on their proposals for a wildcat sculpture. Those who attended the public presentations were invited to submit comments and recommendations to the Art Program Committee. The committee deliberated and awarded the commission to Matthew Gray Palmer, an accomplished animal sculptor from Washington State.

Once the artist was selected, a contract was negotiated, a granite rock was secured as the base for the bronze sculpture, the site was prepared, landscaping was designed, and the Alumni Association raised private funds for the project.

In October of 2006, the UNH wildcat sculpture was installed in front of the Whittemore Center, the University's athletic center on Main Street in Durham. It was dedicated during Homecoming Weekend and, almost immediately, became a treasured addition to the campus landscape, a source of university pride, and a popular meeting place for students, visitors, and alumni. Although the process was long, it engaged the ideas and visions of many people from our community. It enabled the Alumni Association to commission a sculpture of very high quality by one of the finest wildlife sculptors working today and it resulted in a work that will have a timeless appeal to generations of UNH students and alumni.

The members of the Committee for Campus Aesthetics were pleased to have a role in shaping the process of this first commissioned sculpture and hope it will be the first of many public works of art that will enhance our campus.

Case Study: Sustainable Building Design
DOUGLAS BENCKS

When it comes to the design and construction of buildings, sustainability can mean many different things, and while most colleges and universities are engaged in "sustainable design," definitions vary widely from campus to campus. At the University of New Hampshire, sustainable design has come to mean a very holistic way of thinking about the process and end product of well-integrated planning, design, and construction. We pursue a set of clear principles and detailed strategies with every building project, sometimes with great success, and sometimes with great limitation. What is most important is that we are developing a rigor that is beginning to be applied across all projects and not just the chosen green buildings.

Historical Approaches

Current practices are not the result of a linear path forward, but followed a more erratic evolution that began with mixed results at a time before the terms "sustainable" or "green" were applied to design.

For example, in the 1970s, the university installed a 200-foot-long array of solar panels on the roof of the chemistry building to provide hot water. Unfortunately, the system failed after only a few years and was never fixed. It remains a very visible element on top of the building, its only purpose to support and cloak a long series of exhaust stacks. In the mid-1980s, a building addition for our two-year technical school included many design ideas that are still considered progressive: light shelves in computer labs, a south-facing Sun space for passive solar energy collection, natural convection ventilation in the large lecture hall, and a wall insulation system that provided a thermal barrier well above any standards of the day. Unfortunately, the elements of the building that required daily user adjustments were never managed properly, creating overheating, a lack of fresh air, and glaring light that led to covered windows and more artificial lighting. Most significantly, the building envelope failed after ten years and had to be replaced completely — not a sustainable design by any definition.

Becoming more cautious after these failed "experiments," in the early 1990s UNH began focusing on small, incremental, energy-efficiency projects such as light fixture replacements, motor upgrades, and pneumatic heating controls. At the same time, standards were put in place to ensure that all future major construction projects were energy efficient and were designed and built to be both enduring and easy to maintain.

Defining a Sustainable Approach to Building at UNH

In 1997, the Office of Sustainability was established and a year-long process began to both broaden and deepen the efforts for sustainable design. It soon became apparent that, in addition to the many operational aspects of design that needed to be included — energy, careful use of materials, environmental health, the ecology of the site — it was also important to understand what it takes to make a building part of the campus, reinforcing the meaning and sense of place. We discovered that there was much we could learn from our oldest buildings. The earliest buildings on our campus dating from 1893 to 1940 used local materials — brick, slate, granite, and wood; a central heating plant that was the most efficient way to heat the campus; and large, double-hung window openings and tall spaces to allow daylight as the primary light source and to allow good ventilation. The building forms were based on historical references that articulated the role of a university to carry forward the wisdom of the ages to the citizens of tomorrow. They assured students, faculty, and visitors that this is a place with a strong sense of continuity and stability that can be relied upon for generations to come. To put it simply, people recognize it as a collegial environment.

In comparison, the modern movement that began to appear on campus in the 1940s rejected the past and said it was no longer important to learn and apply the traditional and historical design principles. Buildings were stand-alone objects, each one a cocoon to maintain comfort without regard for location or efficiency. Often, buildings of this era had low ceilings and relied on artificial lighting and mechanical systems to provide light and air. They were designed with an attitude that applying technology and cheap energy were better than relying on methods that are tailored to local conditions. And just as significantly, the modernist philosophy preached that buildings should be stripped of all historical references, becoming pure, unclothed machines for living. The results frequently created inhumane objects and energy gluttons that appeared to have been randomly dropped from space like the monolith in Arthur Clarke's *2001: A Space Odyssey*.

As we began to develop our own set of sustainable design principles that would guide us in the twenty-first century, we recognized that the early campus buildings were based on a design system that was much older than those buildings and can be traced back through the great architects of the late nineteenth century and the Renaissance to the classical Roman era. These concepts were first stated by the Roman architect Marcus Vitruvius Pollio, referred to as Vitruvius, whose writings are the oldest-known from any architect. His treatise, called *On Architecture*, presented a "complete system of architecture." For Vitruvius, there were three chief concerns — *firmitas*, *utilitas*, and *venustas* — within which everything else fit. In 1624, an English writer, Sir Henry Wotton, articulated this approach as "Well building hath three conditions — Firmness, Commodity and Delight." The challenge of good design is to always balance these three, never allowing one to be subsumed by the others.

We took this as the framework that we needed to organize our sustainable design approach, which integrates all design factors. This becomes an all-inclusive way to describe good building design, rather than thinking about sustainability or green design as an add-on to what we typically do (see sidebar).

This framework allows us to consider all aspects of design within a holistic set of goals. These goals are inclusive of the more typical requirements of building programs, codes: ADA, ASHRAE, and EPA regulations. They incorporate the climate and biodiversity criteria that commonly are identified as the goals of sustainability. They address the needs of the wider community and the built context, and interject the intangible significance of forms and space that make it humane and alive. Together, the framework provides a

University of New Hampshire Sustainable Design Framework

Based on the precepts of Vitruvius: *firmitas*, *utilitas*, and *venustas*
- FIRMNESS: How the building goes together
  A building should be enduring and resist the elements without waste, using economy of structure and materials without extravagance.
- COMMODITY: What the building does
  A building should serve the functions, comforts, and health of people while fostering community and sensitivity to its surroundings.
- DELIGHT: Why the building lives
  A building should engage people with forms and spaces that attract, inspire, or simply touch people's hearts and minds so that they want to *be there*!

All of these must be in balance, never allowing one to subsume the others.

comprehensive definition of good contemporary design that will serve the campus community for generations to come.

With these principles and goals, we have established a detailed set of strategies to apply to all projects big and small, new construction and renovations. These strategies are taken from several systems for creating high performance buildings, including LEED, Green Building Advisor, and BEES, and added those of our own that speak to the fundamental principles of enduring construction, ease of maintenance, and humane design. We maintain a broad set of potential strategies, but tailor them to the realities of our campus, traditions, and culture. And we continue to be cautious in pursuing novel and cutting-edge components and methods because of the inherent long-term risks.

At the same time, we constantly look for small, low-risk opportunities to explore such possibilities to see if they may be suitable over the long term. We look for ways to apply our goals and strategies on small, incremental renovation projects: replacing lights, reusing and refinishing old doors, keeping as much of the existing room layouts as possible, and rehabilitating the old radiators with new automated controls. We have done a detailed analysis of the most sustainable bookcases for our campus (wood bookcases made by our carpentry shop using wood from our New Hampshire forests). We developed and constantly refine a comprehensive set of construction and renovation standards that make our buildings more enduring and easier to maintain. We have a comprehensive Campus Master Plan, Landscape Master Plan, and Utility Master Plan that guide our decisions for each individual project. We include the background and ability to provide truly integrated design services, energy modeling, and a commitment to our sustainable design goals in our selection criteria for design consultants. All of this has provided some significant success, but the constraints of funding, schedules, and old habits create constant obstacles that can be overcome only by a strong, focused commitment to achievable goals for each project. We have learned to avoid trying to apply a fixed set of goals and strategies, and rather relied upon our constant principles to guide each project team.

Conclusion

Sustainable design is the only option for entities like colleges and universities, where there is a campus with its own set of traditions that builds and renovates facilities that won't be sold off, that will need to be operated and maintained efficiently for as long as possible, within a larger context that needs to be safe, healthful, and attractive. Enduring, efficient, high performance, adaptable, engaging, and meaningful are the principles that need to guide every project. For the University of New Hampshire, this is overlaid by our culture of New England frugality, using every resource to its greatest extent, looking for the best long-term value, and being cautious with building experiments that may not hold up over the long life of a building.

Case Study: Moving the Kingsbury Mural
DOUGLAS BENCKS

In the summer of 1950, just prior to the opening of the newly built Kingsbury Hall, the late professor of the arts John W. Hatch was commissioned by the university to paint a mural in the Kingsbury Hall Engineering Library — a mural that spoke of the newly discovered atomic energy as either a key to the future or the downfall of humanity. The artist once called this mural "a cross section of our contemporary state of technology." Now, over half a century later, as the university moves onward with an expanded and renovated Kingsbury Hall, the mural's message and meaning are far from outdated.

In the center of the mural, Hatch painted a double-edged sword of reason bearing downward from an eye of conscience, splitting both the painting and the atom in half. On the right side of the mural, under a hand spread out in friendship and giving, the atom is used toward a positive future, one of community values, education, and fertile lands. On the left, under a closed fist, is its destructive counterpart. Here, the mural predicts that the new technology will breed war, resulting in a collapse of communication, infrastructure, and humankind. The scene is strongly reminiscent of a post-apocalyptic Earth. Restored and relocated to this more prominent location in 2006, John Hatch's mural will be viewed by many for years to come; his message of the promise and dangers of atomic energy will ring true for future generations.

Moving the Mural

In 2003, the State of New Hampshire funded an addition and complete renovation of Kingsbury Hall. The project required demolition of parts of the existing building that were inadequate for renovation, including the library where the mural was located. Moving a mural painted on plaster applied to a 6-ton, 4-inch-thick cinderblock wall from the second floor to the first floor would be very difficult and risky. Severe cracking or a complete failure of the plaster was a real possibility. However, the university made the commitment and set aside money to relocate and preserve the mural, an important step in preserving this piece of university history and a significant work of public art on the campus.

Moving the Hatch mural was a true collaboration of art and technology. The university hired a nationally renowned painting conservation firm to move the mural and repair the damage caused by stress, weather, vandalism, and the ravages of time. The process required months of planning, two weeks of physical preparation and stabilization of the work, and finally, two full days and the help of ten workers to physically move the work. The final step of restoring the mural took several additional weeks.

Preparation for the move involved adding a plaster background to the 4-inch-thick concrete wall to increase the strength of it. Two layers of compounds and rice paper were added to the mural face to protect its surface during transport. Because of the mural's size, it was decided that the safest thing to do was to cut it in half without disturbing the integrity of the painting. Each half weighed about 6,000 pounds.

Each section was lifted using a block-and-tackle-like device and attached to a set of trolleys suspended from a track of I-beams on the ceiling. The mural wall, originally on the second level, was then trolleyed 140 feet to an opening in the floor and lowered to the ground level, where it was wheeled through the old Kingsbury to the new south wing, suspended from a second I-beam, and slid into place. A portion of the mural will stick out beyond the curve of the wall to represent visually the fact that the mural came from another place.

The final step was the restoration of the mural. The protective layers were removed and any damage done to the mural in transport was repaired. The cut line that splits the mural wall in half was painted over, and faded colors were brightened. For restoring the mural, everything added to its surface is reversible. The hope, though, is that the restoration will be enduring.

Case Study: Sustainable Buildings — Do You Want Fries with Your Building? No Thank You!
DOUGLAS BENCKS

As we discuss the idea of sustainable design and construction with various campus and community constituents, we frequently hear skepticism that it will be cost effective, and that it truly will be in the institution's best interest. As we have described previously, many strong rationales make sustainable design and construction compelling, but sometimes a simple example gets the message across to the widest audience. The following is one we have used in many forums to build broad support.

Creating sustainably designed and constructed buildings is like developing a healthy life style. It can be accomplished in varied ways and for each individual it will be different. For some, a healthy life style may mean being a vegan and eating only the most carefully grown and prepared foods, rock climbing, and having minimal material needs. For others, it may be eating moderately sized meals of things like salmon and peas, walking every day, and using public transportation to commute to work. There are many definitions of a healthy life style, but no matter what, it has to fit the needs and circumstances of the individual. The challenge is to avoid slipping into the "fast food" mentality, which may seem inexpensive and quick, but generally not a good long-term value. Fast food might make you feel good right now, but at what cost later on?

Sustainable building design and construction are no different. Unfortunately, the building industry is full of the "fast food" attitude, and the buildings that are produced may be sparkly and clean at first appearance and often oversized, but within a few years they are tired, out-of-style, energy hogs that are difficult to maintain. This requires another infusion of "fast food" design, and our built environment becomes out of shape and overweight. Truly sustainable design creates buildings that last longer, require less maintenance, use less energy, and have less impact on natural systems. Many solutions are available to make this happen. For some projects, the latest ideas and technology may be a good fit, but for others more common, but highly effective means may be the right answer.

It's easy to say "I want to be healthy" or "I want a sustainable building," but it is the day-to-day habits and the knowledge of what will really work that creates success. Crash diets don't make a life style healthy, and a couple of meetings to identify "green" features don't make a building sustainable. The keys to developing a healthy life style or a sustainably designed building, are a strong commitment to achievable goals, a methodology with specific strategies to meet those goals, and the determination to remain constantly focused, and not give in to the urge for fast food or crash diets.

CHAPTER 4

Creating the Intellectual Basis for Sustainability

Research and Scholarship

John Aber and Cameron Wake

Research and scholarship on university campuses result more from the interests, experiences, and abilities of the faculty than from university policies. The questions and ideas that faculty choose to pursue are less subject to overall university guidance than issues of the curriculum, operations, or even engagement. More contact and interaction with faculty at other campuses and institutions tends to occur in areas of scholarship than the other three CORE activities. How then does sustainability-related inquiry happen on campuses and how can research support the goal of campus sustainability? The research portfolio of a university is perhaps the most valid expression of the research interests, abilities, and passions of the faculty. Conversely, the intensity of activity generated by focused research programs, through engagement of faculty, staff, and students, helps to generate a campus culture that emphasizes those areas where research is most active. However, it is certainly the case that universities can encourage or inhibit faculty initiative by creating, or failing to create, supportive administrative structures and budget models.

University Strengths

The University of New Hampshire has a long history in environmentally oriented research. Initiatives undertaken reflect both the coastal location of

PHOTO: Students are engaged actively in research across campus. These students are part of the CREAM program described in the Food and Society sections of this chapter and chapter 2. *Photo courtesy of UNH Photographic Services.*

the campus and national trends in environmental research, as well as a solid national standing in environmental research in general. For example, the Institute for Scientific Information recently ranked universities in terms of publication impact in different fields by measuring the frequency with which publications of university faculty were cited by their peers. By this metric, UNH was ranked among the top five universities in the country in both Geosciences, and Ecology and Environmental Science. No other university was present in the top five in both lists. UNH is also heavily focused in environmental areas in terms of externally funded research. Over the last ten years, well more than half of total grant funding was in the area of environmental sciences, defined broadly to include terrestrial, atmospheric, aquatic, and marine environments. Few institutions would list NASA and NOAA as their two largest sources of external research funds.

UNH also has been represented in several national and international study groups aimed at defining either the future course of environmental research or the application of knowledge to policy. UNH faculty have held leadership roles in the Millennium Study, the first national and sector-based environmental assessment, and policy-setting studies on the future of global research for both NASA and NOAA. These efforts extend to emerging or nontraditional areas as well, such as organic dairy culture, open ocean aquaculture, and to policy and educational efforts, as outlined in the sections that follow.

Unique Characteristics

While UNH has clear strengths in environmental and sustainability research, many other universities could claim this distinction as well. Are there characteristics of this type of research that are unique to UNH, or that represent best-practice approaches to increasing the impact of the work that is done, in terms of application to sustainability? What lessons might there be here for the broader university community?

Universities express their goals and aspirations in part by the structures and organizations established to lead the university forward. UNH has made accelerating commitments in research on sustainability and the environment over several decades. These include the second-oldest Hydrology program in the country, and a university-wide Marine Program established and first funded in 1973. More recently, UNH established its first University Institute in 2006, the Institute for the Study of Earth, Oceans, and Space (see the section on Climate and Energy in this chapter), which houses several major environmental research initiatives. A university-wide Ph.D. program in Natural Resources and Earth System Science, formed in 1989 on the basis of faculty enthusiasm, has become the largest doctoral program on campus, and spans the disciplines from biogeochemistry and remote sensing to environmental policy and ethics (see the Climate and Energy section in chapter 2).

The most direct institutional statement in support of sustainability-related programs was the formation of the nation's first endowed, university-wide Office of Sustainability Programs in 1997. This office was renamed the University Office of Sustainability and moved to the Provost's Office in 2007, and is now led by the campus Chief Sustainability Officer.

Another dimension of the research enterprise at UNH relates strongly to the sustainability theme, expanding significantly on the traditional land-grant university role in extension. "Outreach scholarship" is a rapidly growing approach to bringing the activities of research universities off-campus to the world at large (see chapter 5, Culture and Sustainability). The critical distinction between outreach scholarship and traditional extension is the involvement, from the beginning, of partners from the communities served by the research. While traditional extension activities bring the results of completed research to identified user groups, outreach scholarship engages those groups from the beginning in the definition of the problem and in the design and execution of research, to ensure relevance and acceptance of the results. Examples of outreach scholarship presented in this chapter include the work of the Carsey Institute, oyster bed restoration, and the Organic Dairy Research Farm.

Many other examples of outreach scholarship can be found on campus and are described in other sections of this book. UNH faculty provided the initial scientific lead for the international GLOBE program, which enlists high school students and teachers around the world in environmental monitoring and analysis work linked through the internet. A regional program (Forest Watch, see chapter 5) applies the same principles more locally. An aquatic effort with a similar focus, the Lay Lakes Monitoring Program (chapter 5), has acquired decades-worth of water-quality data for dozens of lakes across the state, made possible by teams of volunteer sample collectors statewide.

Finally, sustainability emphasizes the analysis of whole systems, so relevant research tends to be interdisciplinary. UNH emphasizes broad cross-boundary research. Two examples would be a unique look at the history of marine fisheries in the Gulf of Maine, with a history professor and a natural resources professor as co-investigators (the HMAP program, described in the Biodiversity and Ecosystems section of this chapter), and a new NIH initiative combining large-scale remote sensing with the prediction of the occurrence and spread of infectious diseases.

In regard to interdisciplinarity, one of UNH's most important weaknesses may be a hidden strength. As a traditionally underfunded state institution, an ethos of cross-department and cross-college cooperation in research has emerged. People are UNH's most important asset, and interdisciplinary cooperation tends to be more easily accomplished where the need for collegiality is high and the administrative structure tends to be lean.

✒

Research on Biodiversity and Ecosystems

Focus and funding in the area of ecosystems and biodiversity are reflected in the participation of UNH scientists in most of the major ecosystem research initiatives over the last two decades. These include the National Science Foundation's Long-Term Ecological Research (LTER) program, where UNH scientists participate in the several site-level programs across the country, and the nascent National Ecological Observing Network (NEON) with active participation in planning and oversight, including National Academy review panels and the current Board of Directors. UNH faculty have been engaged in several major National Aeronautics and Space Administration global-change programs, including regional initiatives in the Arctic and the Amazon, and in process-focused programs on carbon cycling and remote sensing of ecosystem dynamics. Recently, UNH has developed strong partnerships with several National Oceanic and Atmospheric Administration (NOAA) agencies responsible for basic research in atmospheric and marine sciences, and with application and management of air and ocean resources. UNH faculty have played a major role in development of new projects with NOAA, and also through participation in study groups defining the agencies' research direction.

The case studies presented here demonstrate several characteristics of UNH research related to the sustainability of populations and ecosystems. The Cooperative Institute for Coastal and Estuarine Environmental Technology (CICEET) engages managers of estuarine systems and other stakeholders in the definition of research goals, and then funds a competitive process to develop the information needed to meet those goals. The History of Marine Animals program is a wonderful example of widely cross-disciplinary research, as the techniques and sources traditionally employed in historical research are used to answer a fundamental scientific question in fisheries research. The Stormwater Research Center is a CICEET-initiated project that provides innovative approaches to minimizing the impacts of storm runoff on water quality. The work on oyster bed restoration has been carried out in close collaboration with management agencies and nonprofit environmental groups as well, and has involved teams of volunteers that both help get the work done and gain educational experiences along the way.

Case Study: Cooperative Institute for Coastal and
Estuarine Environmental Technology
RICH LANGAN AND DOLORES LEONARD

Every year, new residents and visitors pour into coastal areas, and with them comes development. New homes, roads, parking lots, and industries enrich local economies, but they also compromise the very qualities that make coastal living so attractive: clean water, thriving ecosystems, and the natural beauty that arises from the interface of land and sea. Poorly planned development routinely is cited as a contributing factor in the decline of water quality, the degradation of coastal habitats, and dramatic fluctuations in the water resources necessary to nourish coastal communities and the ecosystems upon which they depend. Such impacts are magnified in a time of climate change, when rising sea levels and increasingly frequent and severe coastal storms cause widespread erosion and flooding.

In this context, the decisions we make today about how to use and manage coastal natural resources have lasting implications for the future. The stakes are high, particularly when calculated in terms of potential lost property, infrastructure damage, habitat degradation, reduced economic opportunity, and increasing threats to human health and safety. The good news is that the United States research and technology development engine is highly capable, possessed of significant resources and intellectual capital that can be marshaled more effectively to provide tools that coastal resource managers can use to describe and address problems on the coast in an effective and sustainable way.

To help build a bridge between science and the practical needs of coastal management, UNH and the National Oceanic and Atmospheric Administration (NOAA) established the Cooperative Institute for Coastal Environmental Technologies (CICEET) in 1997. From its home on the UNH Durham campus, CICEET develops, demonstrates, and implements tools to detect, prevent, and reverse the impacts of coastal pollution and habitat degradation on coastal ecosystems and communities nationwide. As a needs-based organization, CICEET works with coastal resource managers nationwide to identify their priority environmental challenges and then to analyze the obstacles — technical, social, political, and regulatory — that stand in the way of solutions. If this analysis reveals that new or enhanced technology could help address a priority challenge, CICEET designs a targeted, competitive grants program to meet this need.

Working through the mechanism of a competitive grants program allows for the best minds and institutions across the country to be engaged in developing solutions to coastal management problems. These competitions also serve as an opportunity for CICEET to build a network of scientists and coastal managers that bridges academia, government, private industry, and nongovernment sectors. CICEET uses this network to ground-truth the needs assessments that establish research priorities for the institute's grants competitions, to inform the panels that review proposals, and ultimately, to steward CICEET-funded projects so that they can have maximum benefit for the larger coastal management community.

CICEET's principal partner in this process is the National Estuarine Research Reserve System (NERRS), a network of twenty-seven protected estuarine areas around the country. Each NERRS site is a NOAA/state partnership, established for long-term research, education, and stewardship. In the NERRS, the understanding of local scientific and management needs combines with a strong national network that makes the reserves ideal places for CICEET-sponsored project teams to develop, refine, test, demonstrate, and deliver tools and technologies that can be applied to address coastal problems.

Since its inception, CICEET has invested in more than 170 environmental technology development and demonstration projects through its competitive funding programs, which have yielded dozens of field-ready tools. CICEET-sponsored tools encompass a wide range of technologies and methods. These include sophisticated instrumentation, such as a robotic early-warning system for red tide and an integrated remote-sensing and multibeam sonar modeling system to map the seafloor in turbulent coastal waters, to innovative, social science–based approaches to linking science-based information to local decisionmakers. CICEET makes information about all of its projects available to coastal managers through its website, demonstrations, training, outreach, and an evolving technology utilization program.

CICEET also works through strategic investments that leverage the environmental science capacity at UNH. The university's Stormwater Center, highlighted in this chapter, is one of CICEET's most successful programs, providing a unique national resource for stormwater managers who must design programs that comply with tightening water-quality standards and protect their communities in a time when what used to be "the storm of the century" is a regular occurrence. Recently, scientists from UNH's Environmental Research Group developed a test bed for sediment remediation technologies in New Hampshire's Cocheco River with support from CICEET. In both the UNH-based programs and its competitively funded projects,

CICEET supports the training of graduate students and postdoctoral scholars in disciplines associated with the CICEET mission.

Just as the scientists on CICEET-sponsored project teams strive to bring the best-available science to bear on their work, CICEET works to improve its process of advancing research into application on behalf of coastal management. Ten years of experience offers ample opportunity to learn what works and what doesn't. A profound lesson for CICEET's staff has been that for every success, there is a technology with great merit that is not used. When the intended user is not an engaged participant, projects aimed at addressing the needs of coastal management can stumble on a number of unforeseen barriers, including insufficient resources to use the proposed solution, as well as unfavorable political, social, and regulatory climates in which to implement it.

On the other hand, projects that actively engage intended users from the identification of a problem to the demonstration of a solution are more likely to identify and account for such barriers, and thereby have a much greater chance of producing a tool that can be implemented effectively. As a result, CICEET's funding opportunities increasingly have engaged the point of view and the participation of intended users. This is exemplified by CICEET's Living Coasts Program, which seeks to provide coastal communities with more effective tools to grow in a way that preserves water quality, protects natural areas, and improves quality of life. Under this program, thirteen teams in twenty coastal states are working with committed community partners to address priority land-use issues such as comprehensive planning, natural resource protection, the need to balance economic and ecological health, and stormwater management.

CICEET recently has augmented its focus on intended users by building a collaborative process, one that allows for all stakeholders to have a voice into its competitive grants program. Often referred to as "collaborative research," this approach is particularly appropriate for addressing the problems of coastal management, which more often than not dwell at the interface of natural and social systems. CICEET is also committed to continual program improvement; therefore, strategic planning, measuring performance against carefully established metrics, and adaptive management are integral to operation of the program.

Case Study: The History of Marine Animal Populations

ANDREW ROSENBERG, JEFF BOLSTER,

KAREN ALEXANDER, AND BILL LEAVENWORTH

Interdisciplinarity is a hallmark of sustainability-related research at UNH. The challenges of creating a sustainable world rarely fall neatly into the bins of knowledge constructed by departments and colleges on university campuses, and instead require innovative combinations of academic expertise. An historical perspective also can be important in drawing value from traditional practices while pursuing new technologies and behaviors.

The History of Marine Animal Populations (HMAP) program represents just such an unusual combination of fisheries ecology and historical research designed to recreate presettlement population characteristics of commercial fisheries, and to document the downward trends in numbers over time. It forms the historical component of the Census of Marine Life program, a billion-dollar, multidisciplinary, collaborative project involving about a thousand scientists from more than seventy countries. The goal of the Census of Marine Life program is to understand how and why the diversity, distribution, and abundance of marine life in the world's oceans changes over the long term.

HMAP is international itself, involving researchers from Roskilde University (Denmark), Hull University (England), Murdoch University (Australia), and UNH, and involves teams of historians, archaeologists, marine ecologists, biologists, and fisheries scientists who analyze historical and environmental data relating to the use and management of marine animal populations over the last two thousand years.

Consistent with other projects at UNH, HMAP has major outreach, training, and communications components. The project convenes workshops and summer schools and maintains an open and transparent website, in addition to contributing to scholarly journals and meetings.

The UNH portion of HMAP has focused on the cod fishery off the coast of New England and the Maritimes, where the goals and ambitions of fishermen, fisheries managers, and those concerned about marine ecosystems are often in bitter conflict. A key part of this debate is the question of what constitutes a completely recovered cod population, with some claiming that the relatively high levels estimated in the 1980s (high by twentieth-century standards) represent full recovery and should be the baseline population and target for management.

Combining expertise in historical research with the perspective of experience gained through the National Marine Fisheries Service, HMAP researchers have discovered and brought together historical records going back to the mid-1800s and used them as a mathematical basis for estimating cod populations. By acknowledging nineteenth-century fishermen as accurate observers of the environment, the project also encourages a dialogue between contemporary scientists and fishers on the state of the marine ecosystem from which better management policy eventually may result. The success of the project also opens up the potential for others applying similar methods in reconstructing populations of commercially harvested species.

The target of the UNH HMAP program was the federally subsidized, but unrestricted, New England cod fishery of the mid-1800s. Records of fishing schooners of this period provide a rich and previously untapped source for basic data on harvest effort and success, as well as interesting anecdotes.

Archival records of New England cod-fishing vessels between 1852 and 1866 can report daily catch, vessel location, depth of water, and the condition of the sea floor, as well as familial affinities among the crew and communications with vessels fishing nearby. Fishing agreements list vessel size, homeport, crew names and residences, and total catch weight. The combination of daily catch statistics, observations at sea, and geographic location with social, cultural, and demographic data discloses communitarian knowledge systems, information networks, and decisionmaking processes operating within ecological and social contexts. Data from archival fisheries records were evaluated historically and modeled with Geographic Information Systems (GIS) software, tracking changes over time in the distribution of fishing vessels, their homeport, familial and social affinities, and biological indicators for cod stock.

The results of the HMAP project have been profound. Once a dominant species, cod populations have declined by as much as 96 percent since the 1850s. Putting this in perspective, today, sixteen small schooners of the pre–Civil War era could hold all adult cod currently estimated in the once-rich Scotian Shelf off Nova Scotia. This historical analysis indicates that recent levels of biomass and catch may grossly underrepresent the productive potential of commercially important species in these once-rich fishing grounds.

Managing the remnants of the ocean's resources is a critical issue worldwide, but exactly what constitutes a healthy fish population remains controversial. The HMAP project attempts to provide accurate assessments of historical populations and productive potential to aid in rebuilding these fisheries. The historical perspective has proven crucial to the task, and the inter-

disciplinary approach taken at UNH in its contribution to the project is an excellent example of our approach to sustainability research.

Case Study: The Stormwater Research Center
TOM BALLESTERO

The Stormwater Research Center serves as a primary example of the characteristics of research programs at UNH that support sustainability. Established with NOAA funding through the CICEET program (see the first case study of this section), the primary mission of the center is the protection of water resources through effective stormwater management. Currently, the center is acting as a unique technical resource for stormwater practitioners by studying a range of issues for specific stormwater-management strategies, including design, water quality and quantity, cost, maintenance, and operations.

New Clean Water Act Phase II rules require that local governments develop stormwater programs. In response, many organizations have or are now developing plans and actions to achieve desirable water quality and storm volume reduction. Although many of the stormwater-management devices are based on sound theory, there is no requirement that they undergo independent, third-party scientific testing, and a three-year study of nine seacoast sites in New Hampshire showed that traditional stormwater technologies failed to reduce at least one water-quality parameter two-thirds of the time.

The center has designed and constructed and now runs a facility that provides the controlled testing of stormwater-management structures and technologies, as well as educational and outreach programs that involve professionals engaged in stormwater management. The field research facility serves as a site for testing stormwater-treatment processes, for technology demonstrations and workshops. The testing results and technology demonstrations are meant to assist in the planning, design, and implementation of effective stormwater-management strategies for resource managers.

One of the high-profile projects of the center is a multi-year study of a porous asphalt parking lot at our field site on campus. Parking lots made of this material reduce surface runoff significantly by allowing direct percolation of rainwater and melting snowwater through the material, avoiding the need for ponding basins and reducing peak flow events. Data and observations indicate that porous asphalt is a viable, cost-effective approach to treating water quality and reducing the volume of runoff. The system performed exceptionally well in winter and proved itself to be as durable as conventional

asphalt. It also appears to require as much as 75 percent less road salt for deicing.

The porous asphalt experiment is one of several low-impact development (LID) stormwater systems that have been tested over a diverse range of seasonal conditions. What we have observed disproves common assumptions that LIDs do not fare well in the harsh winters that are common in cold climate regions. In fact, all of the LID stormwater approaches we have monitored — biorentention systems, tree filter, the porous asphalt parking lot, sand filters, and gravel wetlands — demonstrated excellent water-quality treatment and peak flow reduction year-round.

This evaluation is made possible by the field facility, which includes fifteen different management systems that undergo side-by-side comparison testing under strictly controlled conditions. The facility also offers a platform for technology demonstrations and workshops as well as specialized training opportunities. In addition to the primary field facility, the center has other sites available to study approaches that need more space or present unique conditions.

The Stormwater Center involves a range of participants. Our Technical Advisory Board provides advice and expertise, and includes industry representatives, state and federal regulators, academics, and local government officials. Vendors, manufacturers, regulatory agencies, system designers, and the thousands of entities required to comply with the Clean Water Act benefit from Stormwater Center research. All are encouraged to comment on the facility and testing methods.

Case Study: Oyster Restoration — Planning, Research,
and Implementation in New Hampshire
RAY GRIZZLE

Populations of the eastern oyster (*Crassostrea virginica*) are in long-term decline throughout its range, including the New England states. Causes for the declines vary but in most cases, including New Hampshire, disease and human harvesting are major factors. Oyster populations in New Hampshire today are only a small fraction of what they were even a decade ago. Some reefs are completely dead and most are severely degraded. Management historically has focused on fisheries and aquaculture, but more recently the oyster's ecological importance has become widely recognized. The reef structures that oysters naturally form provide important habitat for many other

species. A healthy oyster reef can filter large volumes of water as the oysters feed on suspended particles such as phytoplankton, thereby providing measurable improvements in water quality. Oyster reefs also can provide a buffer against shoreline erosion. Thus, management agencies in many areas have ongoing restoration plans that target the "ecosystem services" oysters provide as well as their value as a human food resource.

Since 1999, researchers at the University of New Hampshire have partnered with federal, state, and local government agencies, conservation organizations such as The Nature Conservancy, and local citizen volunteers in efforts to restore our dwindling oyster populations. Most of the work to date has consisted of experimental-scale projects to test different restoration methods. This work has involved introduction of young oysters from disease-resistant broodstocks, tests of several different reef-structure designs, the impacts of constructed reefs on water quality, and how oysters interact with eelgrass to affect water quality.

Two community-based programs also have been started. One enlists volunteers to grow young oysters in cages off their docks, after which they are used in oyster restoration projects. The other is a shell recycling program that provides a drop-off site for local harvesters to return the empty shells from the oysters they consume. The shell is used mainly in oyster larvae-settlement experiments and eventually is returned to the estuary with young oysters attached. Thus, the natural cycle of oyster shell is completed. These two programs provide opportunities for citizens to become involved in the overall restoration effort in meaningful ways. So far, the experimental-scale projects have resulted in improvements in degraded reefs affecting over 4 acres of bottom area.

More recently, the focus has turned to full-scale restoration projects and estuary-wide planning efforts. In 2006, the Great Bay Estuary Restoration Compendium, a major planning document, was published. In 2007, the New Hampshire Estuary Restoration Partners organization was formed to facilitate and coordinate estuarine restoration activities in general, which to date have included salt marsh, eelgrass, diadromous fish, and oysters. The Partners organization consists of a diversity of individuals representing all levels of government, NGOs, interested citizens, and scientists at the University of New Hampshire. There is great interest in ecological restoration activities in New Hampshire, and the ongoing efforts represent an extraordinarily diverse collaboration of participants. One of the major goals is to restore the eastern oyster to its historical role as a "keystone" species providing important ecosystem services as well as a resource for humans to harvest and enjoy.

Research on Climate and Energy

UNH has been ranked among the top five universities in the country for publication impact in both the Geosciences, and in Ecology and Environmental Science by the Institute for Scientific Information (ISI), the only institution to achieve a top-five ranking in both areas. This recognition, based on the frequency with which colleagues cite papers published by UNH scientists, exemplifies the strength of the research enterprise across campus in areas related to climate and energy. UNH faculty have led major programs in the recreation of former climates and atmospheres from ice core samples gathered from around the world, and for regional to global measurements of greenhouse gas concentrations and dynamics. Research into alternative methods of producing energy is also increasing, with a major regional conference on the topic held in the summer of 2008.

This section presents four examples of research efforts that cross boundaries on campus and link the discovery process with student learning, while bringing considerable amounts of external support to the research enterprise. The Institute for the Study of Earth, Oceans, and Space (EOS) focuses on the Earth as a biogeochemical system driven by the energy of the Sun. Understanding climate change on Earth and "space weather" caused by Sun/Earth interactions are major research areas. The Environmental Research Group (ERG) encompasses several programs in environmental and sustainable engineering, including waste and material recycling, water quality and treatment, stormwater management, and coastal and estuarine protection and restoration. Faculty from ERG have been primary drivers for continued student participation, with notable success in the annual Waste-Management Education and Research Consortium contest. UNH student teams have come away with the top prize in this national contest several times. Finally, a number of faculty with expertise in energy and climate issues have provided technical expertise in the formation of science-based policy statements at the state and regional level.

Case Study: The Institute for the Study of Earth, Oceans, and Space
DAVID S. BARTLETT

The Institute for the Study of Earth, Oceans, and Space (EOS), UNH's largest research enterprise, traces its origins to far-sighted thinking in two quite different venues. In the early 1980s, the national research community was beginning to plan for studies in the new field of "global change." A 1983 National Research Council report, *Toward an International Geosphere-Biosphere Program — A Study of Global Change* (Washington, D.C.: National Academy Press) concluded that this new field "transcends the bounds of specialized, scientific disciplines and the scope of limited, national scientific endeavors." It called for the initiation of a cooperative, interdisciplinary effort addressing solar/terrestrial relationships; Earth, ocean, and atmospheric sciences; biogeochemical cycles; and human interactions to make more rapid progress than was possible through traditional, specialized studies.

At the same time, UNH was considering ways to reorganize its space science, marine science, and elements of Earth sciences with the dual objectives of aligning its program with the emerging national trends in interdisciplinary research and fostering a goal "to develop some research and educational programs of a national and international reputation." EOS was established in September 1985, soon occupied a newly constructed research building, and drew affiliated faculty from multiple departments: physics, mathematics, Earth sciences, and natural resources. Its early leaders noted and pursued the alignment of disciplines with NASA's emerging initiatives, including the proposed "Earth Observing System," and the use of different terms but the same "EOS" acronym was not entirely coincidental. NASA was then and remained for many years after the principal source of funds for "global change" studies, both nationally and at UNH.

Space science research has a long history at UNH, originating with faculty expertise in physics along with the convenience of placing heavy cosmic ray detectors in "low Earth orbit" — namely, atop Mount Washington via the haul road to the summit. Marine science was a large but widely dispersed area of faculty research. Strong, but relatively small research programs in ice-core paleoclimatology and computer modeling of Earth systems were clearly complementary elements for inclusion in the new institute.

The institute was founded with the idea that, after an initial period of review, it ultimately would become a graduate "school" offering its own M.S. and Ph.D. degrees in Earth, ocean, and space science. Its financial basis was simple: The Institute was to be supported entirely by grants and the accompanying institutional overhead, not affecting the financial structure of any other university element. New faculty, both tenure-track and "research" (i.e., salaried from grants), were recruited in several strategic areas not represented among the university's existing strengths, including atmospheric chemistry, terrestrial ecosystems, remote sensing, and large-scale hydrology. For a variety of reasons, the transition to a school never occurred, but in 2006 EOS became UNH's first "University Institute," conferring on EOS the status and many of the responsibilities of a college or school, but without granting degrees. The current goal is for UNH to create a small number of additional such institutes, using elements of the EOS model, to enhance and provide increased visibility and student opportunities in areas of existing research strength.

Since 1986, the number of EOS-affiliated faculty has grown from 17 to 56. Total funding has always represented 30 to 50 percent of the rapidly increasing pool of external, primarily federal, research support. Major federal sponsors include the National Aeronautics and Space Administration (NASA), the National Science Foundation (NSF), the National Atmospheric and Oceanic Administration (NOAA), and the Department of Energy (DOE). Research areas include solar physics; climate records in snow, ice, and other proxies; atmospheric chemistry and dynamics; field and modeling studies of biogeochemical cycles; large-scale hydrologic modeling; physical, chemical, and biological oceanography; and remote sensing for monitoring and assessment of marine and terrestrial environments and human interactions.

EOS has become a flagship element of the university's growing reputation and, with its continuing emphasis on studies of what was once termed "global change," is an important incubator for elements of sustainability across campus, across the state, and across the region. The institute makes important contributions to supporting and mentoring undergraduate and, especially, graduate students in multiple departments and in the university's interdisciplinary Ph.D. program in Natural Resources and Earth System Science.

What was once a rather single-minded focus on basic research has expanded to include numerous applied programs of education and outreach related to community concerns about climate change, environmental degradation, and sustainable living. EOS faculty lead programs in Global Learning to Benefit the Environment (GLOBE) and Forest Watch, engaging pre-college students and teachers in studies of their local and global environments. The AIRMAP project is an important element of NOAA's efforts to unravel the complexities of atmospheric chemistry and climate in the Northeast, as well as to provide continuous monitoring of air quality for the citizens of New England. The Coastal Ocean Observing Center and Northeast Consortium programs provide monitoring of the dynamic environment of the Gulf of Maine, and provide venues for involvement of local fishermen in marine research and public education about coastal and marine environments. EOS staff created the New Hampshire Carbon Challenge to provide citizens with motivation and tools to reduce household carbon emissions. Most recently, EOS has developed a strategic partnership with the University Office of Sustainability on an engaged scholarship project titled Carbon Solutions New England (CSNE), a regional collaboration working toward a clean energy future.

In many ways, the concept of "sustainability" is the twenty-five-year-old offspring of "global change." The establishment of EOS twenty-five years ago also helped lay the foundation for sustainability as a recurrent theme at UNH. It was made possible by a combination of foresight on the part of university faculty and administrators, strong alignment with emerging national and international scientific priorities, and the willingness and ability of existing and new faculty to rely on competitive research funding to support the enterprise.

Case Study: The Environmental Research Group
KEVIN GARDNER AND TAYLOR EIGHMY

Environmental engineering is concerned with mitigating human impacts on the environment and minimizing risks to human health arising from human activities and waste products. Over time, the field has evolved from an "end-of-pipe treatment" focus on processing or isolating wastes, to an "up-stream" approach that minimizes waste creation in the first place (for example, recycling electronic components is more economical when electronics are designed to be recycled). Central to this evolution has been the development of a systems-level approach to analyzing problems associated with our impact on the environment and humankind. The term "sustainable science and engineering" has come to define this systems-level view of the human/environment system.

The Environmental Research Group (ERG), founded in 1987, and one of the largest organized research centers at UNH, integrates its research and engagement activities under this paradigm. ERG is part of the College of Engineering and Physical Sciences, and has as its mission improving human and environmental health, mitigating human impacts on the environment, training qualified engineering professionals for the workforce, and serving society locally and internationally. ERG performs high-impact applied and fundamental research related to critical environmental science, engineering, regulatory and policy issues, and fosters the intellectual growth of graduate and undergraduate students through innovative, multidisciplinary research.

Faculty in ERG have primary expertise in the fields of environmental and civil engineering and are associated with the Department of Civil Engineering. Areas of specialization include:

- coastal and estuarine environments: impact mitigation and remediation;
- stormwater management, treatment, and low-impact development;
- material recycling, industrial ecology, and waste management; and
- water treatment technologies.

ERG was created by an entrepreneurial group of individuals who recognized the value of interdisciplinary research groups and the need to pool resources and expertise in order to address truly challenging environmental issues. It was clear at the time, and remains so today, that the single investigator/single laboratory research paradigm was not capable of addressing our most pressing environmental issues.

Formation of ERG was facilitated by an administrative structure and individuals within that structure that provided the flexibility needed to create new groups and centers easily. Equally as important was an appropriate financial structure that allowed provision of critical support capabilities for a major research center such as this. To be successful, this type of endeavor requires the attention and efforts of a director and requires support staff for administrative, computational, and professional reporting purposes. The traditional college and department structures need to be supplemented with cross-department, cross-college research centers that can be agile in their formation and transformation in response to opportunities and challenges, and it this approach that has allowed ERG to be successful.

ERG has developed a number of research centers in response to opportunities and environmental challenges. Currently, the group has four major research centers that reflect faculty expertise within ERG, recognition of important environmental issues with research needs, and successful grant writing. These include:

- The Recycled Materials Resource Center, funded by the Federal Highway Administration, Environmental Protection Agency, and individual state departments of transportation;
- the Coastal Response Research Center, funded by the National Oceanic and Atmospheric Administration;
- the UNH Stormwater Center, funded from the Cooperative Institute for Coastal and Estuarine Environmental Technology; and
- the Water Treatment Technology Assistance Center, funded through the U.S. Environmental Protection Agency.

These centers provide a rich diversity of interest and expertise, while maintaining a sharp focus on sustaining the integrity and health of our natural environment and mitigating society's impact.

This combination of interdisciplinarity and problem-oriented focus provided the basis for the development of the Sustainable Science and Engineering Ph.D. Fellowship Program. This program was created within ERG with critical funding provided through a competitive process by the UNH Vice President for Research and Public Service and the UNH Graduate School, which was matched with funds from ERG, ERG research centers, and the College of Engineering and Physical Sciences. This is a perfect example of why ERG has been successful in the UNH environment: In order to grow in this critical new field, a decisive new initiative was developed using funds combined from a number of sources. This success has allowed ERG to move forward in the integration of its research areas in recognition of their contribution to the theme of sustainability and sustainable civil infrastructure.

The first doctoral fellows in the Sustainability Science and Engineering program are working to develop tools to measure the overall sustainability of municipalities and metropolitan regions and how changes in planning and zoning may alter the course of a community toward a more sustainable form and function. Included in this analysis are basic physical characteristics of a region and how they dictate infrastructure requirements, as well as metrics related to environmental impact and social health. An example is a project to determine the relative sustainability of different stormwater-management and low-impact development techniques and technologies.

In general, fellows are focused on the scientific analysis of sustainability paradigms to provide an objective evaluation of technologies or concepts historically considered only in a heuristic manner. This is one of the critical roles that the growing field of Sustainability Science and Engineering provides to our society and the larger debate over how to move toward a more sustainable way of life. The flexibility, resources, and responsiveness of ERG have fostered this paradigm-shifting research and helped UNH respond to this grand challenge of our times.

Case Study: Multidisciplinary Design Competition
JENNA JAMBECK AND KEVIN GARDNER

The International Environmental Design Contest is an annual student competition hosted by Waste-Management Education and Research Consortium (WERC), a consortium for Environmental Education and Technology Development at New Mexico State University. Beginning in 2000, UNH has assembled a multidisciplinary team drawing undergraduates from Environmental Engineering and the Whittemore School of Business, as well as Civil Engineering, Environmental Science, Earth Science, and English. Our student teams have won first or second place in their chosen category each year, and on four occasions have won contest-wide awards for innovation and for the sustainability of their solutions.

We attribute this success in large part to our ability to put together successful and truly integrated multidisciplinary teams. The student teams and the projects proposed reflect the sustainability culture of the campus and the relative ease of interdisciplinary work at UNH. Solutions developed revolve around themes of industrial ecology, recycling, and alternative energy.

The 2007 team, called MicroCellutions, Inc., consisted of seven environmental engineering students, one civil engineering student, and four business students. MicroCellutions, Inc., won the Intel Award for Innovation, the third winning team from UNH in the award's five-year history. The 2005 team won this award for a task sponsored by the Department of Energy for the removal of CO_2 from the atmosphere for less than \$10/ton. In 2003, UNH won this award for a low-cost, sustainable technology for home point-of-use and small water supply arsenic removal from drinking water. The 2007 team also won first place in its task group, and filed an invention disclosure to protect intellectual property developed by the students and faculty advisor. The description of the project is best provided by the excerpt from the report written by the students describing their conceptual full design based upon successful demonstration in the laboratory:

> In a world of finite resources and rapidly declining fossil fuel reserves, society must employ an integrative energy strategy to provide a more sustainable future. As a responsible member of the global community, MicroCellutions, Inc. is advancing renewable energy technologies by designing a single-chamber, open-air microbial fuel cell (MOR-2007) that successfully converts cow manure directly into electricity. The MOR-2007 is designed to reduce maintenance, operational difficulty, energy requirements, odors, chemical oxygen demand, and phosphorus, while minimizing the impact of current manure management practices on air and water quality. Residuals from MOR-2007 can be easily composted to provide bedding or land applied to cropland providing essential nutrients for plant uptake. This cyclical approach to nutrient management on the farm minimizes costs for additional fertilizers and bedding materials. MicroCellutions' innovative technology

and design, along with their education of farmers about microbial fuel cell (MFC) technology through public outreach, will provide dairy farmers with an alternative and sustainable manure management system.

This technology was proven at the bench scale and electricity was produced successfully from cow manure both in the laboratory at UNH and at the competition in New Mexico. The faculty advisor since has received competitive external funding to continue research on this promising technology, and one of the students from the team is conducting this research for her graduate thesis.

Case Study: Regional Climate Assessments —
Supporting Informed Public Policy
CAMERON WAKE

Reducing our collective greenhouse gas emissions and adapting to our changing climate have become two of the key societal issues of the twenty-first century. Providing an assessment of the potential impacts of climate change is now a central and well-recognized activity of the research community, with no better example than the four assessment reports produced by the Intergovernmental Panel on Climate Change. While climate change is certainly a global challenge, most of the impacts are experienced locally. Assessment of the impacts of climate change on a *regional* scale has proven to be a valuable tool for providing scientists, policymakers, private sector decisionmakers, not-for-profit organizations, and the general public with the best available science upon which to base informed choices concerning adaptation and mitigation strategies.

Two regional assessments have provided decision-relevant information across New England and the Northeast United States. The first assessment was begun in 1997 as part a broader National Assessment of the Potential Consequences of Climate Variability and Change that was supported by the U.S. Global Change Research Program. The New England Regional Assessment (NERA) was led by two UNH faculty members and involved stakeholders from a wide range of sectors. After numerous workshops, meetings, research, analysis, and review, the final report provided information not only on New England's changing climate, but also on the potential impact of future climate change on regional forests, regional water, human health, and the region's economy. This document became *the* reference for discussions of climate change in the region and helped inform the Climate Change Action Plan that eventually was adopted by the New England Governors/Eastern Canadian Premiers in August 2001. In addition, these findings were integrated into the larger national report that was presented to the U.S. Congress in 2000.

The second regional climate assessment focused on the Northeast was initiated by the Union of Concerned Scientists and involved more than fifty independent scientists and economists. It was designed to provide opinion-leaders, decisionmakers, and the public in the nine-state region (from New Jersey and Pennsylvania northward to Maine) with the best available science upon which to base informed choices about climate-change mitigation and adaptation. A UNH faculty member was the co-leader of the climate team that assembled and tested the projections for future climate change. These data were then provided to teams investigating the specific impact on key sectors in the region (coastal, marine, forests, agriculture, winter recreation, health, and water). The results of this three-year collaboration include the Northeast Climate Impact Assessment (NECIA) Synthesis Report that was released to considerable media attention and is now serving as the basis for a robust climate-change dialogue among scientists, policymakers, private-sector decisionmakers, and the public across the region; and a series of fourteen scientific papers that provide the primary technical underpinnings for the NECIA Synthesis Report.

Research on Food and Society

It is worth repeating here that UNH exists in an unusual position for a land-grant institution relative to food production. With relatively small amounts of federal funding due to its low agricultural production, and with the relative absence of major national and international commercial players in the state, UNH has the flexibility and campus culture to pursue alternatives to conventional agricultural practices. Compared with our farm-belt colleagues, we can support only a very small set of programs on agricultural production, but because of our unique position, those programs can be "outside the box" and provide innovative ideas and new solutions to a degree that is out of proportion to the funding available. A key characteristic of this approach is that it does not stop at the farm or even the store, but carries through to indicators of health, nutrition, and wellness on campus.

The four case studies presented here demonstrate the breadth of topics that this innovation can cover and reflect the integration among diverse approaches that typifies the sustainability initiative on campus. UNH has established the first commercial-scale Organic Dairy Research Farm in the country. This precedent-setting commitment has involved faculty from many departments and strategic support from the university administration and a number of private-sector partners. The Atlantic Marine Aquaculture Center has taken on the socially and technically challenging task of developing environmentally acceptable methods for off-shore aquaculture. The Community Food, Nutrition and Wellness Profile is a first effort at developing criteria and collecting data on the nutritional aspects of the food-delivery services on campus, in the broader context of institutional sustainability. Direct links among the development of new varieties of vegetables, student participation in growing and harvest, and use of the produce in university dining halls complete a cycle of research, education, and production.

Case Study: The UNH Organic Dairy Research Farm
JOHN E. CARROLL AND TOM KELLY

The UNH Organic Dairy Research Farm is our nation's first organic research dairy at a land-grant university, and a central piece of the university's pursuit of national leadership in sustainability. At the same time, it has proven a valuable resource supporting the growth of the organic dairy industry in

New England and nationally — and organic dairying is growing. Over 20 percent of the dairies in Maine are now organic. Vermont alone has 209 such dairies. Demand for organic dairy products has risen dramatically and supply in the region is falling short of demand. Yet organic farmers of all types, dairy and otherwise, are a population that has been underserved by major land-grant universities, as have grass-based livestock operations of all sorts. This creates an opportunity for a land-grant university to contribute to the health and integrity of family farms and rural communities through developing science and education that supports agroecological, sustainable agriculture enterprises.

Goals of the Organic Dairy Research Farm

The UNH Organic Dairy is, first and foremost, a grass-based dairy designed for serious and substantial research on intensive rotational grazing, a method based on constant movement of grazing animals from paddock to paddock in a manner that benefits the soil and the pasture grasses as well as the animals. Forage from the 100-plus acres of certified organic pastures is supplemented, particularly in winter, by the provision of certified organic forage and grain grown on university farms. As a result, UNH's Organic Dairy is becoming a center for research on grazing and forage production.

Major advantages of organic, pasture-based dairy production include reduced energy inputs and reduced greenhouse gas emissions. A goal of energy independence will make the farm a site for research into alternative methods for producing and using energy.

In this and other ways, the organic dairy is linked directly to UNH sustainability efforts in food and nutrition curricula and research, climate change and carbon reduction challenges, biodiversity initiatives, on-farm systems research, and energy security and conservation. The dairy represents nutritional qualities, reduced energy inputs and thus reduced carbon emissions, greater biodiversity on pasture and cropland, an invitation to self-contained systems research, and reduced energy dependence. Use of the dairy for teaching is growing steadily each semester as more classes and individual students make use of this unique resource for education, research, and outreach.

UNH's Organic Dairy has generated a great deal of public interest and press attention. This university organic dairy is now well known across the United States and in Canada. In addition to U.S. visitors, delegations have come twice from Canada's first and only university organic dairy at Guelph University's Alfred College Campus in Ontario, and formal cross-border collaboration is now beginning. Collaboration is also soon to begin with the Nova Scotia Agricultural College, Canada's Atlantic Pasture Research Group, and the Organic Agriculture Research Centre of Canada, and a broader Canada–U.S. Organic and Grazing Dairy Conference soon will be hosted by UNH. Regional and national interest and support are reflected in the Dairy's advisory panel, which includes representatives from major commercial organic producers and processors as well as regional organic dairy practitioner groups.

On the home front, UNH and the University of Maine at Orono (UMO) are now engaged in advanced joint research for which the UNH organic dairy provides a unique resource. This work focuses on different systems for managing the pasture-herd system to improve forage quality and animal health. There is also plenty of scope for UNH collaboration with the neighboring land grants of Vermont (particularly on organic dairy) and Massachusetts (particularly on grazing).

One of the greatest forms of recognition is emulation. In addition to the number of other university dairies and dairy programs keeping an eye on developments at UNH, something interesting has happened in the private sector in UNH's own backyard: a new start-up organic (and biodynamic) dairy based on grazing Jerseys and inspired by and modeled after UNH. Nearly all organic dairies in New England are conversions from existing conventional dairies, but this new one is unique, for it is an entirely new start-up from scratch and fully certified from day one.

Getting It Started: Financial Realities and a Sustainable Solution

The project began in 2004 with a meeting organized by the Office of Sustainability with UNH faculty and staff, a representative from Stonyfield Farms, the New Hampshire Commissioner of Agriculture, and an organic dairy farmer from nearby Maine who was part of the Organic Valley Farmer Cooperative. That meeting concluded with three primary questions. First, herd health: What are the real health conditions under organic productions systems? Second, is transition from a conventional to an organic production system for individual dairy farm enterprises economically viable? And third, what are the long-term economic prospects of the organic milk market? Based upon these questions and a follow-up meeting with UNH faculty and staff, two two-day field trips were organized to visit eleven organic dairies in Vermont and Maine. The goal of the trips was to separate "fact from fiction" on organic dairy production systems. The visits confirmed that good management is a key variable in any type of production system, but more importantly, it revealed that organic producers could benefit greatly from the nutritional expertise of UNH faculty and that UNH faculty and staff could benefit from the soils and grazing expertise of many of the producers.

Following the "field trips," senior UNH faculty member Chuck Schwab and Sustainability Director Tom Kelly met with Gary and Nancy Hirshberg of Stonyfield Farms to discuss plans for an organic dairy research herd at UNH. Over the next two years, plans evolved from a barn adjacent to the existing on-campus conventional dairy for a small organic demonstration herd, to an organic dairy research farm located at the university's Burley-Demeritt Farm six miles from the main campus with nearly 200 acres of diverse topography and soils along the federally designated Wild and Scenic Lampry River. The decision to develop the research dairy at Burley-Demeritt was due in part to a meeting with colleagues from the University of Maine to explore regional collaboration. Today, organic milk is being shipped, research is being conducted, and students are learning at the farm. In addition to multiple research grants, the organic dairy has raised $1.8 million in external funding from industry and individuals.

Larger Implications

Very significant progress has been made at UNH to support the notion of a coming agricultural renaissance in the state and region. Faculty, students, and staff at UNH have proposed and supported a revival of sustainable, organic agriculture, along with allied efforts in nutrition and food systems. Similarly, one can find both expertise and strong interest and commitment in the UNH Foundation and the University Office of Sustainability. The most likely scenarios for energy prices and climate change suggest that grazing- and grass-based organic dairying represents the future of the dairy industry in New England.

Garrison Keillor has written, "Dairy farming was what permitted very industrious people to earn a living on poor land; it's fundamental to our culture." Dairying is indeed fundamental to the New England culture and has been practiced here for over three hundred years, grass-based and largely organic, by very industrious people. It has been sustainable, it is sustainable, it will be sustainable, provided we conduct our dairy farming in a sustainable manner. The University of New Hampshire and its unique Organic Dairy Research Farm hope to help show the way.

Case Study: The Atlantic Marine Aquaculture Center
RICH LANGAN AND DOLORES LEONARD

Fifteenth-century explorer John Cabot's report that the schools of cod in the waters off Newfoundland were so thick that they slowed the ship may be the greatest fish story ever told. Yet, while some may take issue with the probability of such an event, one thing is certain: The abundance that inspired such hyperbole has ebbed. As with many other commercial seafood species in the Gulf of Maine and around the country, the cod stocks have declined dramatically. At the same time, consumer demand for seafood is on the rise. Americans now consume an average of 16.6 pounds per person each year. Our taste for seafood cannot match that of the Japanese, but it has been growing at a steady clip, and now far exceeds what we can produce domestically. As a result, we import. Nearly $8 billion of the $11 billion Americans spend on seafood each year goes to imported products, making the growing U.S. trade deficit for seafood second only to that of oil.

What distinguishes the United States from those countries that are able to sell us more and more fish is a willingness to embrace aquaculture as a means to satisfy growing demand. Global aquaculture production has increased by approximately 10 percent annually since 1980 and now plays an integral role in filling the widening gap between wild seafood supply and demand. Four million metric tons of the imported seafood Americans eat has been farm-raised in another country, where we cannot ensure that it has been raised using sustainable practices that protect the environment or the consumer. By contrast, the U.S. aquaculture industry is small and takes place exclusively on land or in sheltered, near-shore waters. These approaches are limited in what they can produce. Land-based operations are restricted by rising real estate and energy costs, while near-shore farms must find their place in waters crowded by competing activities. Evidence also suggests that large-scale, near-shore finfish production can have severe environmental consequences when farms are poorly sited or managed.

In 1997, a group of scientists at the University of New Hampshire asked a fundamental question: If aquaculture operations moved much further offshore, could U.S. production be expanded in a way that would mitigate the environmental impacts associated with near-shore operations? They knew that for offshore aquaculture to succeed, significant technical and operational challenges would have to be addressed. They also knew that those challenges would have to be answered in a way that would satisfy consumers, environmental groups, industry, scientists, and marine resource managers. Funding from the National Oceanic and Atmospheric Administration gave them the opportunity to explore that question. They formed the UNH Open Ocean Aquaculture Project and built an offshore facility where they could test their ideas. In 2006, that project became the Atlantic Marine Aquaculture Center.

Today, the center's interdisciplinary team of marine biologists, ocean engineers, benthic ecologists, and technical operations professionals work closely with commercial fishermen, coastal communities, private industry, and fellow marine research scientists to develop technology and know-how to raise native, cold-water finfish and shellfish in exposed oceanic environments. The center's goal is to provide the research and development necessary to stimulate an environmentally sustainable offshore aquaculture industry in New England and nationwide. The heart of this work is a 30-acre field site, located 6 miles from shore in New Hampshire State waters, and suspended in 180 feet of water. There, UNH scientists are putting potential solutions to the challenges of offshore finfish farming to the ultimate test — the extreme weather and waves of the Gulf of Maine. This unique, fully permitted facility has provided a platform on which the project team has demonstrated that it is possible to raise native finfish species in submersible cages, and native shellfish on submerged longlines in an exposed ocean environment.

Over ten years, the center's work has focused on the implementation of management practices to prevent or mitigate potential environmental impacts; the development of tools to advance engineering design and assessment; the deployment and evaluation of engineered systems, including moorings, cages, feeders, and remote observation and operations systems; and the development of rearing techniques for a number of native marine species. In the process, they have demonstrated that, with the proper engineering design, systems to farm finfish such as cod, haddock, and halibut can be installed, maintained, and operated in the harshest oceanic conditions. The growth rates, feed conversion, and health of several native species raised offshore have been excellent, indicating a high potential for commercial production.

The blue mussel culture component of the program already has made the leap from R&D. The first commercial enterprise using UNH's offshore, submerged aquaculture technology is a small-scale farm licensed to a New Hampshire fisherman in 2006. The growth performance and quality of these mussels far exceeds those produced in near-shore farms. Combined with the relatively low capital costs for startup, offshore mussel culture is a clean, environmentally sustainable and economically attractive alternative for the region's fishing industry and for fishermen hard hit by unstable capture fisheries and increasingly restrictive fishing regulations. Center scientists estimate that the area from Cape Ann, Massachusetts, to Cape Elizabeth, Maine, could yield as much $40 million in commercial mussel production per year.

Implicit in the center's goal of clean, sustainable, open-ocean aquaculture is the importance of creating infrastructure and systems that weigh lightly on the environment. Scientists take the environmental pulse of the surrounding ecosystem four times each year. With a high-powered winch, they extract box core samples from the bottom to gauge the abundance and diversity of the animals that live burrowed in the ocean floor. Video shot by a camera towed above the bottom's surface provides a window on still another community of organisms. The composition of the sediment also is the subject of scrutiny. The water column is sampled periodically by an environmental monitoring buoy, which measures waves, water temperature, salinity, dissolved oxygen, nutrients such as nitrogen and phosphorus, chlorophyll, and particulate matter. The monitoring program has shown little or no change in environmental conditions, indicating that with properly sited farms, appropriate system design, and sound management and husbandry practices, the environmental impacts of offshore finfish culture are negligible. Scientists will continue to monitor environmental conditions carefully as they scale up the operation to raise commercial-size populations of fish.

The future of offshore aquaculture in the United States is perceived by many to be at a tipping point. Four commercial aquaculture facilities are currently operating in state-regulated waters where conditions approximate a truly offshore environment. At the same time, the National Offshore Aquaculture Act to permit operations in the waters of the federally regulated Exclusive Economic Zone (EEZ) is pending in Congress. Yet, while commercial success and advances in technology strongly suggest a positive future for offshore farming, uncertainty and controversy over the industry's long-term environmental sustainability have mired this legislation in conflict and cast doubt over its future. Reaching consensus will require not only the resolution of certain technical challenges but also of the perceived environmental impacts. Concerns over sustainable feed ingredients, escapes from cages, and carrying capacity of offshore environments must be addressed if open-ocean aquaculture is to realize its economic potential. Continued public support for research, technology development, and demonstration at near-commercial scale is critical to resolving these issues and paving the way for a new model for seafood production in New England.

Case Study: The UNH Community Food, Nutrition, and Wellness Profile
JOANNE BURKE

National trends indicate a loss of agricultural capacity, a growing awareness of the impact of industrial food systems and food environments, alarming increases in rates of obesity and type 2 diabetes and a persistence of food insecurity faced by many Americans. Locally, compelling questions have emerged regarding the current status of the UNH campus, including the food, nutrition, and wellness practices of its students and staff.

In response, faculty and staff from University Office of Sustainability (UOS), the Department of Animal and Nutritional Sciences, and University Dining Services have begun development of the UNH Community Food, Nutrition, and Wellness Profile (UNH-CFNWP).

Traditionally, food sustainability assessments have focused on food production, purchasing, marketing, composting, and recycling. Missing from many sustainability discussions, evaluations, and strategic plans are the consequences of food and community environments on nutrition and health outcomes.

Using the UOS lens, as part of its Food and Society Initiative, the goal of this project is to profile the food, nutrition, and wellness status of the UNH population utilizing farm, food, health and nutrition, campus environment, resources, and economic indicator data. Faculty and staff from Cooperative Extension, the Department of Natural Resources and the Environment, the Office of Health Education and Promotion, the Organic Garden Club, and many others are sharing their insights and data with those working on this first report. Since UNH at Durham is comprised of a community of students, staff, and faculty that is larger than most New Hampshire towns, it provides a potentially unique opportunity through which trends can be identified, practices reviewed, problems targeted, and interventions tested.

Profile staff have begun to identify quantitative and qualitative indicators appropriate to the purposes of the project. Selected specific examples of the type of "farm" data include, but are not limited to, quantifying data on woodlands and farms, descriptions of both our conventional and organic dairy farms, and highlights of the student organic gardening club. "Fork" or food environments information relies on existing data from UNH Dining Services, including determination of the types and quantities of foods purchased locally and regionally, and menu analysis of selected recipes and vending choices. Food stamp use and requests for food assistance on campus serve as indicators of food insecurity.

Nutrition and health outcomes are being investigated primarily as part of the Young Adult Health Risk Screening Initiative. Over one thousand students from diverse majors at UNH have agreed to participate in this research as part of an introductory Nutrition and Wellness course. Three-day food records are recorded electronically by students, combined with direct measurements of height, weight, fasting blood glucose and lipids, and blood pressure. Life-style and wellness practices are also assessed via survey. Additional health data for the UNH-CFNWP have been made available through collaboration with the Office of Heath Education and Promotion. The environment component will assess transportation practices, physical activity, and economics as well as research and curriculum that focus on food nutrition and wellness.

This pilot report is designed to begin a process of assessment, identification of data gaps, and a process of meaningful dialogue while providing a benchmark for future evaluations. Thoughtful reflection on the initial findings will better position the university community to assess more comprehensively, respond more effectively, track progress more extensively, and initiate innovative solutions more confidently. Subsequent reports will represent a continuous, collaborative effort by all those vested in promoting a healthy, sustainable UNH community and beyond.

Case Study: From Campus Farm to Dining Hall
JOHN MCLEAN

A land-grant university such as the University of New Hampshire has an implicit responsibility to educate and serve the agriculture industry within the state and region. With regard to food production, these endeavors have fallen largely on the shoulders of the Environmental Horticulture Program within the Department of Plant Biology, with research support from the New Hampshire Agricultural Experiment Station and outreach provided by Cooperative Extension. During the past thirty years, research conducted at the Woodman Horticultural Farm and Kingman Research Farm mostly have targeted efforts that benefit small-farm, retail marketing and local agriculture. These efforts have produced many new and more sustainable agricultural technologies that have assisted local farmers, including use of row covers, high tunnels, new types of mulch groundcovers, development of a plasticulture strawberry production system, better insect- and disease-management strategies, and better disease-resistant varieties of vegetables.

The Woodman Horticultural Farm, in particular, has made a conscious effort to work within the university to educate students and bring an awareness of agriculture to the university community. Labor needs at the research farms and greenhouses are met by hiring UNH students from a variety of majors and backgrounds. Students are able to experience first-hand the operation of a farm from seeding to consuming the finished product. Because much of the research at the Woodman Horticultural Farm has been to reduce inputs such as labor, sprays, and energy, while still producing a high-quality product, students get to see how new, sustainable methods are being used to grow produce. Also, in cooperation with the dining halls and Hospitality Services, many projects that start in the fields end up on the plates of those who dine at the University of New Hampshire.

For example, in the summer of 2007, the commitment of the College of Life Sciences and Agriculture and UNH Dining Services to agriculture and sustainable practices was highlighted by an effort to raise an acre of squash specifically to be used in the dining halls at UNH. A faculty member in the Plant Biology Department had developed a new variety of kabocha squash named Thunder. The faculty member and the Woodman Farm crew planted and grew this acre of the new variety, providing valuable production data on the new strain, as well as a bountiful yield of very high-quality winter squash. In conjunction with the UNH Dining Services, the squash was processed by a major food supplier, Costa, and then delivered to the university to be served in the dining halls. The information obtained from this project may in turn make it feasible for the dining halls to obtain some of their future food needs from local growers. Existing programs to use UNH-grown apples in the dining halls and the Harvest Dinner Initiative reinforce the collaborative link between the university's agricultural college and Dining Services.

Research on Culture and Sustainability

Research on culture and sustainability blends at UNH with initiatives that enhance a campus culture that is supportive of research and creativity in general. Increasing student awareness of the cultural opportunities on campus and in the region and helping them experience these resources are seen as integral parts of creating that culture, so the University Office of Sustainability (UOS) supports a program that takes students to major performances in the Boston area. UOS also sponsors programs as diverse as the Celebrity Series, which brings top performers to campus, and the University Dialogue.

Three case studies discussed here represent the diversity of approaches taken to doing research on the cultural aspects of sustainability and sustaining a campus culture that supports research and scholarship. UNH supports one of the largest and most comprehensive Undergraduate Research Conferences (URC) in the country. This annual, week-long signature event highlights original research, scholarship, and creative work by students produced in close mentoring relationships with faculty. The Carsey Institute brings Outreach Scholarship and interdisciplinarity to the problems of poor and rural communities in several parts of the country, with the goal of providing solutions to structural issues limiting sustainable development. In the "Growing a Green Generation" project, we see an essential university service (child care) provided in a research setting (the Child Study and Development Center) that engages children in long-term inquiry through the innovative use of gardening.

Case Study: The Undergraduate Research Conference — A Key Ingredient in the Sustainable Learning Community
ELEANOR ABRAMS

The annual Undergraduate Research Conference (URC), a celebration of academic success, has become a signature event at the University of New Hampshire. Students present the results of research, creative, capstone, and service-learning projects at more than twenty events across campus during the week-long conference. In 2008, more than eight hundred students presented original work through the URC. Feedback from student participants indicates that the URC is often one of if not the most memorable event of their academic careers at UNH.

The URC is designed to highlight student research, scholarship, and creative presentations. The purpose of the conference is to encourage student learning and an appreciation for their disciplines. Other benefits for our undergraduates immersed in the research process include promoting critical thinking, encouraging collaborative learning, refining communication skills, enhancing organizational skills, and developing feelings of competence. One of the most important benefits for our students is that they have the opportunity to experience what it would be like to be a professional in their chosen field through interacting with faculty members and colleagues with similar interests. The URC experience encourages the development of a mentoring relationship between faculty and student. Previous research on faculty mentoring explains the mentoring relationship as a seasoned professional counseling, guiding, and tutoring a protégé who is either a newcomer to or a trainee in the profession. This interaction not only motivates students to pursue a job or graduate school, but also provides them with personal contacts who help open doors to other opportunities beyond graduation and build the students' confidence. In fact, research experience, presentations, and publications are valued by employers and graduate schools.

Like many other institutions of higher education, the University of New Hampshire for many years maintained two or three department and college-wide conference events for their undergraduate students. These events were small and often sparsely attended. In 2004, our URC began to expand dramatically. With a small influx of resources and leadership from the Office for the Vice President for Research and Public Service, the first step in revitalizing the URC was expanding the URC Planning Committee from a faculty-only advisory committee to a working team that includes professionals from many parts of the university, including Editorial and Creative Services, Multimedia and Instructional Design Services, the Parents Association, the Hamel Center for Undergraduate Education, and the UNH Foundation. This new interdisciplinary working committee was energetic and creative, and developed several innovative ways to raise the profile of the URC on campus.

The most powerful new approaches include:

- A dedicated web site for the event (http://www.unh.edu/urc);
- an online registration system for the students and faculty;
- a professionally designed conference program;
- a nationally recognized keynote speaker;
- URC Student Awards of Excellence;
- a media recruitment campaign aimed at presenters and mentors;
- a second campaign used to attract conference guests.

All of these elements serve to support the already wonderful college and department events.

The URC Planning Committee also plans and hosts several university-wide events to encourage interdisciplinary research, including the Interdisciplinary Science and Engineering Symposium, the Naked Arts event, and the Vice President's Symposium.

Through these efforts, the URC has been extended from a one-day event to a week-long celebration of student inquiry and creativity. The UNH Undergraduate Research Conference has grown from attracting fewer than two hundred to over eight hundred student presenters. Three university-wide events currently are held as well as twenty department and college-wide events. Guest attendance from inside and outside the university community has increased dramatically. Undergraduate research conference guests including legislators, prospective students, and community residents who mingle with university faculty, staff, and students. In addition, the past three conferences have hosted a nationally known author as a keynote speaker, selected not only for their ability to draw an audience but also for their meticulous interdisciplinary research.

A unique aspect of the URC at UNH is a scholarly assessment of the impact of the experience on students and faculty. Contact information collected as part of the online registration has allowed for wide distribution of a follow-up survey to URC participants that assesses impacts and also identifies concerns. Responses from URC alumni and current participants indicate that their participation in undergraduate research has a significant and positive effect on their educational and postgraduate experience. The URC experience increased student confidence and presentation skills and in many cases influenced their graduate school and/or career choices. Participants also reported a sense of pride in being able to plan, implement, and report their research to peers, faculty, and family members.

Student responses also clearly indicated that mentoring made the research more fulfilling by providing a linkage to professional practice and opportunities for students to enter graduate programs or the job market. These results are in line with published findings indicating that graduate students who have faculty mentors are more confident about their roles as professionals, more satisfied with their graduate programs, more successful in graduate school, more productive, have better publication records, and ultimately are more viable job-market candidates than those without mentors.

Many research questions require students to view the world through cultural perspectives that are different from their own. They often need to synthesize two or more disciplines to investigate the complex, real-world questions they want to answer. Interdisciplinary understanding arises from understanding each discipline's approaches, assumptions, and tools, and then combining these in novel ways that advance our understanding of a complex issue. Experienced faculty mentors help students cross the borders into other disciplines and become the cultural brokers by which the students enter the disciplines in the search for answers. The URC supports several university-wide events to encourage and support students to participate in interdisciplinary research.

An example that might best demonstrate the kind of effective, interdisciplinary research that finds an outlet through the URC is the work of UNH Students Without Borders (SWB). UNH SWB students traveled with two faculty advisors to Niger to build a low-technology pumping system. A sustainable water-extraction system was needed to irrigate community gardens. The SWB team was able to design a culturally acceptable, easily understood, sustainable, and efficient system that successfully delivered the 2,000 gallons per day needed for the garden. This project was presented at the URC Interdisciplinary Science and Engineering Symposium and also at a national research event. The students won awards for their innovative engineering design at both events.

URCs can be used as a vehicle to educate undergraduate students about ways to search for answers to complex problems, stimulate new knowledge, and develop new technologies. Hosting interdisciplinary events, sponsoring nationally known speakers whose research tackles complicated societal problems, and honoring faculty and students who are involved in research can help undergraduates learn how to live as literate and democratic citizens.

Case Study: The Carsey Institute — Building Knowledge to Support Opportunity for Families in Sustainable Communities
MIL DUNCAN

Families and communities are encountering profound economic, demographic and environmental changes. Globalization means that the old economy based on manufacturing that supported a broad middle class is no longer viable, and the United States has not yet developed policies to ensure that the new economy of services and technology can provide this support. The impact of a globalized world is compounded by significant demographic shifts, as aging baby boomers begin to retire and new growth from foreign-born workers and families reshapes neighborhoods and communities across the country. Finally, dramatic environmental forces, especially climate change, are reshaping the energy, food, and transportation systems of the future. Understanding the challenges and opportunities these three large changes present requires a dynamic, collaborative, interdisciplinary team, with strong ties to community leaders, that is supported by flexible, core support encouraging entrepreneurial approaches to policy and applied research. The Carsey Institute is building a responsive and rigorous research program because these elements are available at the University of New Hampshire.

In 2002, UNH alumna Marcy Carsey endowed the Carsey Institute, seeking to develop a center for policy and applied research that would be a strong voice for families and communities by providing solid, grounded, independent research to inform decisionmakers and engaged citizens, and guide policy and practice in the changing environment of the twenty-first century. UNH leaders brought together those already working on children, youth, and family issues with experts in sustainable resource development, and sought out others in the fields with practical family and development experience as well as a deep understanding of civic culture and the dynamics of community change.

The Carsey leadership team partnered with regional and national philanthropic leaders interested in building opportunities to support a strong middle class and to encourage inclusive, sustainable communities in rural areas and small cities across New England and the nation. In three years, the institute has grown from one staff member to a dozen, and developed interdisciplinary programs engaging some forty faculty members working with graduate research assistants and undergraduate interns. The research and outreach programs are supported through grants and contracts that totaled $1.5 million in 2007, from about fifteen foundations and organizations that work on families, community and environment in rural communities and small cities.

Several factors have been key to the Carsey Institute's success to date. First, the institute combines a passion for research that makes a difference for families in rural communities and small cities with a commitment to rigorous, peer-reviewed research methodologies. Second, our commitment to providing useful resources to communities and policymakers means that we work closely with nonprofit, business, and government leaders, activists, and funders to ensure that we understand their research needs and can disseminate our work effectively. Third, to ensure we are an accessible resource, we publish our work in a lively, frequent policy and issue report series, and provide a range of timely indicators on social, economic, and environmental trends on rural America, northern New England, and New Hampshire's North Country.

While many have called for the integration of a commitment to positive social change with rigorous, independent scholarship, effective and lasting implementation of this approach to research is rare. On the one hand, advocates for change who conduct research often do not prioritize their funds to support sophisticated research and are reluctant to disseminate research results that do not fully support their mission or policy objectives. Carsey researchers ask questions that are grounded in real social issues and important for understanding and even guiding change, and they do so using sophisticated data sets and methodologies, and report the findings fully. On the other hand, scholars in an academic setting are not rewarded with tenure and promotion if they spend too much time on policy and applied research compared to publishing in their field's premier peer-reviewed journals. Carsey has worked to support scholars who publish in their discipline's top journals and, at the same time, who write more accessible outreach pieces for lay audiences eager for their expertise. The institute benefits from generous faculty interested in seeing their work put to use and from the university's true commitment to outreach.

Carsey staff and faculty researchers do not hang out in the ivory tower. They attend meetings where nonprofits discuss economic changes, asset building, or changes in forest communities. They hear up-to-date accounts of how families are coping and what challenges community leaders struggle to address, and these encounters help set the research agenda. They conduct research to inform new program development and evaluate existing initiatives. They interview community leaders, workers, and program participants, and synthesize what they hear, putting it in the context of the best and most current thinking in the field. They organize and facilitate strategic thinking sessions with leaders in a range of fields, from fiscal policy for low-income families to those working at the intersection of smart growth and affordable housing, to formulating a new national rural policy agenda. They meet with congressional and legislative staff and representatives, and formulate research agendas that speak to their day-to-day pressures. Foundation leaders and the organizations they fund seek out the Carsey Institute to provide timely, sophisticated analyses to frame discussions for their board and staff and move strategic planning to new levels based on those analyses.

Carsey's published reports, an indicators database tracking social change, and an active communications program ensure that the research Carsey conducts reaches those who can use it, and helps those immersed in changing circumstances see their own problems and opportunities in a broader perspective.

Two examples of Carsey work illustrate this approach to research and outreach on community sustainability. The Community and Environment in Rural America (CERA) research project seeks to build knowledge and awareness of socioeconomic trends and policy opportunities in communities where natural resources have long played an important role in the local economy. Our work explores the potential of working-landscape development strategies to build diverse, resilient local economies in rural and small-town America. We examine the dynamic interplay of changing social, economic, and environmental factors and the implications for ecologically sustainable economic development policies. Phase I CERA research focuses on selected groups of counties in four forested regions: the Northeast's Northern Forest, Central Appalachia, the Pacific Northwest, and Alabama. The research methodology underway includes a large-scale survey of public perceptions and experiences, as well as the collection of secondary data on regional socioeconomics and forest types, uses and management.

We have partnered with regional and national foundations and the practitioners they support to ensure that our research informs and helps track practitioners' efforts on the ground. For example, in Central Appalachia, Carsey is working with the Central Appalachian Network, a multi-state association of rural development organizations, to test the hypothesis that sustainable development options for regional economic development offer viable and beneficial alternatives to the current resource extractive practices. In one element of this work, Carsey's diverse interdisciplinary team of researchers is assessing the potential services and economic values that can be generated by maintaining an undamaged regional ecosystem. Preliminary analyses reveal that very positive benefits for regional water supplies and global climate change can be obtained through expanded watershed and forest conservation efforts.

Similarly, Carsey scholars working in New Hampshire's North Country and neighboring Vermont, Maine, and Quebec, have partnered with the Neil and Louise Tillotson Fund of the New Hampshire Charitable Foundation to track changes in the region, to inform and evaluate the work of the fund's grantees and initiatives, and to provide strategic thinking and national perspective to guide the fund's leadership as well as civic leaders in local communities. The fund has launched an ambitious effort to invest strategically in the region to transform it from "managing decline" to "sustainable development." This effort includes an active website offering up-to-date indicators of socioeconomic and environmental conditions, biannual surveys of more than fifteen hundred adults to track community change, a longitudinal panel study of youth who were seventh and eleventh graders in early 2008, ongoing evaluations of specific family and job development programs, and strategic leadership development with nonprofit leaders in the region. We publish reports periodically from the research and meet with local leaders to share results and learn more about their needs and concerns.

The integration of outreach and listening with sophisticated scholarly expertise and rigorous methodological techniques is what makes the Carsey Institute an unusual resource for decisionmakers coping with the enormous sustainability challenges of the twenty-first century. Land-grant universities have a long-standing commitment to outreach, but this outreach often is conducted as programs, too often unconnected to ongoing research. Venues and occasions have existed for scholars who are experts in a given field — medicine and health, history and politics, sociology and psychology — to share what they and their colleagues understand about important current topics or issues. They write op-eds, give presentations at meetings, or are interviewed by the media. But rarely are these efforts built into a research institute's program, as part of its everyday approach to its work, and shared by the entire team of researchers. Carsey is building the capacity to conduct and share timely, deeply informed and very rigorous applied and policy research for people in communities to use as they encounter economic, demographic, and environmental challenges and make decisions to position themselves to succeed in building a more sustainable world.

Case Study: The Growing a Green Generation Project
JOHN NIMMO

Beginning in the summer of 1999, early childhood teachers from the UNH Child Study and Development Center (CSDC, an integrated child care, education, and research center) came together with plant biologists and farmers from the university to invent and field-test experiences that could lead to children, infants through kindergarteners, having a more intimate and meaningful engagement with the natural world. Named the "Growing a Green Generation Project" because of our desire to engage our youngest citizens and their emerging role as stewards of the Earth, these efforts have been supported by annual funding from the Anna and Raymond Tuttle Environmental Horticulture Endowment and an interdisciplinary collaboration between the UNH College of Life Sciences and Agriculture (COLSA) and Health and Human Services (CHHS). At the center of these efforts is a demonstration

Children's Garden that acts as a laboratory for curriculum development and research, and provides a place to engage hundreds of UNH students in outdoor early education.

As our adventure has moved forward over the years, we have reflected on the images of the children's garden that have framed our work. First, the garden can be viewed as a play environment in which children create new worlds that use the color, smell, and texture of nature to shape drama and fantasy. It is a place in which children's curiosity and desire to investigate can be provoked by the surprises of the plant world. Using the knowledge of horticulturists, we have been able to present children with experiences that can provoke their imagination, from purple beans to flower pods that explode when touched. Unlike the natural world of the woods, the garden exists because of human interaction with plants. The garden is a focal point for children to develop enduring relationships with adults in our community. While our intent always has been child-focused, we have come to realize that a garden brings with it a rich history of cultural activity that involves the specialized knowledge of horticulturalists, the expertise and sweat of farmers, and the everyday life of diverse families. For instance, the manager of the UNH Farms and Greenhouses, who has led the design and construction of our demonstration garden, has formed relationships with the children over the years as they have observed and participated in his work in the fields. As a result we have focused our research efforts on examining the nature of the relationships between children and important adults involved in the gardening project through interviews with both children and adults. In our garden, adults and children negotiate their roles and skills in bringing a real-life project to fruition. It is okay that children can't do it all by themselves. In raising our expectations of children, teachers have learned that children can be entrusted with garden jobs. They can be given more responsibility with the knowledge that they won't do it the same way as adults. Plants will get stepped on and broken — but these are opportunities for negotiating the work of keeping a garden healthy. The children's work is informed by their collaboration with adults who are passionate about nature, and the impact is reciprocal. As we have learned about plants, our collaborators have also learned about the play and ideas of young children.

While the working garden is at the core of the project at the CSDC, our activities have been reaching a wider audience of educators and parents through a variety of means. The project hosts an annual conference at the CSDC and the COLSA Greenhouses for sixty regional educators on the joys of gardening. CSDC teachers present regionally and nationally and have been published in the premier national journal for early childhood educators. In addition, a curriculum of piloted activities is available on the project's website and in paper format, and the project participates in university-wide efforts regarding sustainability, including the Local Harvest Dinner, University Day, and the student Organic Garden Club, and supports networks such as the New Hampshire Leave No Child Inside initiative.

The essence of our experiences is to connect children to their local ecology and culture in ways that will be memorable, and in so doing, sustain a deeper awareness of their growing identity. Our curriculum emerges from an intimate understanding of the local geography and community. We have come to view the garden as a place of intersection between the natural and the social environment where children can create a meaningful relationship between our cultural work as humans and the complexities and unknowns of the natural world. In this process, adults grow in their understanding of children and become (we hope) advocates of children's rights and voices in sustaining their future as citizens.

CHAPTER 5

Sustaining the Larger Community

Engagement

Jeffrey A. Schloss

This chapter provides diverse examples of how the University of New Hampshire practices engagement in our efforts to foster sustainability on many levels, from well-established programs over thirty years old to relatively new efforts that have arisen based on current concerns. True institutional engagement defies the old models of the land-grant university's public relationship, where consulting, expert testimony, and technology transfer were considered the major forms of public service and outreach. The Kellogg Commission on the Future of State and Land-Grant Universities discussed and defined institutional engagement:

> Engagement goes well beyond extension, conventional outreach, and even most conceptions of public service. Inherited concepts emphasize a one-way process in which the university transfers its expertise to key constituents. Embedded in the engagement ideal is a commitment to sharing and reciprocity. By engagement the Commission envisions partnerships, two-way streets defined by mutual respect among the partners for what each brings to the table.

The Kellogg Commission also listed seven guiding characteristics to define an engaged institution: responsiveness, respect for partners, academic neutrality, accessibility, integration, coordination, and resource partnerships. As you read through the case studies in this chapter, you will see that the programs described herein meet these criteria very well.

PHOTO: Ed and Mary Scheier, former UNH faculty and renowned potters. A description of a show honoring their work is provided in the Culture and Sustainability section of this chapter. *Photo courtesy of UNH Photographic Services.*

Initiatives such as the New Hampshire Lakes Lay Monitoring Program, Students Without Borders, and Cooperative Fisheries Research demonstrate how involving external stakeholders in all aspects of our applied research creates a rapid responsiveness to community needs, a synergy of scientific synthesis, and an efficiency in our outreach efforts. While all of the efforts contained in this volume display a tremendous respect for the partners and stakeholders involved, examples such as Forest Watch, where middle-school educators took the lead in curriculum development, and the Marine Docent Program, where volunteer educators develop their own lesson plans, show how the knowledge and experience of our external partners are integral to program success.

Moving from knowledge to action, especially when it comes to climate change concerns, requires tremendous effort targeted at many different levels. Engagement through Carbon Solutions New England and the New Hampshire Carbon Challenge offer new opportunities for integrating UNH faculty, staff, and students with grassroots organizations and agencies combining technological advances, creating useful analysis tools, and generating the political will to reduce our carbon footprint. In a similar fashion, the New Hampshire Center for a Food Secure Future seeks to better coordinate existing and future efforts among the many interested stakeholders to create a truly cross–disciplinary approach covering the entire food system, from seed to plate to health outcomes.

Dealing with the realities of nutrition, locally produced food, and the need to have our children better understand the farm-to-table process the New Hampshire Farm to School Program coordinates with many agencies and stakeholders to support the small farm operations characteristic of New Hampshire while providing schools with affordable, nutritious produce. Public awareness and public school access to the early and recent history of Africans and American-born Black people in New Hampshire was one of the goals of the effort involving the creation of the Portsmouth Black History Trail. This case study is an excellent example of how effective engagement involving many participants working at a local scale with University support can yield statewide impacts resulting in accessibility to an often under-engaged constituency.

Just as the Operations chapter discusses the opportunity for UNH to serve as the test bed and proving ground of sustainable practices, so too do we rely on internal efforts to advance our engagement methods. If our work in external communities requires complex problem solving and policy development in a civic context, then lessons learned through the use of study circles, as highlighted in the case study called "Deliberations in the Civic Sector," will be useful. As an engaged institution has to nurture and encourage all faculty, students, and staff to become involved in the process and effect a substantial change in the culture of the institution, the Outreach Scholars Academy is a critical program. Student programs like the Organic Garden Club, which arose out of the university's Food and Society Initiative, allow students to engage with a wide segment of the UNH and local communities. The Wild-CAP program also engages students in the decisionmaking that is required to live more sustainably in their own lives and furthers the university's efforts to conserve energy.

Everyone benefits from effective engagement. Research is enhanced. Curriculum is improved and made more relevant, and hence more interesting to our students. Service becomes a two-way process among faculty, staff, and students as well as with our external partners and communities. Recently, much attention from both our funders and our public has been focused on accountability. The programs highlighted in this chapter move from just creating research, scholarship, and outreach outputs to providing true outcomes in participatory education and research, natural resource improvement and protection, and community empowerment. Together, they help to move us closer to a sustainable society.

Engagement in Biodiversity and Ecosystems

Engagement is inherent in the land-grant mission, and in a state as rich in natural resources and systems as New Hampshire, much of the attention is focused on biodiversity and ecosystems. Cooperative Extension in New Hampshire supports a number of programs that engage campus expertise with residents and organizations across the state. While this is not unusual for extension organizations, what may be unique to New Hampshire is the very high degree of volunteer involvement in these programs. Building on a tradition of local control and town meetings, New Hampshire citizens assume that things get done when local folks participate. This commitment to participation can extend to action taken as part of a professional life as well as a civic life.

The four case studies in this section may seem very different in terms of subject matter and location, but they all share one characteristic: substantive engagement by individuals who participate on a voluntary basis and do more than is expected or required. This is an essential part of creating a sustainable society. Appropriately, the first three case studies are model efforts of the university's Land Grant, Space Grant, and Sea Grant Extension programs. The N.H. Lakes Lay Monitoring Program engages residents near many of the lakes in the state in monitoring environmental quality. It also often results in creation of knowledgeable environmental stewards and activists. Forest Watch is a program that engages teachers and students from all levels of the public school system in New Hampshire and beyond in the long-term measurement of tree health in relation to air pollution. It also links those students and teachers into a community and network of classrooms engaged in the same project. The UNH Marine Docent Program has been recognized for its outstanding programs and services that bring a cadre of dedicated volunteers to the task of providing marine and environmental education for students and adults that complement traditional programs.

Engagement in biodiversity and ecosystems at UNH is not restricted to a local, state, regional, or national scope. The mission of the chapter of Students Without Borders established at UNH is to encourage, support, and implement environmentally and economically sustainable technical projects in local and international communities, while developing globally responsible and knowledgeable students. Projects in Niger and Thailand have provided enriching international experiences for its members.

Case Study: The New Hampshire Lakes Lay Monitoring Program —
A Sustainable Model for Engaging Citizen Scientists
JEFFREY A. SCHLOSS

A boat anchors over the deep spot of the lake and the two passengers start lowering a plate-sized, black and white disk into the water to check water clarity. Then they reel out a weighted line, measuring temperature by depth, use what looks like a garden hose to fill a dark bottle, and then pull up the anchor and head back to shore. Unusual behavior? No, just volunteer citizen scientists at work.

The New Hampshire Lakes Lay Monitoring Program (NH LLMP), founded in 1978, was conceived by two University of New Hampshire faculty as a way to involve local residents in detecting long-term trends in lake water quality. It began as a follow-up to a UNH class in which students performed a detailed analysis of a local lake at the request of a neighborhood lake association. The students produced an assessment of the lake that was far more detailed than could be done through state or federal programs. Once word spread through the Lakes Region, a deluge of requests from other associations followed and very soon the founders realized that there would simply not be enough students available to meet this demand.

Drawing on experiences in Minnesota and Vermont, the UNH professors were able to design a set of protocols to allow properly trained citizen volunteers to conduct a core suite of accurate water-quality tests as well as to pre-process and preserve water samples for later analysis at the university. In 1985, through support from the UNH Vice President of Research, the co-directors hired a research scientist (the author) to grow the program, expand monitoring options, and provide quality assurance testing.

Our original outreach intentions were twofold: to provide unbiased data for informed local lake management, and to create an opportunity for participants to gain hands-on understanding of water resource concepts and issues. We didn't anticipate that our statewide "army" of volunteer scientists would prove invaluable in advancing applied research important to lake and watershed management decisions, that our model of citizen science would spread to thirty-five states and a dozen foreign nations, or that that the confidence gained by participating in our program would empower many NH LLMP citizen scientists to get involved in local boards and commissions and effect real change toward natural resources protection.

Challenges

Keeping the program funded and gaining the acceptance of the regulatory community have been major challenges. For its first ten years, support for

NH LLMP came from temporary grants and gifts, some from the university's Water Resources Research Center. Then, in 1989, the university's Cooperative Extension integrated the NH LLMP into its newly formed water resources program, benefitting both parties. Extension was able to expand its outreach, research, and grassroots water-quality program to fulfill a new USDA program emphasis, and the monitoring effort gained a stable source of funding. NH LLMP receives additional funding from participants, state agencies, towns, conservation commissions, community organizations, and watershed or lake associations as well as foundations and the occasional competitive federal grant from the U.S. EPA, USDA, USGS, or NOAA. Contracted laboratory services maintain field and laboratory equipment and support student field and lab technicians.

Agencies initially balked at using citizen-collected data because of a combination of misperceptions regarding the quality of methods and the intentions of the volunteer monitors, as well as the fear that water-quality issues identified could swamp agency capacities. Following the First National Workshop on Citizen Volunteers in Environmental Monitoring held in Narragansett, Rhode Island, in 1988, the U.S. EPA produced a guidance document for state water-quality managers that included comparisons from the NH LLMP and other established volunteer programs showing no significant difference between measurements made by professional technicians and citizen monitors. The tide was turning and the value of citizen monitoring data was being realized.

NH LLMP Data Delivers a Range of Powerful Impacts

Both the approach and the datasets developed through the NH LLMP have and are affecting water resource policy in the state and beyond. As one example, volunteer-driven intensive studies of the drainage area around Lake Chocorua led to a significant reduction of pollutants coming from roadway runoff next to the lake, and gained national attention with recognition as a U.S. Environmental Protection Agency "Success Story" and awarding of a Technical Achievement Award from the North American Lake Management Society. LLMP data also have had a direct impact on other decisions, including:

- Altering siting of a highway around a wetland bordering a lake;
- qualifying lakes to receive federal and state assistance;
- supporting sewer system bonds;
- expanding vegetated buffer zones and shoreline setbacks;

- supporting changes or cancellation of poorly planned, high-impact projects;
- establishment of "No-rafting" zones (dense congregations of moored boats);
- supporting Geographic Information System analysis for multijurisdictional planning;
- setting statewide nutrient criteria and Total Maximum Daily Loading (TMDL) standards.

In addition, we supply the N.H. Department of Environmental Services with our yearly dataset, which they warehouse and distribute along with their own data and use for their biannual reports to the U.S. Congress. UNH faculty also utilize NH LLMP data in their classes, and for studying long-term water-quality trends, informing regional global change assessments, and improving regional weather models.

These are all "value-added" products. Our main intent is to have our volunteer monitors use their data on the local level where they have the chance to influence informed water-quality protection and stewardship.

Volunteers' Questions Spur New Research

After working as lake monitors for awhile, our volunteers began raising some very interesting questions about the health of their lakes and their wildlife. After consulting with state agencies and researchers, we devised methods to start addressing these questions, using our volunteers to provide the lion's share of the person-power needed to monitor the waters. Completed studies range from the documentation of fishery health in a wide range of lakes to the analysis of the impacts of motorized watercraft in relation to bottom composition and water depth.

Conclusion

Our citizen-science approach offers a truly participatory research experience for our volunteers. It arose organically, yet it patterns itself after research engagement models developed for public health and livelihood outreach in developing countries. The model includes the following elements: (1) community members should be involved in the design and implementation of the research projects; (2) the research processes and outcomes should directly benefit the community; (3) community members should be part of the analysis and interpretation of data and should have input into how the results are distributed; and (4) productive partnerships between the researchers and the community members should be encouraged to last beyond the life of the project.

Case Study: Forest Watch — Enhancing Pre-College Understanding of Biodiversity and Ecosystems
BARRY ROCK

In August 1987, Phil Browne, a Concord High School biology teacher, contacted the author looking for ideas from NASA scientists. The Space Shuttle Challenger disaster in 1986 had created a very negative image of NASA in the minds of his students, especially with the loss of one of their teachers, Christa McAuliffe, in that tragedy. Mr. Browne wanted to provide his students with an activity that would reflect positive impacts of the space agency. Initial ideas focused on engaging students in existing research projects on the effects of air pollutants in the White Mountains, but the difficulties associated with long travel times to those remote sites forced us to revise our thinking. We instead devised a program that used a common species — white pine — as an indicator of ozone (smog) pollution and developed a protocol that could be used at nearly any school across the state.

Out of this effort, the Forest Watch program was born in 1991. Starting with six high schools within New Hampshire, the program now includes over four hundred from all across New England, and has become a K–12 science education/outreach program that engages precollege students in hands-on, inquiry-based scientific research aimed at improving our understanding of the impact of ground-level ozone on sensitive forest species. An important part of this development process was early support from the NASA Space Grant Consortium that was being developed at UNH. Another university-sponsored program focused on encouraging state high school students to consider college-level programs in math and science also provided initial funding. These funds covered travel and workshop costs necessary to train the initial six teachers (including Phil Browne).

Goal of Forest Watch

Forest Watch engages the full age-range of precollege students (K–12) in the study of the white pines outside their own classrooms. Students both learn the process of doing science (making observations, generating hypotheses, collecting data, testing hypotheses, and drawing conclusions) *and* generate data of value to scientists studying the biological response of forest species to variations in regional air quality. Students participate by following age-appropriate protocols designed to provide relevant and reliable data sets that educate the students as well. Forest Watch promotes an improved understanding of what sustainability really means; not only do ecosystems become limited in their functioning when one or more ecosystem components is unhealthy, but improving air quality can have a positive impact on those components, even varying year to year.

The Approach

The Forest Watch model involves a train-the-trainer method. Teachers are trained during three- to five-day workshops, and then in turn train their students to follow the data-collection protocols, use field and laboratory measurement tools, and integrate their school's data sets into the annual region-wide white pine survey data set. All of the participating schools' data sets and submitted branch and needle sample reflectance data are then published each year in the form of a Forest Watch Data Book that summarizes all the data.

The species selected for this work was white pine (*Pinus strobus*), a common tree in New England and a known bio-indicator for exposure to elevated levels of ozone. Students measure annual changes in diameter, height, percent canopy closure, and needle retention, as well as common indicators of needle health, including chlorotic mottle (bleached spots) and tip necrosis. The same five trees are monitored each year, and interannual changes are then compared to changes in summertime ozone conditions across the region. Ozone data are provided by both state and regional air-quality monitoring networks. Students can compare a given year's forest conditions with the previous year's conditions and with student data sets from other schools participating in the program.

In the process of studying white pine's interannual variation in response to variations in ground-level ozone during summer months, students collect branch and needle samples as well as recording valuable observational data that are submitted to the university's Forest Watch research scientists in the Complex Systems Research Center, within the Institute for the Study of Earth, Oceans, and Space (EOS). At EOS, a lab-based spectrometer is used to collect spectral reflectance data that provide very detailed information about needle chlorophyll concentrations, cellular conditions and mass, and canopy water content. The spectrometer data are then compared against student data sets in order to validate student data and to provide comparable measurements of year-to-year variation. For example, white pine that are unhealthy one year may be more healthy the next if ozone levels in year two are lower than the levels in year one. This is a very important lesson that students learn through Forest Watch: Ozone levels dropped in the late 1990s, in part due to the Clean Air Act Amendment passed in the early 1990s. As the ozone levels dropped, the health of the five pine trees growing outside the students' classrooms improved in health.

Forest Watch, now in its seventeenth year, is unique in several ways:

- It is relevant, addressing a real air-pollution issue — ground-level ozone;
- ozone damage symptoms are easily quantified, even by primary grade students;
- teachers love the interdisciplinary nature of the program, which touches on basic biology, chemistry, physics, and math;
- lessons learned are readily transferred to human health issues;
- it fits into existing curricular requirements in math, science, and hands-on learning;
- it has now developed a long-term database of significant environmental value.

Three factors have been essential in the success of Forest Watch: the funding to initiate and expand the program, enthusiastic and supportive teachers, and direct involvement of the teachers in the design of the program. Initial Space Grant and UNH funding were critical in providing support for program development; had this not been available, Forest Watch might never have happened. Teacher enthusiasm has driven program growth as word-of-mouth contacts bring teachers from across New Hampshire and the region to the program. Involving teachers in the process of developing Forest Watch activities that were appropriate for the classroom ensured acceptance and practicality of the exercises.

Case Study: The UNH Marine Docent Program
MARK WILEY

Introduction

The UNH Marine Docents are volunteers who staff Sea Grant Extension marine education programs and who are dedicated to the preservation and wise use of marine resources. The UNH Marine Docent program began in 1977 with eight dedicated volunteers who provided a liaison between the public and university marine research facilities. Originally funded with a six-month grant, funding was picked up by the federal Sea Grant College Program in 1978. Since 1986, the UNH Marine Docents have been supported by both New Hampshire Sea Grant and the University of New Hampshire Cooperative Extension.

From its small beginning, the Marine Docent program has grown into a valued leader in coastal and estuarine education. Over 170 Docents are working actively throughout seacoast New Hampshire and southern Maine, teaching in school settings and on boats, educating community groups, and guiding visitors at two local nature centers (the Seacoast Science Center at Odiorne Point in Rye and the Great Bay Discovery Center on Great Bay).

Docents are trained in marine science and formal and informal education methods for two days a week for six months. Additional training occurs at monthly meetings with presentations by UNH professors and other experts. After completing the training, the majority of the Docents work with school-children, taking SeaTrek presentations about the marine and coastal environments to schools, 4-H clubs, and scout groups. SeaTrek Programs cover a variety of marine topics through slide presentations, lectures, field trips, and tours. The programs are designed to increase public awareness of the marine environment.

Successes and Challenges

The UNH Marine Docent program is considered by the national Sea Grant program as a "best management practice" in marine education outreach due to the significant number of students and adult participants who are provided programs at a modest cost. This economic efficiency and the multiplier effect of volunteers facilitating the programs of one professional staff member make the program a model for Sea Grant marine education outreach efforts around the country.

Two significant societal changes challenge the current functioning of the program. First, the nature of volunteering nationwide is undergoing radical change. Retirees, who make up the vast majority of Docent volunteers, are healthier, wealthier, and busier than they ever have been. They have significantly more choices for using their time and are committing their time to volunteer efforts more stringently. This has forced the Docent program to commit to fewer programs to ensure that a sufficient number of adequately trained volunteers are available.

The second major societal change impacting the Docent program is the re-alignment of school programming as a result of "No Child Left Behind." Schools have reduced markedly the number of Docent programs they are bringing to schools and the number of boat-based programs they are attending, due to the increased time dedicated to preparation for statewide assessments and associated performance accountability. In response, Docent programs currently are being closely aligned to statewide science standards in order to justify their use in school curricula.

Case Study: Students Without Borders
JENNA JAMBECK AND KEVIN GARDNER

In the autumn of 2002, students at the University of New Hampshire established Students Without Borders (SWB), a university chapter of the not-for-profit organization Engineers Without Borders-USA. SWB's mission is to encourage, support, and implement environmentally and economically sustainable technical projects in local and international communities, while developing globally responsible and knowledgeable students. The organization is open to all students at the university and consists of both undergraduates and graduate students. Students from a wide variety of majors, including environmental engineering, mechanical engineering, civil engineering, public health, political science, art, and community planning have joined and participated in the group. A relationship has been developed with a community in Thailand. Three trips have been taken to Thailand to install drinking water treatment and distribution systems, waste treatment, and irrigation systems.

Additionally, over the past few years, a relationship was developed with a community school in Niger facilitated through a local nonprofit organization called RAIN for the Sahel and Sahara. The community is a village of the Tuareg people, which is a seminomadic culture that primarily practices animal husbandry for its livelihood. The Tuareg educate their children in cooperation with nonprofits and have built community boarding schools. At these schools, they have gardens that grow crops to feed the children; excess crops can be sold to provide further funding for the school. They are trying to implement drip irrigation throughout the region, but the camel-and-bucket method of water extraction was too slow to fill current cisterns. Gas-powered pumps were explored and began to be used by the people; however, these were both unsustainable and dangerous. A new, more sustainable and efficient water-extraction method was needed.

SWB has taken two trips to Niger; an assessment trip (two students and a professional mentor) and an implementation trip (four students and a professional mentor). The water-extraction system the students designed and built was low impact and completely sustainable; it was a rope-and-washer pump system made from materials that could be found locally in Niger. The guide box for the washers was constructed of concrete and a glass bottle (to reduce friction). The washers were cut from recycled tires by local artisans. The pump is animal powered so children would not have to work and could be in school. The local gardener could teach a camel to walk in a circle turning a wheel (horizontally) that translated power to the pump (vertically). The wheel the camel operated was made from wood atop a post connected to an old car bearing. The rope-and-washer pump extracts water more efficiently than a bucket and camel, yet does not use any other outside energy sources, such as gasoline or electricity. The pump is designed with technology the local people understand and animal power is a renewable resource with which they are comfortable. The pump was built in January 2007 by the students and villagers working closely together. A prototype of the pump that was built in Niger was displayed and operated at the 2007 National Sustainable Design Exposition on the Washington Mall in Washington, D.C. To be able to present at the Expo, the students won a U.S. EPA People, Prosperity and Planet (P3) award, which gave them $10,000 toward their efforts. At the Expo, they presented their ideas for the second phase of the work, and won an honorable mention award for their locally made sustainable design.

Engagement in Climate and Energy

In the future, we may well look back at the years of 2006 to 2008 as the turning point when the United States as a nation finally realized that human-driven climate change (global warming) demanded a collective response. A unique and accelerating series of events has brought us to this point.

At the national and international level, these include the hyperactive 2005 hurricane season and our failed response to Katrina, recognition of the rapid retreat of Arctic sea ice and the impact on polar bears, the popularity and impact of Al Gore's Oscar-winning *An Inconvenient Truth*, the U.S. Supreme Court's ruling that the Environmental Protection Agency has the authority to regulate greenhouse gases, and the release of the Intergovernmental Panel on Climate Change (IPCC) Fourth Assessment Report, followed by the awarding of the 2007 Nobel Peace Prize to Al Gore and the IPCC community. Finally, the summer of 2008 brought us $4 per gallon gasoline.

On a regional level, the Regional Greenhouse Gas Initiative (RGGI) — a cap-and-trade program for electricity producers in nine states in the Northeast United States — moved toward implementation, and the Northeast Climate Impact Assessment published a series of scientific papers and reports detailing the potential regional impacts of our changing climate.

At the state level, the Carbon Coalition pushed the issue of climate change to center stage in the New Hampshire Presidential Primary as 164 towns passed a resolution requiring action on this issue at town meetings across the state.

At UNH, we self-identified as a climate-protection campus, installed a co-generation plant, established the Energy Task Force, decided to pipe landfill methane gas from the Turnkey Landfill to power the UNH co-generation plant, were awarded EPA Energy Star rating for several buildings, and passed the one million person ridership in a year on Wildcat buses (See chapter 3 on Operations).

The four case studies in this section exemplify the role that students, faculty, and staff have played in important initiatives at each of these scales. Carbon Solutions New England is a partnership among UNH people and several nonprofit, business, and governmental organizations whose aim is to reduce the greenhouse gas footprint across the entire region. The New Hampshire Carbon Challenge has similar goals, and is aimed at the more than 200 towns, 164 of which have approved resolutions to reduce their own greenhouse gas emissions. The WildCAP discount program brings this idea to campus, with a focused program to encourage students to use only Energy Star appliances in all residence halls. Finally, university expertise has been tapped by two statewide commissions on energy and climate change that will determine New Hampshire's direction in these areas, and students in one class have had access to these activities, and simulated the task force process.

Case Study: Collaboration for a Low-Carbon Society —
Carbon Solutions New England
CAMERON WAKE

The scientific evidence is now clear: We must achieve an unprecedented reduction in the emissions of heat-trapping gases over the next decade to begin to stabilize our climate system. In light of the transformational response required to reduce our emissions significantly while sustaining our quality of life, the question for UNH is "How can we help solve the problem?" One of the stumbling blocks for land-grant and state universities, highlighted in the 1999 Kellogg Foundation Report on Engaged Institutions, is that while society has "problems," our institutions have "disciplines" and in focusing on excellence driven by peer review, we have "lost sight of our institutional missions to address the contemporary multidisciplinary problems of the real world."

One response to the challenge of overcoming compartmentalization and helping solve the carbon problem has been to build upon previous relationships and formalize a strategic partnership among the University Office of Sustainability, the Institute for the Study of Earth, Oceans, and Space, and the UNH Foundation to promote collective action to achieve a clean, secure energy future. We agreed upon three guiding principles for our effort:

- Building a low-carbon society demands an entirely new level of collaboration among a wide range of stakeholders, including the private sector, government, nonprofits, churches, and universities;
- our analyses and products would all be publicly accessible, transparent in purpose, method, and reasoning, and valuable for creative problem solving;
- we will focus our efforts regionally on New England, as emissions-reduction strategies and solutions, in many ways, will be driven by action at local-to-regional scales.

New England is a spatial scale at which we can be effective, and it is uniquely positioned to demonstrate an effective regional response due to the substantial entrepreneurial and intellectual resources available in the region.

What is Carbon Solutions New England?

Carbon Solutions New England (CSNE) is a public-private partnership, organized through the University of New Hampshire, to promote collective action to achieve a clean, secure energy future. A common set of regional indicators and milestones is required to provide decision-relevant information for a diverse set of stakeholders to coordinate action and track progress. To address this need, we will develop open-source analyses, products, and related databases, all web-accessible, that provide credible information on our progress toward reducing greenhouse gas emissions. This information provides a common reference point for policymakers, business, the media, non-profits, and educators. A collaborative process of focused working groups, annual assessments, and biannul summits will sustain dialogue and coordinate action across sectors and institutions.

Achieving significant emission reductions while sustaining our quality of life requires a transformational response. Our goal is to unite leaders from the public, private, and nonprofit sectors to collaborate at an entirely new level to build a low-carbon society while sustaining our unique natural and cultural resources. The transformational change required to build a low-carbon society demands collaboration among the wide range of stakeholders previously listed. Leaders from these sectors will join a collaborative learning community that will benefit all participants by producing products that are publicly accessible, transparent in purpose, method, and reasoning, and valuable for creative problem solving. Participants also will benefit from a process focused on learning and innovation that adds value to both individual and collective goals while pursuing a long-term public good.

CSNE already has secured seed funding from the New Hampshire Charitable Foundation to build our lead partnership network and conduct a series of rapid appraisals of the region's carbon cycle, the potential for renewable energy, the economic impact of state and regional policies that reduce net carbon dioxide emissions, and existing institutions and initiatives working toward a low-carbon society.

Why Collaborate?

We realized early on that we had to develop new and useful tools and analyses to attract partners and contribute in a meaningful way to regional efforts given the wide range of emission-reduction projects already initiated by cities, states, foundations, and not-for-profits in the region. Following on our initial principles, we reasoned that CSNE must build a regional collaborative that rewards and reinforces participation by:

- Pursuing a public-good project focused on solutions and a collective legacy;
- facilitating a process focused on learning and innovation that adds value to both individual and collective goals; and
- delivering products that are publicly accessible, transparent in purpose, method, and reasoning, and valuable for creative problem solving.

To date, we have been successful in developing a series of partnerships with several New Hampshire and regional organizations. This includes partnering with UNH-based carbon initiatives such as the New Hampshire Carbon Challenge (see the next case study) and building a partnership with Clean Air–Cool Planet (CACP), a not-for-profit based in Portsmouth, New Hampshire, that is finding and promoting solutions to global warming with a focus in the Northeast. UNH has a long history of collaboration with CACP and, due primarily to complementary strengths and areas of interest, our partnership provides the opportunity to have a significantly greater impact on the region as we integrate our efforts to be effective on a continuum of engagement in research and analysis, education, action, and policy. Other developing collaborations include the State of New Hampshire, the Environmental Protection Agency — New England Region, Northeast States for Coordinated Air Use Management (NESCAUM), Environment Northeast, and the Kendall Foundation.

Analyzing Solutions

One of the four main activities of CSNE is the analysis of various strategies to reduce emissions of heat-trapping gases in New England. Following on a seminal 2004 paper published by Stephen Pacala and Robert Socolow ("Stabilization Wedges," *Science* 305, pp. 968–972) that showed we currently have all the tools we need to solve the problem on a global scale, UNH faculty developed the DeCarbonizer (http://CarbonSolutionsNE.org), which allows users to visualize the impact of various strategies to reduce the emissions of heat-trapping gases on a regional level and thereby provide decision-relevant information to decisionmakers, policymakers, and any citizen interested in this issue. Examples include the impact of the RGGI, increasing the fuel efficiency of automobiles, reducing vehicle miles traveled, heating homes with biodiesel, and washing clothes in cold water. More analyses will be added as they are completed and we expect to develop more strategies than are required to reduce our emissions significantly. As a way to integrate our research and analysis into the curriculum, we are teaching classes that focus on identifying and quantifying regional strategies (also called "wedges"). Students perform detailed analyses that are reviewed in detail, they present the results to the university community, and their analyses are added to the DeCarbonizer.

Conclusion

CSNE is a relatively new initiative. We have benefited from initial support from the New Hampshire Charitable Foundation. Our discussions have generated considerable interest and excitement with a variety of people representing a range of institutions who have been working on the issue of climate change in New England. Central to the success of CSNE is effective and mutually beneficial collaboration with external partners to apply relevant knowledge and drive collective action. In this respect, CSNE represents one of many examples of engaged scholarship at UNH (see the case study on the Outreach Scholars Academy in the Culture and Sustainability section of this chapter).

Case Study: The New Hampshire Carbon Challenge
CHRIS SKOGLUND, DENISE BLAHA, AND JULIA DUNDORF

The New Hampshire Carbon Challenge (NHCC) is a UNH initiative committed to providing New Hampshire residents and communities with the information, tools, and support to reduce the carbon dioxide emissions of each household by 10,000 pounds per year. A key objective of the New Hampshire Carbon Challenge is to develop a replicable model for residential outreach using research-based behavioral-change tools that target the root causes of climate change inaction and utilize the networks and community organizations that can foster personal behavioral change.

The NHCC developed out of an enthusiastic response to a presentation by Denise Blaha, of UNH's Complex Systems Research Center, to a Barrington, New Hampshire, women's group hosted by Julia Dundorf. The presentation, on the mechanism, causes, and solutions to climate change, served as a wake-up call to the group, alerting them to the immediacy and severity of the climate crisis and highlighting the vital role that households can play in stabilizing greenhouse gas emissions. An initial challenge by Julia to the rest of the group to identify and lower their carbon footprint lead to a collaboration between Julia and Denise to create the New Hampshire Carbon Challenge that focuses on reducing the energy consumption of households statewide.

Successful Launch

The official launch of the NHCC on October 1, 2006, followed the release of the film *An Inconvenient Truth*. That event raised awareness of the threats of climate change and fostered a desire to take action. For many, however, the film fell short by failing to provide viewers with concrete solutions. The NHCC addressed that shortcoming by emphasizing the connections among energy efficiency and conservation, greenhouse gas emission reduction, and energy cost savings, and was an immediate success. With the passage of the New Hampshire Climate Change Resolution by 164 towns in March 2007 (fully 90 percent of those N.H. towns that had the resolution on the ballot), demand for the information provided by the challenge increased further.

Public reception of the initiative was enhanced by a number of key characteristics. The university, through the Institute for the Study of Earth, Oceans, and Space, served as an incubator by providing the initial seed funding. A dedicated, enthusiastic team of staff, steering committee members, and volunteers (many from UNH) was created swiftly, drawing on concerns for the potential catastrophic impacts of human-induced climate change and on the energy and perseverance of the co-founders. The skills, talents, and energy of the collective group, with backgrounds in climate science, education, behavioral change, grassroots organizing, community building, and political activism, were instrumental to the rapid growth and advancement of the program from an idea in an email to a program with statewide credibility.

Innovative Focus and Design

The NHCC is residentially focused for a number of reasons. Households, when considering home heating, vehicle use, and electricity consumption, contribute at least 40 percent of all greenhouse gas emissions. In spite of the fact that modest reductions in household energy use can significantly reduce residential carbon emissions, this focus area has been underserved until recently by New Hampshire climate-change initiatives.

The majority of behavioral-change campaigns have relied on techniques that are a combination of the quick, easy, cheap, and familiar, resulting in a succession of information-based campaigns that use newspaper articles, brochures, websites, or other traditional means of communication. While such campaigns can generate modest increases in awareness, they have not been terribly effective in changing behaviors. In an age when the general public is inundated with literally thousands of messages every single day, the average person is hard-pressed to distinguish among the messages, let alone act on the ones that might resonate with him or her.

In addition, climate change often is described in catastrophic terms that rob people of a sense of control or hope. The mechanism and causes of climate change are poorly understood, which prevents people from recognizing their connection to the issue. Personal action is limited by the fact that this issue is a collective action problem, a reality that can dissuade personal action in the face of such a global problem. People may not understand that solutions and technologies exist right now. The net result is that while many in society increasingly believe that global warming is real, they also may feel powerless to do anything about it.

To support the adoption of energy-efficiency and conservation measures within the home, the NHCC is developing a comprehensive program that relies on research-proven behavioral-change techniques and climate-change communication strategies. These tools address the key obstacles that have stymied more widespread personal and collective climate-change action and are consistent with Community Based Social Marketing, fostering behavioral changes by normalizing energy efficiency as part of a community's values.

To facilitate the development and testing of the tools that will be implemented across the state, two regional pilots have been established; one located in southeastern New Hampshire (the Oyster River Carbon Challenge) and another in southwestern New Hampshire (the Monadnock Carbon Challenge).

To support these community challenges, the NHCC has developed:

- The NHCC website (http://carbonchallenge.sr.unh.edu/calculator
  .jsp) with an online carbon calculator capable of tracking who is taking
  the challenge and what they are doing to reduce household emissions;
- a Community Challenge Organizers Guide for individuals and organizations who want to implement the Carbon Challenge in their communities;
- electronic newsletters to highlight Community Challenge news, give seasonal tips, and spotlight local "Climate Heroes";
- a Google map showing the distribution of communities that are taking the challenge and the collective reduction in carbon dioxide and

energy dollars saved by residents in those communities (http://
carbonchallenge.sr.unh.edu/maps/challenge_takers.jsp).

Expanding the Challenge

Using the experience gained from over a hundred public presentations to
six thousand residents and collaboration with climate action partners at the
local, state, and national level, the NHCC has developed a variety of tools and
resources to disseminate the Carbon Challenge to municipalities, faith-based
communities, civic organizations, and businesses, and to provide educators
with resources appropriate for school-age children.

Building on the success of their original presentation, the NHCC has
crafted an Employee Carbon Challenge initiative that supports concise, practical presentations to employees on how they can reduce their household
greenhouse gas emissions. These talks enable the Carbon Challenge to reach
more diverse audiences than typically would attend a global-warming presentation at other venues. To increase the NHCC's capacity to spread its message
and programming more rapidly to New Hampshire's 1.3 million residents, the
NHCC is developing a Train-the-Trainer program, partnering with organizations with well-defined networks such as UNH Cooperative Extension and
the National Wildlife Federation. Workshops developed from these collaborations will provide volunteers with the resources and training to give Carbon
Challenge presentations to the communities in which they are vested.

The NHCC has adopted a somewhat different approach to working with
schools, but views schools as a critical piece in the development of a comprehensive program. Sensitive to concerns about blurring climate-change education and advocacy, the NHCC has opted for a more conservative approach.
This has resulted in the development of programs and materials to support
residential CO_2 reduction through existing school environmental or ecology
organizations and collaborating with teachers to develop residential energy-
audit kits that allow students to assess their home's energy efficiency, relate
these observations to the larger problem of global climate change, and reach
conclusions of their own.

Case Study: WildCAP Discount Program
BRETT PASINELLA

WildCAP is a campus-wide program to reduce greenhouse gas emissions (the
name derives from wildcat — the university mascot — and CAP for Climate

Action Plan). The program is organized through the University Office of Sustainability (UOS), and is part of UNH's response to the University Presidents Climate Commitment (ACUPCC).

In 2005, UOS started looking for ways to encourage members of the UNH community to adopt energy-saving appliances and lightbulbs. One program arose out of a partnership with the local business community. Houghton's Ace Hardware is a small, locally owned store with two locations near campus and off-campus housing areas. Student move-in day traditionally has been one of their largest business days of the year, as students and their parents purchase all the last-minute items for their dorm rooms, so Houghton's was eager to explore partnership options.

Many opportunities existed for both parties. A primary concern for both was to build strong ties to the university and the local community and to maintain small, thriving, traditional New England towns in the face of increasing competition from national chain retail stores. Houghton's also saw an opportunity to reach out to college-age customers who were not part of their traditional customer demographic, and to familiarize new students with the stores and their locations as soon as possible after their arrival at UNH.

The first step was to define the products and the discount that would be offered to members of the university community. Houghton's usually did not offer many appliances, and only a few were available to them from their distributor. UOS and Houghton's worked together to determine which available models were part of the Environmental Protection Agency's Energy Star program. In some cases, an Energy Star product was not available in all categories and so available models had to be compared to the Energy Star requirements so that equivalent efficiency could be assured. Additionally, all the products offered had to meet all the requirements of the UNH Housing Office in terms of fire safety and other regulations. Houghton's then worked closely with their distributor to ensure that enough models and units would be available during the move-in period.

To promote the program, links were placed on the UNH Housing web page, which new students and their parents would view when reading the requirements for dorm residence. Houghton's and UOS maintained a table with outreach materials and order forms at all the orientation days held by the university over the summer. As part of one of these activities, a mock dorm room was set up, displaying the energy-efficient options for refrigerators, microwaves, lamps, stereos, clock radios, and other products available through the program. This physical model corresponded to an online virtual dorm room where information and facts about energy efficiency could be viewed by mousing over various icons of typical dorm-room appliances.

Houghton's remains a close university partner, but the appliance-purchasing program has changed with the closure of their store in Durham. Two stores in adjacent towns remain, and the University Office of Sustainability is now working with Housing, Residential Life, and other offices and partners to find a new way to offer energy-efficient mini-appliances, electronics, and other sustainable products to the UNH community.

Case Study: Informing Public Policy — Engagement on Climate with the State of New Hampshire
CAMERON WAKE

New Hampshire state government often has relied upon expertise at UNH to inform the development of public policy and UNH faculty have a long history of collaboration around the issues of climate and energy. This has included collaborative research and briefings for the House Science, Technology, and Energy and Senate Energy Committees, and Department of Environmental Services staff. In particular, faculty have provided expertise on the impacts of increasing the renewable energy contribution to electricity production, and on designing state responses to climate change. Students also have played a role in a discovery learning setting that shadowed a statewide task force.

On the electricity production issue, a UNH Management professor and a colleague performed research on the economic impact of pursuing a Renewable Portfolio Standard (RPS) and on the implications of the state of New Hampshire signing onto the Regional Greenhouse Gas Initiative (RGGI). Their findings have been cited widely as key studies that provided decision relevant information to state policymakers.

In December 2007, Governor Lynch created the Climate Change Policy Task Force that, in conjunction with the Department of Environmental Services (DES), was asked to develop a Climate Change Action Plan that establishes climate-change goals and recommends meaningful steps to meet those goals. Representation on the task force includes state politicians, leaders from state agencies, and individuals representing general commerce and industry, environmental groups, forestry, science/academia, public utilities, municipal government, and the insurance industry. In addition to serving as the science/academia representative, UNH faculty have provided the task force with an overview of the science and impacts of climate change for New Hampshire based on research that was done at UNH and as part of the Northeast Climate Impacts Assessment. Carbon Solutions New England (CSNE; see the first case study in this section) is providing technical assistance to quantify the potential greenhouse gas reduction, implementation costs, and potential cost savings of a variety of greenhouse gas reduction strategies that the working groups have identified. Ultimately, the Climate Change Task Force will provide final recommendations based on the strategies selected by its working groups and the detailed analysis done by CSNE. The resulting Climate Change Action Plan should provide a grounded, detailed roadmap for the state to grow its economy while reducing its greenhouse gas footprint.

During the spring semester in 2008, a Freshman Honors Discovery class was offered that essentially mirrored the task force process. Student groups were established to perform analyses in the areas of interest of several of the task force working groups. To provide the students additional background material, several task force members spoke with the class as did the chairman of the task force, DES Commissioner Tom Burak. Each group of students presented its findings at the Undergraduate Research Conference (see the section on Culture and Sustainability in chapter 4). In addition, the students had to complete the process of presenting, discussing, and deciding among the solutions developed. A final report was compiled, including URC posters, student papers, and the results of the discussions and votes, and was presented to Commissioner Burack.

Engagement in Food and Society

As a land-grant university, UNH has long been involved in food- and agriculture-related engagement efforts. UNH Cooperative Extension, which "provides New Hampshire citizens with research-based education and information," is a clear example of this. With programs on agriculture, aquaculture and fisheries, food and nutrition, food safety, and gardening, and programs like 4-H and the Family Home and Garden Education Center, Cooperative Extension is an important resource for the state. In addition to UNH Cooperative Extension, efforts to engage the broader community in issues of food, agriculture, and nutrition are numerous. Many research undertakings at UNH have direct engagement functions. For example, the UNH Organic Dairy Research Farm (see the case study in the Food and Society section of chapter 4) is an education center as well as a research center, providing organic dairy farmers and farmers considering transitioning to organic with essential, science-based production and management research. Other efforts, like the UNH Organic Garden Club highlighted in this chapter, demonstrate how students engage with the broader community through their student organization. Three other examples provided in this section—the New Hampshire Farm to School Program, Cooperative Fisheries Research, and the New Hampshire Center for a Food Secure Future—reveal how solid partnerships between the university and stakeholders throughout the state, including state government, nonprofits, and businesses, can build important collaborations to address food, agriculture, and nutrition issues in unique, innovative ways.

Case Study: The New Hampshire Farm to School Program
ELISABETH FARRELL AND LYNDA BRUSHETT

Introduction

According to the Farm to School website, farm-to-school programs are those that "connect schools and local farms with the objectives of serving healthy meals in school cafeterias, improving student nutrition, providing health and nutrition education opportunities that will last a lifetime, and supporting local small farmers." These programs are a response to a variety of trends facing students and local agriculture, including excessive weight gain in children, food industry consolidation, and loss of local agricultural infrastructure. Farm-to-school programs respond to these trends by reestablishing a local market connection between farmers and schools and linking that connection to broader educational goals.

Farm to School Takes Root in New Hampshire

In 2001, a working group representing the food system was brought together by an informal group, the New Hampshire Coalition for Sustaining Agriculture, to explore farm-to-school connections. This working group included staff from the UNH Office of Sustainability (UOS), UNH Cooperative Extension, N.H. Department of Agriculture Markets and Food, Resource Conservation, and Development councils, Natural Resource Conservation Service, the N.H. Department of Education, a school food-service buying group, Agriculture in the Classroom, Project Food, Land and People, and an apple grower and a dairy farmer. The group undertook initial research on the kinds of products used in cafeterias and the kinds of products that New Hampshire potentially could provide. Apples emerged as a product that was both a staple item on school menus and a traditional, albeit threatened, part of New Hampshire agriculture.

A USDA Sustainable Agriculture Research and Education proposal was submitted and awarded in 2003 to UOS in cooperation with the N.H. Coalition for Sustaining Agriculture for a three-year pilot New Hampshire Farm to School Program (NH FTS). The pilot focused on developing a business and educational model that would integrate N.H. apples and cider into as many N.H. K–12 schools as possible.

Impacts and Outcomes of the Pilot Program

Working with existing apple-distribution and school-procurement systems was integral to the success of the NH FTS pilot program. Offering schools N.H.-grown apples and cider created a cost-effective entry point for farmers and schools to make a market connection: Farmers got a fair price for an undervalued product and a steady, easily accessible market, and schools got a nutritious, locally grown food and an educational opportunity. Three wholesale producers and one retail grower agreed to launch the program. The program was designed to continue through the winter as long as quality supply was available, with schools receiving start-up and close-down notices. Because of this pilot program:

- Over half the schools in the state were able to make the farm-to-school connection by purchasing N.H. apples and cider for their cafeterias;
- seven apple growers developed schools as a new wholesale market, one regional apple wholesaler launched a new product for schools, and one grower expanded his cider operation;
- food-service directors were provided with a simple way to make a desired change; and
- educational materials that could be integrated easily into on-going activities in the classroom and the cafeteria were created and collected.

And, because the economics of this program worked for everyone — schools, distributors, and growers — the program is both successful and sustainable.

Expanding the Options

With one successful model in place, NH FTS decided to pilot a new farm-to-school project with a different approach. Focusing on school districts in the Seacoast region of the state, the Get Smart Eat Local 10-District Project was designed to use direct connections between schools and farmers to expand the variety of fresh, locally grown products on school menus.

The project began by conducting a detailed assessment of opportunities and barriers for getting New Hampshire–grown, local food into the target public schools. Meetings with food-service directors covered staff and kitchen facility capacity to use fresh, seasonally available farm products, menus and nutritional requirements, quality and volume needs, price points and delivery procedures. With these needs in hand, the project organized farmer-information sessions through county Cooperative Extension Educators, supported by press releases to local and agricultural media and visits to local farmers' markets.

While each meeting attracted interested farmers, discussion revealed that a farm-to-school market would not work for many direct-market farms because: (1) farmers had good and sufficient outlets for their products through farmers' markets, farm stands, pick-your-own, Community Supported Agriculture outlets, and other direct sales; (2) farmers enjoyed spending their time at these markets; (3) prices charged per item and sales volume obtained from those outlets covered income and profitability expectations; and (4) demand for products at these outlets exceeded supply.

However, by tapping into the farmer-to-farmer network, NH FTS was referred to a farmer who grew vegetables for wholesale markets and who potentially would be a good fit for the program. The 30-acre operation grows a variety of produce, including potatoes, tomatoes, lettuce, carrots, zucchini, and cucumbers. The grower's expertise in wholesale marketing meant that prices were competitive with what the public schools expected through their regular ordering. This, combined with the fact that he had enough product to service all the schools in the ten districts and that he could deliver, made him a prime candidate for the program. He was more than willing to forgo the trip to Boston to make local connections.

Outcomes of the Get Smart Eat Local 10-District Project

The pilot project helped establish the personal relationships and commitment to a common goal that led to the successful creation of a farm-to-distributor-to-school system. Ongoing discussion facilitated by the NH FTS program coordinator allowed the parties to work out challenges, from harvesting schedules and crop failures; to coordinating orders, farm pick-up, and school deliveries; to fluctuating items and quantities. Everyone is enthusiastic about these first connections. Crop planning has begun for next year and all elements are in place for a 2008 program start-up with spring lettuces.

The program offers benefits to everyone involved: The farmer is provided a guaranteed market with a profitable margin, enabled production expansion, and reduced delivery travel time and expense; the distributor is able to provide schools with products they wanted at price points they needed, in appropriate quality, quantities, and packaging, leading to an expansion of his business; and the schools are able to upgrade food quality without adding cost, as well as to learn an appreciation for great taste and multiple values of eating local.

Conclusions

Farm-to-school connections provide an innovative way to help rebuild the local agricultural infrastructure while improving the quality of food offered at schools. Making and sustaining the connections takes a long-term commitment based on trust and respect. As a land-grant university, UNH is in a unique position to help advance these relationships while fulfilling its research and engagement missions. Future goals of the program include linking more directly with UNH curriculum to involve students in the program, as well as undertaking more research studies on the challenges and opportunities of the farm-to-school system.

Case Study: Cooperative Fisheries Research — The Innovative Fisherman
KEN LAVALLEY

Many who are not familiar with today's commercial fishing industry still perceive the fisherman as Ernest Hemingway's "old man and the sea" who struggled for the greatest catch of his life. Although similarities may exist between the persistence of Hemingway's idealized fisherman and today's professional, the days of harpoons and hand-lines are gone. Today's fisherman has to be more than just "wise with the ways of the water."

Following the dramatic decline in Gulf of Maine and Georges Bank fish stocks during the early 1990s, New England fishers have faced a daunting list of regulations that dictate the gear they can use, the number of days they can fish, and even how much fish they can land. To combat these limitations and preserve fishing as a means to make a living, many fishers have evolved into innovative collaborators with university scientists all along the New England coastline. It is not unusual now to find the wheel house of a fishing vessel equipped with satellite internet access, global positioning systems to navigate and track fishing grounds, and hydroacoustic imaging systems to "see" the gear while fishing; and to find marine scientists using that same vessel as a platform for research. What started out as a "taxi" service for academia soon developed into an equal partnership between the fishing and science communities. As a result, the research capacity of academic institutions has increased and the application of scientific methods has led to rapid innovations in the effectiveness of fishing gear while allowing overfished stocks to rebuild.

Building Sustainability through Cooperative Fisheries Research

Two organizations have been crucial in supporting and building capacity for cooperative research in the Gulf of Maine: The Northeast Consortium (NEC), funded by NOAA and based at the University of New Hampshire, and the Cooperative Research Partners Program (CRPP). The NEC was established in 1999 to encourage and fund effective, equal partnerships among commercial fishers, scientists, and other stakeholders, and to engage in cooperative research and monitoring projects in the Gulf of Maine and Georges Bank. Four institutions make up the NEC: UNH, the University of Maine, the Massachusetts Institute of Technology, and Woods Hole Oceanographic Institution. The NEC has funded more than 171 cooperative research projects, involving over 395 commercial fishing vessel captains and owners, 32 fishing industry organizations or businesses, and over 264 scientists from 57 research institutions and state and government agencies.

The Northeast Regional Office of the National Marine Fisheries Service (NMFS) developed the NOAA Northeast Cooperative Research Partners Program (NECRPP) to support and promote collaborative research among New England's commercial fishing industry, marine science, and fishery management communities. The NECRPP focuses on research questions identified by the Northeast Fishery Science Center as well as the New England Fisheries Management Council. The information is then used to enhance the data on which fishery management decisions are made. Since 2000, NMFS and NECRPP have supported more than 60 short- and long-term fisheries projects. Together, the Northeast Consortium and NMFS have funded more than 200 projects totaling more than $30 million.

Collaborative Research in Sustainable Fishing at UNH

New Hampshire fishers currently are engaged in a number of projects with UNH scientists, which include the exploration of cod genetics, monitoring phytoplankton and nutrients to detect ecosystem change, assessing benthic impacts of fishing gear, field testing whale-entanglement mitigation strategies, and fishing gear conservation engineering. Central to all of these projects is the idea that the fishers — who work with gear on the water for a living and have an innate understanding of which designs will work and which won't — and scientists — who bring new technologies and approaches to bear — work as equal partners to develop improved gear and techniques.

Eliminating bycatch in the northern shrimp fishery. Shrimp trawlers in the Gulf of Maine were harvesting large numbers of juvenile groundfish as bycatch, and the fishery was in danger of being closed entirely. Fishers worked collaboratively with a group of regional scientists to evaluate grate systems that would allow juvenile fish to escape from the net while shrimp would pass through a window-like grate of bars and be retained by the net. The success of this design resulted in the reopening of closed areas and the continuation of the seasonal fishery.

Sustaining whale populations: Mitigating fixed-line entanglements. Concerns over the entanglement of endangered whales in fixed gear has been a driving force behind increased demands on fishers to modify their equipment and their fishing practices, often at great cost. Between 2000 and 2004, the National Marine Fisheries Service verified reports of 147 entanglements, 29 ship strikes, and 276 mortalities of whales along the East Coast. Entanglements can occur, for example, with a ground or end-line from a lobster pot or fixed gear, either by catching in the whale's baleen while the animal is swimming forward or by wrapping around the whale's body. A private industry group working with New Hampshire lobstermen developed two devices that will cut the fixed line when it is encountered by a marine mammal. This group in turn worked with an ocean engineer at UNH to evaluate these devices. One outcome of this research was the development of an artificial right whale flipper, a low-cost means of testing devices that will eliminate large whale and marine mammal entanglement mortalities in the Gulf of Maine.

PULSE: Cooperative monitoring of the Gulf of Maine ecosystem. Shifts in the Gulf of Maine marine ecosystem have the potential to trigger changes that can affect everything along the food chain from phytoplankton right up to herring and juvenile cod. The Partnership for Pelagic Ecosystem Monitoring of the Gulf of Maine, started in 2001, engages teams of New Hampshire fishers and scientists to sample zooplankton, phytoplankton, hydrography, and nutrients at four fixed nearshore and offshore stations off the coast. The goal is to develop a long-term history of seasonal changes in plankton organisms. This kind of data eventually should help fishery managers predict how many fish the ecosystem is capable of supporting.

Evaluating marine protected areas. Since 1997, several shallow-water features in the Gulf of Maine, known to be productive fishing grounds, have been closed to allow fish stocks and benthic communities to rebuild. A team of scientists and commercial fishers has been deployed to determine the effect of this closure. The scientists bring technical expertise in benthic habitat ecology, satellite imagery, bathymetric mapping, and video analysis to the table, while the industry participants have identified historically fished and nonfished habitats and have retrofitted vessels for oceanographic sampling. A major accomplishment of the project to date has been the development of a high-resolution, bathymetric map providing unprecedented detail on seabed topography in the study area, which will be crucial for future marine protected-area delineation and modifications to existing regulations.

Conclusion

The cooperative research process has been very successful in bringing management, scientists, and fishers together. As with anything, the process is not without its limitations; however, as we continue to build trust and cooperation between these historically opposing groups, the fisheries will continue to rebuild and the longevity of the industry and the sustainable harvest of the resource will be supported.

Case Study: The Organic Garden Club
REBECCA GRUBE

Each winter, a dedicated group of UNH students is hard at work ordering seeds, filling out organic certification paperwork, and planning for the next summer's harvest. These students belong to the UNH Organic Garden Club (OGC). Each year, the OGC produces a diverse crop of organic vegetables and makes sure they reach a wide segment of the UNH community.

The OGC was first envisioned in 2001 by faculty and staff participants in the UNH Food & Society Initiative, which aimed to "integrate the ethics, science, technology, and policies of civic agriculture and community food security into the university's identity and practices." They focused on the idea of developing a student-run campus-community farm that would enhance the university's experiences with organic and sustainable food production. A 2-acre parcel of land on the west side of campus was secured, and interested faculty, staff, and students began to discuss their goals for the site. Over the next two years, the initial vision was realized as the plot was certified organic, the first cover crops were planted at the site, and the UNH Organic Garden Club (OGC) was formed in 2003.

The OGC is student-run, with students managing day-to-day farm operations as well as all outreach activities. This provides an excellent opportunity for developing leadership skills. For example, former OGC leaders Bill Errickson and Lauren Buyofsky continue to use these skills in their current positions managing an educational farm and teaching small-scale organic farming and sustainable living.

One of the keys to the OGC's success is active involvement by a diverse group of stakeholder advisors. For example, John McLean, manager of the UNH Woodman Horticultural Research Farm, brings twenty-plus years of experience farming and teaching agriculture to students. The advisory group also includes local farmers, faculty and staff in the departments of Natural Resources and Plant Biology, UNH Dining Services, the Office of Sustainability, and the UNH Child Study and Development Center.

One of the challenges faced each year by the club is the availability of labor, since most field work needs to be done during late spring and in the summer, when the fewest students are on campus. Despite offering many advantages, the fact that the OGC is student-run also poses challenges, since student leaders do not have long tenures. With frequent transitions in leadership, it can be difficult to maintain the long-term vision and consistency that is required for careful land stewardship and soil building. Shifting priorities from year to year make it hard to stay on course with long-term objectives.

The Organic Garden Club, first recognized as a student organization in 2003, now has over a hundred members and was honored with the title of Student Organization of the Year in 2007. This rapid success is due to several factors, not the least of which is the focus on community service and cooperation. An example is the Garden Project, a partnership with another student organization, Students Without Borders, to design and build a shed and water cistern on the garden site.

The OGC is an active part of the campus community and cooperates to increase the presence and awareness of local organic food at UNH. In 2004, OGC members established the tradition of using their produce to prepare free monthly dinners for the Durham community and for those in need at the Cross Roads House, an emergency and transitional shelter in Portsmouth, New Hampshire. Students, faculty, and staff purchase vegetables seasonally from the vibrant OGC farmstand that is held weekly in the center of campus. Other produce is donated to local food banks or sold to the local supermarket, Durham Marketplace. UNH Dining Services has been a key partner and supporter of the OGC. They routinely purchase, prepare, and serve produce grown by the club, and in many cases have featured it as locally grown or UNH-grown (such as at the annual Local Harvest Dinner).

Case Study: New Hampshire Center for a Food Secure Future
ELISABETH FARRELL

In 1979, Maynard C. Heckel, then Director and Associate Dean of UNH Cooperative Extension, introduced a report containing recommendations for New Hampshire food policy that addressed statewide issues of food insecurity and loss of food production capacity. The result of significant internal and external stakeholder participation, the report detailed a visionary strategy for addressing these issues. However, the actions that followed have yet to meet many of the challenges that were outlined. In 2005, funding awarded to the University of New Hampshire's Office of Sustainability (UOS), Department of Animal and Nutritional Sciences, and Cooperative Extension by UNH's Office of Research and Public Service Discretionary Fund enabled the development of a strategic planning process to address these challenges, as well as others identified since the 1979 report was issued.

A subcommittee comprised of UNH investigators and external partners from government and nonprofit agencies, including the New Hampshire Food Bank and the New Hampshire Department of Agriculture, invited key stakeholders to conduct a comprehensive planning process. The goal of the process was to inform the development of a center that would address the need for coordinated, comprehensive action linking agriculture, the food environment, and health and nutrition in our state and region. This approach was unique in that it dealt with the systemic nature of the entire food system, from seed to plate to health outcomes, and determined that a cross-disciplinary approach would be required to make truly sustainable interventions. In-depth discussions by the committee included research into the current status of food security in the state and a SWOT (strengths, weaknesses, opportunities, and threats) analysis, as well as public sessions for gathering perspectives from agricultural representatives, dieticians, grocers, and others. Out of this process emerged a strategic plan for the establishment of the New Hampshire Center for a Food Secure Future (NHCFSF), from which the following description has been drawn.

NHCFSF was launched officially in 2006 with a mission to advance a renaissance of New Hampshire food culture from farm to table, promoting food systems that support sound nutrition and healthy sustainable communities. The vision of NHCFSF is to:

1. Educate stakeholders in our food community about the interconnected aspects of food security and develop communication strategies that provide this education.
2. Advance local, state, and national policies that promote a food secure future.
3. Serve as a clearinghouse for dependable data and resources on topics related to food security.
4. Conduct independent research, education, and training on food security.
5. Create linkages and provide networks for those working on the fragmented aspects of food security to come together under a common mission.

While the need for this integrative work remains critical, finding adequate funding to support NHCFSF's work has been a challenge. An advisory council meets regularly to guide NHCFSF as it seeks funding opportunities, engages with stakeholders, and implements some of the goals identified in the strategic plan, including establishing a quarterly newsletter and researching the status of the food system in New Hampshire and the region. In 2007, NHCFSF received seed money from the New Hampshire Charitable Foundation to develop a food security indicator and communications tool. As of this writing, the tool is in development and is anticipated to be released in its initial form in the fall of 2008.

Engagement in Culture and Sustainability

Recreating a culture of engagement between land-grant institutions and the society in which they are embedded has become a widespread initiative. Realization that traditional Extension activities were only part of the solution has led to a re-evaluation of how universities engage and enrich their surrounding communities. Engagement should not be limited to just the Extension faculty but should encompass the full range of faculty talent the university has to offer. This requires a substantial organizational commitment to integrate research with outreach. The phrase "outreach scholarship" captures the nature of this new endeavor, really a rebirth of the traditional linkage between campuses and constituents, and adds an important emphasis on engaging those with a stake in the outcome of any project at the beginning, in the definition of the project, and throughout the research program. It also benefits and rewards those faculty who integrate community service into their scholarly activities.

At the same time, a campus needs to look internally at the culture it creates, and assess whether that culture sustains open dialogue and diverse representation of points of view.

The four case studies presented here display the two-sided nature of this aspect of sustainability. "Deliberation in the Civic Sector" discusses the role that study circles have played in engaging citizens in problem solving and policy development, and examines how this approach has been used at UNH. "Building a Sustainable Community of Engaged Scholars" describes the innovative approach taken at UNH to the definition of outreach scholarship and the role that a particular program, the UNH Outreach Scholars Academy, plays in the development of a culture of engaged scholarship. The Portsmouth Black Heritage Trail is the outgrowth of cooperative efforts of UNH faculty, a number of local nonprofit organizations, and a dedicated community activist, while the Scheier Project values the sense of place that can be generated by telling the story of two dedicated campus artists and teachers.

Case Study: Deliberation in the Civic Sector — The Role of Higher Education in Sustaining Democracy
BRUCE L. MALLORY

In the fall of 1997, the University of New Hampshire launched what would become the first of a continuing series of campus-wide deliberative dialogues.

Using the study circles model of sustained dialogue, the author and an ad hoc group of faculty and staff engaged seventy-five members of the community to examine the question, "Are freedom of speech and a non-threatening environment mutually exclusive on campus? Gender, power, and difference at UNH." The purpose of the project was two-fold. First, we hoped to defuse tensions on campus in the wake of a prolonged and divisive adjudication of a faculty member some of whose students accused him of using sexually harassing and intimidating language in his lectures. Second, we wanted to draw on the wisdom of the community, through an intensive and semistructured dialogue process, in order to modify the university's policies on discriminatory harassment so as to better resolve future complaints. The experience proved to be meaningful to participants and useful in generating specific recommendations for policy changes. The ad hoc and spontaneous nature of the study circles led to a sense that they could be an effective tool for addressing subsequent difficult community issues.

Since 1997, the university has supported campus-wide study circles on a host of topics, including:

- "University or polyversity? The promise of conflict in the UNH community";
- "What is the impact of alcohol on our community? A conversation for everyone about education and expectations";
- "The compelling interest of diversity: How should UNH meet its educational and civic responsibilities to foster an inclusive campus community?"

These projects, along with other forms of dialogue that have addressed race, campus safety, and governance issues, have been critical to the university's ability not only to sustain but to foster a democratic, participatory culture.

Sustaining democracy is no small challenge in general. In the context of a large, complex research university that values autonomy over interdependence, individual over collective achievement, and the recognition of status distinctions (by faculty rank or staff classification, for example), merely practicing democracy is a challenge. In this way, UNH is not unlike any other bureaucratic organization where efficiency and hierarchical power arrangements trump concerns for democratic processes. Shared or participatory governance in universities is too often characterized by what Benjamin Barber calls "thin democracy," in which a few elected or appointed individuals are assumed to represent the will of the community. But our work at UNH has been an effort to build "strong democracy," in Barber's terms, where most of the citizens (faculty, staff, students) feel and behave in ways that demonstrate authentic civic engagement. Our goal is to offer an alternative to the traditional forms of engagement on campus, often limited by who participates (e.g., only faculty or only students), who sets the agenda (often one person or a small group in authority), and how business is conducted (haphazardly with no agenda, or rigidly with a fixed agenda, driven by an artificial time limit, after which participants come away with a sense that little was accomplished).

The use of sustained dialogue models, in conjunction with traditional forms of university governance processes, can expand the number of participants, allow time for much deeper examination of the issue at hand, and produce concrete recommendations for action that a significant number of community members feel committed to. Perhaps as important as these instrumental results, the use of sustained dialogue models can shift the culture in the direction of greater interdependence among university constituents, greater equity of participation among those who hold differing statuses, and greater accountability on the part of those charged with implementing recommendations that emerge from the process. Ultimately, we hope that the use of more participatory approaches to community problem solving and governance matters will impress upon our students that their obligations as citizens can be realized in a similar fashion. That is, we believe that a campus that sustains itself through deliberative democratic practices is more likely to produce future citizens who will strengthen and sustain the democracy in which we live.

The experience at UNH with sustained dialogue as a means to strengthen and sustain community is not unique. Over the past several years, the author, working with colleagues at other colleges and universities, has brought the civic engagement movement that Barber, Harry Boyte, Thomas Erlich, Peter Levine, David Schoem, and Iris Marion Young have been describing for the past decade onto a number of campuses. We have done so partly in response to concerns expressed by Ernest Boyer in 1996:

[W]hat I find most disturbing . . . is a growing feeling in this country that higher education is, in fact, part of the problem rather than the solution. Going still further, that it's become a private benefit, not a public good. Increasingly, the campus is being viewed as a place where students get credentialed and faculty get tenured, while the overall work for the academy does not seem particularly relevant to the nation's most pressing civic, social, economic, and moral problems.

At a number of campuses, study circles have been the choice of dialogue tool (e.g., UNH, Wagner College, Manhattan College, La Guardia Community College, Mount Holyoke College). Others utilize intergroup dialogue (University of Michigan, University of Massachusetts, Arizona State University, University of Washington). Still others draw on the National Issues Forum approach (Franklin Pierce College, Regis University, the University of Pennsylvania). National organizations such as the Deliberative Democracy Consortium, the National Coalition for Deliberation and Dialogue, Everyday Democracy, and AmericaSpeaks are all now working to foster sustainable, participatory dialogue in communities and on campuses.

In 2007, UNH sponsored a national gathering of scholars and practitioners in higher education working to create sustained dialogue. The result was the creation of the Democracy Imperative, located at UNH, whose mission is, "To improve public life and advance deliberative democracy in and through higher education" (see http://www.unh.edu/academic-affairs/democracy/). The Democracy Imperative provides resources to campuses in four areas: curriculum development, shared governance practices, community-university relationships, and research on deliberative dialogue. Essentially, deliberative, democratic practices are a necessary part of addressing the challenges detailed in this volume. If we are to create sustainable universities that themselves generate critical knowledge for resolving the immediate problems of climate change, sustainable food systems, biodiversity, or the homogenization of culture, we need concrete, accessible, low-technology tools for doing so. The approaches to deliberation described here are one such set of tools.

Case Study: Building a Sustainable Community of Engaged Scholars — The UNH Outreach Scholars Academy
JULIE E. WILLIAMS, ELEANOR ABRAMS, AND CHRISTINE SHEA

In 2001, the University of New Hampshire began a series of university-wide conversations about the institution's engagement mission. National reports from the Kellogg Commission and others had exposed a critical national need for higher education to renew its commitment to its public purposes. Jeremy Cohen and Rosa Eberly, writing in 2006, captured this need in an essay entitled "Higher Education, Democratic Capacity and Public Scholarship" that described the centrality of public scholarship and engagement to the nation's democratic values. They stressed that public scholarship must be centrally connected to, not set aside from, teaching and learning — describing what they termed a "curriculum of consequence." As new or redefined terms, both engagement (or engaged scholarship) and public scholarship were not defined clearly for most academics.

Led by the first author and a team of UNH faculty and staff, the discussions that began in 2001 were designed to provide clear definitions of this new form of scholarly work, and to connect this endeavor with two critically important institutional priorities: developing the university's first Academic Strategic Plan (2002) and providing leadership for engagement in the ten-year accreditation review.

This effort built on earlier work by smaller groups of UNH faculty and staff, and, in particular, a process undertaken in 2000 by UNH Cooperative Extension (UNHCE). The Strategic Plan that emerged became a model for others at the university. However, the 2001 conversation about engagement was the first systematic, university-wide endeavor undertaken with a range of faculty, extension educators, staff, and administrators to link engagement strategically to the institution's overall mission, goals, and future priorities. This significantly elevated engagement, and the scholarship of engagement, and for the first time explicitly articulated the critical role of the UNH faculty.

As a consequence of these university-wide dialogues, engagement and outreach became one of five goals in the university's academic strategic plan, and "engagement through research and scholarship" became one of only three priorities highlighted for advancement in the accreditation review. The hope was to link engagement further to the work of the faculty and to the core institutional missions: research and scholarship.

Perhaps most importantly, the term "engagement," which had held varied meanings for different people and in different settings across UNH, for the first time was defined institution-wide. In the 2003 NEASC report, engagement was defined as "a mutually beneficial collaboration between the University of New Hampshire and external partners for the purpose of generating and applying relevant knowledge to directly benefit the public."

With the plans written, engagement defined, and broader goals and strategic priorities articulated, the leadership team began to ask several critical questions, including:

- How do we move from rhetoric and lofty goals to practical reality and specific actions?
- What specific actions and strategies might be best utilized to help advance the engagement mission within the University of New Hampshire culture?

- How do we attract greater numbers of faculty and develop their capacity to lead the engagement mission?
- What enabling mechanism might begin to demonstrate to faculty the critical link between engaged scholarship, research, and teaching to build a sustainable community of engaged scholars?

The Outreach Scholars Academy

The UNH Outreach Scholars Academy was developed in response to these critical questions. The initial purpose of the academy, initiated in 2003, was to serve both as an enabling and recruiting mechanism to help faculty learn about engaged scholarship and as a structure to lead a range of engagement efforts. More specifically, the academy is a faculty professional-development program designed to enhance, support, and advance the work of tenure-track, research, extension, and clinical faculty. Faculty members participate in a semester-long series of workshops based on a curriculum led by external and internal experts. They participate in interdisciplinary discourse, interact with peers, receive feedback from coaches, meet with federal agency program officers, and develop a collaborative project. Although the specific curriculum and time commitment have been modified over time, face-to-face workshops typically occur once or twice a month for four to six hours and team and individual assignments typically are set.

Participation in the Outreach Scholars Academy is an honor and faculty must be nominated by deans, department chairs, or academy alumni. Nominations are followed by a formal application process, letters of support, and a review process to determine the appropriate class composition. To date, more than sixty UNH faculty members from a range of academic disciplines and academic ranks have participated in the academy.

Over the last four years, the specific goals of the academy have been modified based on evaluation data and the inclusion of new curriculum areas. The goals are to:

- Enhance individual faculty members' ability to move from a focus primarily on outreach and service to peer-reviewed engaged scholarship;
- enhance knowledge about how to engage effectively with external partners in mutually beneficial partnerships;
- contextualize the national conversations about engagement and outreach scholarship to the UNH context and develop a common understanding of engagement as a form of scholarship;

- implement the engagement and outreach goal in the UNH academic strategic plan; and
- Build a sustainability community of scholars who possess the knowledge and commitment to advance engagement as a form of scholarship.

Building a Sustainable Community of Scholars

The Outreach Scholars Academy has resulted in the development of a community of engaged scholars — about sixty UNH faculty members — who have a renewed understanding of engagement, and who support and assist colleagues, advance institutional engagement goals, and help support broader goals of the administration. Success has resulted from the work of a few dedicated faculty members and administrative leaders who were committed to engagement, and understood the necessity of building a sustainability community of scholars.

The academy has been an interesting challenge and a balancing act. At times, its very existence was in doubt and it was unclear whether and how the academy might continue. In the initial two years, sustaining the academy required that proponents consistently advocate for and gain the commitment of both mid- and top-level administrators who agreed to help challenge the status quo, and who were willing to risk challenging others. In the most recent two years, the academy has thrived. It now connects a large and growing number of faculty members committed to engagement with the strategic vision, future plans, and priorities of mid-level leadership — and to senior administrative goals, priorities, and financial commitments. The academy model also has garnered significant national attention and interest recently, after several presentations at national conferences, a journal publication, and the development of an interactive website.

In 2007, at the request of several members from three prior academy classes, a new alumni program was developed: "the Outreach Scholars Academy Lunch and Learn" series. This series will meet three or four times each year and alumni will have ongoing opportunities to learn about the work of their colleagues. In the first 2007 meetings, dozens of alumni (from each of three years) participated in the lunch-and-learn discussions. New intellectual and social connections already have begun to occur across cohorts. Further, the zeitgeist among a number of academy alumni is that "giving back" and helping new faculty join this community of scholars is important. Requests for assistance by academy administrative leadership and requests for participation in new initiatives typically result in positive responses from alumni members. This positive approach further supports this relatively new community of scholars.

When it initially was designed in 2003, the Outreach Scholars Academy was thought to be a specific implementation step to help realize the promise of engagement and engaged scholarship at UNH. At present, the academy has become an enabling mechanism through its alumni and its symbolic position, to energize and support a growing community of engaged scholars who are committed to advancing engagement and engaged scholarship locally, nationally, and internationally.

Case Study: Portsmouth Black Heritage Trail
VALERIE CUNNINGHAM

In 1995, the Portsmouth Black Heritage Trail was inaugurated as a self-guided walking and driving tour of twenty-four sites located within the city limits of this historic New Hampshire seaport. The trail reveals that Africans and American-born Black people have lived here from the period of colonial slavery through the Civil Rights Movement of the Sixties and to the present. These long-forgotten stories invite further inquiry by local historians and scholars into the previously ignored practices of slavery and de facto segregation in northern New England.

The small nonprofit organization that founded the trail was composed of a cross-section of community activists and professionals of all ages, including three UNH professors. Initially, in addition to fundraising, the emphasis was on developing the most effective way to get this long-neglected dimension of the New Hampshire story into local classrooms. Mark J. Sammons, then-director of Educational Programs and Historic Research Projects at Strawbery Banke Museum, volunteered to help amateur historian Valerie Cunningham transform her independent research into a resource book for public school teachers and students. The New Hampshire Charitable Foundation made it possible to place the books, free of charge, in all the city schools and area public libraries. Guiding the organization and editing of this first publication generously was provided gratis by UNH Professors John Ernest and David Watters of the English Department and Jeffrey Bolster of the History Department, all of whom have continued to serve as advisors and board members to the trail.

The trail has helped raise public awareness of African-American organizations across the state. And these organizations want to interact with the university community, to welcome student and faculty participation in their various activities, while the university is eager to attract more community members to the campus. Having strong relationships with the African-American community is of critical importance to the well-being of the university and is particularly important for recruiting faculty and students to this campus.

A significant opportunity was created in 2004 when Provost Bruce Mallory accepted a proposal by Professors Ernest, Watters, and Bolster to create a position for Black Heritage Partnerships that could link the campus to the African-American community. Cunningham, president of the trail and a well-known community activist, would coordinate the Partnerships, collaborating with African American Studies to link students, faculty, and staff with activities in the Black community. Again, the Charitable Foundation recognized the value of sharing cultural and scholarly resources and co-sponsored funding for the first three years.

Black Heritage Partnerships has complimented work begun by the Black Heritage Trail through service projects, independent study, and internships that enrich student and faculty experiences of what it means to be in New Hampshire. This initiative demonstrates how a commitment to sustainable thinking, despite modest resources, can model civic and corporate responsibility for our future.

Case Study: Four Hands, One Heart — Ed and Mary Scheier
Documentary and Exhibit
TOM KELLY

The Scheier project took the form of a documentary on the lives of Ed and Mary Scheier, who were at the forefront of American studio pottery beginning in the 1940s and who taught ceramics at UNH for twenty years. In addition to the film, which was a collaboration between the University Office of Sustainability, the UNH Dimond Library, the Currier Gallery of Art located in Manchester, New Hampshire, and independent filmmaker Ken Browne, the project also included the construction of display cases for an ongoing exhibition of Scheier pottery throughout the Dimond Library and a collaboration with the Freshman English program to introduce faculty and instructors to the pottery and the Scheier's story for use in their teaching. The premier of the film at UNH brought together more than two hundred faculty, students, staff, alumni, and community members to celebrate the great legacy of Ed and Mary Scheier.

The Scheier project originated in programming by the University Office of Sustainability to contribute to ongoing community building efforts through the cultivation of a sense of place for all members of the UNH community. UOS saw sense of place as an integral part of a quality of life that is experienced at the community or landscape scale. Difficult to define but unmistakable when experienced, "sense of place" in the context of sustainability conveys a discernable level of harmony between nature and culture and a strong community identity rooted in a common purpose and shared experience. One approach that UOS took to the goal of cultivating a sense of place was captured in the saying "if you know the story of a place, you can find a place in the story." In other words, while universities have many boundaries and large numbers of relatively transient members of their community (four years can be an awfully short time) an overarching narrative or set of narratives about the story of the place, if authentic and systematically conveyed, can contribute to a strong sense of place and allow all members of the community to "find their place in the story."

After a series of meetings with administrators and faculty, a consensus emerged on the value of developing a program around "finding a place in the story." Of the many suggestions that were made, the use of a common book for all incoming students was identified as one worth pursuing. As a result of collaborative work that already had begun between UOS and the Arts and Society Program (see *The Promise of the Sun* story in the Culture and Sustainability section of chapter 2), a catalogue that had been written for a 1995 show of the work of Ed and Mary Scheier at the Currier Gallery of Art was identified as an excellent possibility. Extremely well researched and written, the catalogue's narrative of the Scheiers' lives introduced the reader to the Depression era, Roosevelt's Works Project Administration, the evolution of the crafts movement in the early to mid-twentieth century — including the establishment of the League of New Hampshire Craftsman — and, of course, the intertwined lives of Ed and Mary Scheier that happened to include twenty years of teaching at the University of New Hampshire. While investigating the possibilities of printing several thousand copies of the catalogue with the Currier Gallery of Art, its director, Susan Strickler, shared an emerging documentary project with filmmaker Ken Browne focused on the life of Ed and Mary Scheier.

The rest, as they say, is history. With the co-sponsorship of UOS and the Dimond Library, filmmaker Ken Browne worked with UNH and the Currier Gallery to craft a beautiful film, *Four Hands, One Heart*, which was aired on more than one hundred Public Television stations across the country. Today, the Scheiers' work is on permanent display at the university's main library and the film continues to be used in classes. The film highlights the contemporary link between sustainability and art and the tremendous impact that these two great artists had on everyone around them in the UNH community. Mary and Ed passed away in March 2007 and April 2008 respectively: Mary, just days short of her hundredth birthday and Ed, less than a year later, at the age of ninety-eight. Their extraordinary lives add an important chapter to the history of our place at UNH. We can take great pride and inspiration in knowing that we share that story with them and if we are successful, so will future generations of students, faculty, and staff.

How the Sustainability Ethic Developed at UNH, and the Next Phase of Our "Journey to the Future"

Sara Cleaves, Tom Kelly, and John Aber

How do we in higher education make our work fundamentally about sustainability? How does sustainability relate to higher education's core values and mission? What can sustainability offer scholars, practitioners, and students, and how can what we undertake on campus advance sustainability at the regional, national, and international levels?

In this book, we have presented some initial answers to these questions by describing the University of New Hampshire's unique sustainable learning community educational model; a model we use to integrate sustainability into our mission and identity and to help us cultivate a critical and creative global sustainability outlook in our students and ourselves. The sustainable learning community model focuses on four key systems. These four systems — biodiversity and ecosystems, climate and energy, culture, and food — are integrated as educational initiatives focused on institutional practices across what we refer to as the core functions of the university: curriculum, operations, research, and engagement (CORE). Together, the four-systems approach integrated throughout the CORE activities of the university support educational innovations that cultivate the perspectives needed to enhance quality of life, both on and off campus, generation after generation.

This book presents a wide variety of case studies and lessons learned in our continuing effort to transform UNH into a sustainable learning community, but two questions have not been answered yet: How did the campus come to embrace sustainability in the first place, and where will our journey take us next?

PHOTO: Courtesy of UNH Photographic Services.

History of Sustainability at UNH: The Early Years

Earlier chapters have suggested a number of diverse reasons why UNH might have been poised to accept sustainability as a core value and goal. The location of the campus may have tended to attract faculty, students, and staff who valued a high level of environmental quality. The relatively underfunded nature of the campus meant that energy shocks, particularly in the 1970s and now in this decade, created strong financial incentives to reduce energy use and increase efficiency (the garbage-to-energy and solar applications of the earlier era were unsuccessful but educational initiatives). A culture of interdisciplinarity led to the formation of cross-campus units of the kind required to support environmental teaching and scholarship (the first of these, the Institute of Natural and Environmental Resources, was disbanded not too long after it was formed, but others have thrived). All of these, and perhaps the absence of large, competing interests, like a medical school, helped focus the campus on environmental topics in the broadest sense, from academics to operations and outreach.

This growing interest in living, studying, and teaching about our environmental setting took one very tangible form through the formation of a grassroots leadership group of faculty, staff, and students, many in the College of Life Sciences and Agriculture. Under the leadership of then-Dean Bill Mautz, this group came together often to discuss how to advance what came to be called sustainability at UNH, and a white paper was developed laying out the principles and groundwork for making this happen. The movement was strong enough to draw the attention of the UNH Foundation, which was soon to kick off a $100 million capital campaign for the university and, unbeknownst to them at the time, receive a generous offer from a visionary alumnus.

Development of the Office of Sustainability Programs: One Donor's Generosity and Vision

UNH crossed a crucial threshold in our journey to a sustainable future with the establishment of an endowed sustainability program. The approach taken by that program has been instrumental to involving *all* parts of the campus in implementing sustainability goals and programs and developing an inclusive and forward-looking framework, with measurable outcomes.

When the late Oliver Hubbard, an alumnus of the class of 1921, came to the university wanting to donate funds, he came with a particular vision in mind. He did not want his donation to create yet another building or endowed faculty position. Rather, Hubbard wanted his donation to bring faculty, staff, and students together — across disciplinary, departmental, and college boundaries — to create a fundamental change in the way the university operated and affected the state. The UNH Foundation suggested sustainability to Hubbard as a growing movement on campus that met his criteria, and in 1996 Hubbard donated $6 million to create the first endowed sustainability program in higher education in the nation.

The stated purpose of Hubbard's visionary gift was to stimulate collaborations across disciplinary lines and to enhance quality of life and the human relationship to the natural world through education. According to a university trustee who helped secure the endowment, Hubbard recognized sustainability as a concept that could change the entire university long-term.

A committee comprised of senior administrators, faculty, staff, and students from across campus began a national search for someone to direct this unique program, and founding director Dr. Tom Kelly was brought on board in July 1997. During his first year, the endowment for the program increased from $6 million to $10 million. Over the course of the next ten years, Dr. Kelly and his staff developed the unique vision of the sustainable learning community, the combination of the four initiatives intertwined with the four functions (or CORE) that have become the operational framework for the sustainability program on campus, and the outline for this book.

Work on the four initiatives is advanced through working groups in each area comprised of campus representatives (faculty, students, and staff) from each of the four functions. Each working group has a primary commitment:

- **Biodiversity Education Initiative (BEI).** Commitment to being a biodiversity protection campus that promotes ecological and public health through the protection of biodiversity and ecosystem integrity.
- **Climate Education Initiative (CEI).** Commitment to being a climate protection campus that pursues reductions in carbon emissions through sustainable energy and emissions-reduction policies, practices, research, and education.
- **Culture & Sustainability Initiative (CAS).** Commitment to being a cultural development campus that promotes a culture of sustainability through a dedication to community, diversity, citizen engagement, public arts, and the conservation and sustainable development of cultural and natural resources.

- **Food & Society Initiative (FAS).** Commitment to being a sustainable food community that promotes healthy food systems from farm to fork to health and nutrition outcomes.

To accomplish this vision and mission, the program encourages staff and partners to:

- **See it.** Facilitate cross-disciplinary partnerships through the common ground of sustainability that strengthen the university's responsiveness to environmental, economic, and cultural challenges.
- **Build it.** Develop and support university-wide decisionmaking mechanisms, tools, and policies that make UNH a model sustainable learning community.
- **Live it.** Initiate, lead, and collaborate on innovative teaching, research, and outreach initiatives that engage the university in building a sustainable learning community.

As the program began to take shape, advisory and working groups were formed and vision papers were written for each initiative. New communications efforts, like a program website and newsletter, were developed to bring the program's message to the campus community. Most importantly, a variety of new efforts were initiated to catalyze change across the four core areas of curriculum, operations, research, and engagement. These ranged from a new Earth Sciences course that engaged students in negotiating greenhouse gas strategies for the university, to sustainable landscaping standards, to a university-wide lecture series addressing critical issues where bioscience and technology converge to impact the environment and human health. In fact, many of the efforts described in chapters 2 through 5 of this book have been initiated, catalyzed, or supported by UNH's sustainability program.

The director of the program summarized the results of the first year of operation by saying:

Sustainability is a new chapter in the story of UNH that combines the strengths of tradition and the creativity of innovation. It builds on UNH's enduring commitment to preparing leaders in all professions to face the unique challenges of their generation and responds to the unprecedented need for the next generation to balance economic viability with ecological health and human well-being.

Transformation into the University Office of Sustainability: The Ten-Year Tipping Point

When the sustainability program was first established, the director's stated goal was for ten years of intense effort to bring the program and the campus to a tipping point at which the campus community would embrace sustainability as its own, much more than just the name of a particular office on campus, and the next phase of UNH's sustainability leadership would begin. That tipping point was reached in July 2007 when newly appointed UNH President Mark Huddleston altered the name of the program as well as the title and reporting structure of its director. The new name, the University Office of Sustainability (UOS), reflects the cross-campus mission of the office. The director became the Chief Sustainability Officer, one of the first in the country to carry that title, and the position now reports to the Provost and Executive Vice President, rather than to a college dean.

The last two years in particular have seen Oliver Hubbard's original intention to support collaboration across all parts of the university to improve education, research, and ultimately quality of life for communities in the state and region come to life. Support has been generated at all levels in the university system, including top campus administrators, and even up to the level of the board of trustees (without whose active support and investment the co-generation plant and landfill-gas pipeline could not have happened). Sustainability has been embraced as one of the central organizing principles around which UNH understands and executes its mission, and has emerged as a critical educational and research topic and a strategic area of focus for new curricula, research, fundraising, and communication efforts. Again, the outcome of this campus-wide cultural acceptance of sustainability as a core value is expressed in the stories contained in this book.

The Next Phase

If we have successfully captured the flavor of what has been accomplished at UNH in the area of sustainability, then what of the future? The challenge of sustainability has increased significantly in the last decade. Accelerating climate change, dramatic increases in energy prices, and the resultant impact on food prices are just some of the changes that have placed many communities across our state and region, and indeed across the country and world, in a precarious state. In many cases, these vulnerabilities are increasing. Responsive education and research that supports the ability of communities to sustain a high quality of life require the kind of collaboration across colleges and departments that Oliver Hubbard envisioned.

Two initiatives currently in the planning stage would take UNH to the next level as a sustainable learning community: (1) Developing the UNH Sustainability Academy, and (2) Expanding on the concept of the Energy Task Force (see the Operations chapter) to enhance the integration of sustainable thinking into campus decisionmaking.

The Sustainability Academy

Educators long have envisioned a "university without walls" that would advance quality of life through teaching, research, and engagement without regard to departments or disciplines. A Sustainability Academy at UNH could be the vehicle for creating this kind of broadly multidisciplinary institution, while also meeting the founding mission of land-grant universities and Oliver Hubbard's desire when he endowed the nation's first university sustainability program. The UNH Sustainability Academy would facilitate collaboration from all parts of the university and build on UNH's significant strengths in sustainability teaching, research, and engagement — from Earth system and environmental science, food systems and agriculture, and energy and waste management to sustainable communities, education, and the arts. The overarching goal would be to draw together and focus multidisciplinary knowledge on strengthening the resilience of communities to sustain a high quality of life for generations to come, and then make that knowledge available to a wide range of students and stakeholders across the university, state, and region.

Sustainability-related credit and noncredit programs and certificates would be offered at the undergraduate, graduate, professional, and citizen levels. Examples could include certificates in green building or sustainable community development, trainings on greenhouse gas emissions inventories or communicating sustainability effectively, or workshops on community gardening or household carbon-reduction strategies. Certificates, minors, majors, Master's, and Ph.D. programs also could be developed in sustainability itself and in key systems of sustainability, such as food (see the case study on UNH's new undergraduate dual major in EcoGastronomy in the Food and Society section of chapter 2 as one example that already exists). Each participant's educational experience could be enriched further through a sustainability

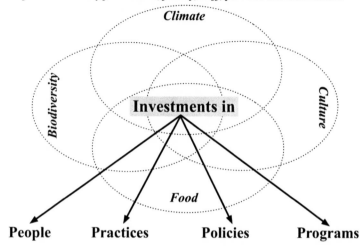

UNH Sustainability Academy

*Investing resources to scale up the reach and impact of integrated scholarship
for sustainability for students, faculty, staff, partners and stakeholders*

FIGURE 6.1. Conceptual diagram of the UNH Sustainability Academy. *Tom Kelly, December 2008*

internship program, conferences, and lecture series for the entire community, including alumni and other external stakeholders, study-abroad experiences, service learning opportunities, and more. The overarching mission
tying all of these offerings together would be a dedication to offering learning
that responds to the sustainability challenges we face and empowers students
with knowledge and opportunities to make a difference.

Sustainability Task Forces and Executive Council

UOS is also working with the UNH administration to explore innovative
administrative arrangements that draw knowledge together from across the
university to focus on the practices of the UNH community and the programming of the UNH Sustainability Academy. Currently, a structure that builds
upon the sustainable learning community framework and the success of the
UNH Energy Task Force is being considered (see discussion of this task force
in the Climate and Energy section of chapter 3). Under this approach, three
new campus-wide task forces that build on existing committees would join
the already existing Energy Task Force, and together would advance initiatives in biodiversity, climate, food, and culture (see figure 6.2). All four groups

Sustainability Task Forces

FIGURE 6.2. In the first year of operation, each of the four task forces will perform a preliminary assessment of its area across curriculum, operations, research, and engagement, and work with the other task forces and the Sustainability Executive Council to develop a strategic plan for the Sustainability Academy. The task forces will continue to meet in subsequent academic years to assess and refine plans and to carry out programmatic functions related to academic programs, communication and marketing, fundraising, and recruitment. *Tom Kelly, April 2008*

would be advisory to the president, and their leadership would form a Sustainability Executive Council discussed below. The groups would make recommendations related to issues across the CORE functions that relate to the purpose of that task force. The four groups would be:

Biodiversity Task Force. Would build on the existing Land Use Committee (see the Biodiversity and Ecosystems sectino of chapter 3) and be responsible for maintaining biodiversity and ecological integrity on UNH lands; developing tools for assessing, evaluating, and managing biodiversity, ecological integrity, and ecological and public health; and developing ecologically based approaches to landscape design and management; creating mechanisms that support teaching, research, and outreach around biodiversity, ecological integrity, and public health. Their goal would be to guide the university toward a systemic and integrated policy that emphasizes ecological and public health and integrity.

Energy Task Force. Already established and responsible for issues that relate to energy use, including generation, demand management, efficiency, conservation, greenhouse gas mitigation policy and action, and participation in markets related to energy and carbon. Recommendations will be formulated taking into account UNH's signing of the American College & University Presidents Climate Commitment (ACUPCC) and the energy needs of faculty, staff, students, and campus visitors. Their goal is to guide the university toward a systemic and integrated energy policy that emphasizes health and integrity, climate protection and carbon neutrality, efficiency, cost-effectiveness and stability, fairness for all university constituents, consistency with priorities set by the Strategic Academic Plan and the Master Plan, and focus on both the supply and demand characteristics of energy use.

Creative Campus Task Force. Would build on the Campus Aesthetics Committee (see the Culture and Sustainability section of chapter 3) and be responsible for issues that relate to democratic participation, social justice, vibrant communities, cultural heritage, and community arts. Their goal would be to guide the university toward a systemic and integrated creative campus policy and creative campus plan that emphasizes civic discourse, developing and conserving cultural and natural heritage, diversity, exposure to and participation in fine and performing arts, and increasing common, shared experiences for all university constituents.

Food Task Force. Would build on several existing programs (see the Food and Society sections in chapters 2 and 3) and be responsible for issues that relate to civic agriculture, sustainable food procurement, food entrepreneurship, health and wellness, food security, and social justice as related to the food system. Their goal would be to guide the university toward a systemic and integrated food policy that emphasizes health and integrity, efficiency, cost-effectiveness and stability, fairness for all university constituents, and consistency with priorities set by the Strategic Academic Plan and the Master Plan.

The executive leadership of these four task forces would then be brought together into a UNH Sustainability Executive Council (SEC) that would be charged with advancing sustainability at UNH in a systematic and comprehensive way both across the university's "CORE" of curriculum, operations, research, and engagement, and across the university's four sustainability initiatives in biodiversity, climate, food, and culture. The SEC would make recommendations to the UNH president and cabinet on sustainability-related strategic planning, communications, and education and would evaluate progress toward established goals.

A Continuing Commitment

Regardless of what new policies, practices, and programs UNH develops in the coming years, sustainability will remain a fundamental part of the university's mission and identity. Resting upon years of research and work by the global scientific and policy communities, sustainability at UNH will continue to evolve in response to new scientific findings and emerging global challenges and opportunities. Institutions of higher education — especially public institutions with land-grant missions — can have no greater mission than helping their graduates and surrounding communities advance sustainability at home, at work, and abroad.

As the Kellogg Commission states in its 2001 report "Returning to Our Roots: Executive Summaries of the Reports of the Kellogg Commission on the Future of State and Land-Grant Universities":

> Today, the promise of American public higher education must be made whole in a new era and a completely different world. The great international, economic, technological, and geo-political forces reshaping the world are hardly by-passing higher education ... The obstinate problems of today and tomorrow in our nation and world — poverty, family and community breakdown, restricted access to health care, hunger, over-population, global warming and other assaults on the natural environment — must be addressed by our universities if society is to have any chance at all of solving them ... What then, amidst these stresses and demands of our emerging new century, does the term "public university" mean? ... The irreducible idea is that we exist to advance the common good. As a new millennium dawns, the fundamental challenge with which we struggle is how to reshape our historic agreement with the American people so that it fits the times that are emerging instead of the times that have passed.

This is a call to action, and this collection of stories about our university's "Journey to the Future" is one attempt to answer that call.

Contributors

JOHN ABER is a Professor in the Department of Natural Resources and the Environment at UNH.

ELEANOR ABRAMS is an Associate Professor in the Department of Education at UNH.

KAREN ALEXANDER is a Research Scientist in the Institute for the Study of Earth, Oceans, and Space at UNH.

KIM BABBITT is the Associate Dean of Undergraduate Studies and a Professor in the Department of Natural Resources and the Environment at UNH.

TOM BALLESTERO is an Associate Professor in the Department of Civil Engineering at UNH.

DAVID S. BARTLETT is a Research Professor in the Institute for the Study of Earth, Oceans, and Space at UNH.

DOUGLAS BENCKS is the University Architect and Director of Campus Planning at UNH.

DENISE BLAHA is a Research Associate for the Complex Systems Research Center at UNH and is co-founder and co-director of the New Hampshire Carbon Challenge.

JEFF BOLSTER is an Associate Professor in the Department of History at UNH.

RIA BREJAART is an Affiliate Assistant Professor in the Department of Natural Resources and the Environment at UNH and Academic Director of the EcoQuest Education Foundation.

LYNDA BRUSHETT is a consultant to the New Hampshire Farm to School Program at UNH.

JOANNE BURKE is a Clinical Assistant Professor in the Department of Molecular, Cellular, and Biomedical Science and is Director of the graduate-level Dietetic Internship Program at UNH.

ROSEMARY CARON is an Associate Professor of Health Management and Policy at UNH and Program Director of the Master's of Public Health Program at UNH-Manchester.

JOHN E. CARROLL is a Professor in the Department of Natural Resources and the Environment at UNH.

PAUL CHAMBERLIN is an Assistant Vice President of Energy and Campus Development at UNH.

SARA CLEAVES is the Associate Director of the University Office of Sustainability at UNH.

BERT COHEN is an Adjunct Professor in the Department of Natural Resources and the Environment at UNH.

DREW CONROY is a Professor at the Thompson School of Applied Science at UNH.

VALERIE CUNNINGHAM is the former Coordinator of Community Black Heritage Partnerships at UNH and currently serves as Executive Director of the Portsmouth Black Heritage Trail, Inc.

JOANNE CURRAN-CELENTANO is a Professor in the Department of Molecular, Cellular, and Biomedical Science at UNH.

DONNA DOWAL is the Director of Admissions for the UNH–EcoQuest New Zealand Program at UNH.

MIL DUNCAN is the Director of the Carsey Institute at UNH.

JULIA DUNDORF is a co-founder and co-director of the New Hampshire Carbon Challenge.

ROBERT ECKERT is a Professor in the Department of Natural Resources and the Environment at UNH.

TAYLOR EIGHMY is the Interim Vice President for Research at UNH.

PETER ERICKSON is an Associate Professor in the Department of Biological Sciences at UNH.

ELISABETH FARRELL is the Culture and Sustainability, Food and Society Initiatives Program Coordinator at the University Office of Sustainability at UNH.

KEVIN GARDNER is an Associate Professor in the Environmental Research Group at UNH.

RAY GRIZZLE is a Research Professor in the Department of Biological Sciences at UNH.

REBECCA GRUBE is an Extension Associate Professor in the Department of Biological Sciences and a Specialist in Sustainable Horticulture Production for UNH Cooperative Extension.

JOHN L. HART is a Professor at the Thompson School of Applied Science at UNH.

MICHELE HOLT-SHANNON is the Administrative Director of the Discovery Program at UNH.

GEORGE HURTT is an Associate Professor in the Department of Natural Resources and the Environment, and at the Institute for the Study of Earth, Oceans, and Space at UNH.

JENNA JAMBECK is a Research Assistant Professor in the Environmental Research Group at UNH.

DAVID KAYE is an Associate Professor in the Department of Theatre and Dance at UNH.

TOM KELLY is the Chief Sustainability Officer and the Director of the University Office of Sustainability at UNH.

NANCY KINNER is a Professor of Civil and Environmental Engineering at UNH.

RICHARD LANGAN is the Co-Director of the Cooperative Institute for Coastal and Estuarine Environmental Technology and Director of the Atlantic Marine Aquaculture Center at UNH.

KEN LAVALLEY is an Extension Specialist in Commercial Fisheries Technology for Cooperative Extension at UNH.

BILL LEAVENWORTH is the primary Environmental Historian for the UNH Gulf of Maine Cod Project.

TOM LEE is an Associate Professor in the Department of Natural Resources and the Environment at UNH.

DOLORES LEONARD is the Communications Manager of the Cooperative Institute for Coastal and Estuarine Environmental Technology at UNH.

RICK MACDONALD is the Assistant Director of University Hospitality Services at UNH.

BRUCE L. MALLORY is the Provost and Executive Vice President at UNH.

JOHN MCLEAN is the Manager of Farms and Greenhouses at UNH.

JOHN NIMMO is an Associate Professor of Family Studies and the Executive Director of the Child Study and Development Center at UNH.

MATT O'KEEFE is a Campus Energy Manager in the Energy Office at UNH.

BRETT PASINELLA is the Biodiversity Education Initiative and Climate Education Initiative Program Coordinator for the University Office of Sustainability at UNH.

STEPHEN PESCI is Special Projects Director, UNH Campus Planning.

BARRY ROCK is a Professor in the Department of Natural Resources and the Environment at UNH.

ANDREW ROSENBERG is a Professor in the Department of Natural Resources and the Environment at UNH.

JEFFREY A. SCHLOSS is an Extension Professor in Water Quality for the Department of Biological Sciences at UNH.

CHRISTINE SHEA is an Associate Dean of Graduate Programs and Research at the Whittemore School of Business and Economics at UNH.

CHRIS SKOGLUND is the Program Manager for the New Hampshire Carbon Challenge.

STACY VANDEVEER is an Associate Professor of Political Science at UNH.

CAMERON WAKE is a Research Associate Professor at the Institute for the Study of Earth, Oceans, and Space and in the Department of Earth Sciences at UNH.

MARK WILEY is an Extension Associate Professor at UNH and an Extension Specialist in Marine Science Education for UNH Cooperative Extension.

JULIE E. WILLIAMS is the Associate Vice President for Research and Outreach Scholarship at UNH.

VICKI C. WRIGHT is the former director of the Museum of Art at UNH.

Index

Academic Master Plan, 75
Academic Strategic Plan (2002), 234
ACUPCC (American College & University Presidents Climate Commitment), 128–29, 130, 216
ADA (American Dietetic Association), 83
Adaptive capacity and climate change, 19–20
Advisory Committee on Land and Property Use (ACLPU), 110–11
Aesthetics, xv, 105–8, 114–16, 141–45
African Americans in New England, 196, 237–38
Agricultural Experiment Station, 183
Agriculture: biodiversity and ecosystems, 29–31; climate change role of, 30–31; curriculum and pedagogy, 58, 176–78, 184; dairy programs, 87–89, 176–78; environmental impact of, 27–31; federal subsidies, 28–29; food production, 79, 82, 84, 138, 183–84, 219–22; importance of local action, 32; international assessment, 27, 30–31; land-use issues around campus, 106, 108–12; orientation during The Real Dirt course, 86–87; renaissance in NH, 178; Soul of Agriculture conferences, 79, 80; UNH's unique position vis-à-vis, 175. See also College of Life Sciences and Agriculture (COLSA); Food and society
Agriculture of the middle, loss of, 29
Agroecological approaches, 30
AIRMAP project, 168
Alternative-fuel vehicles, 117, 125–26
American College & University Presidents Climate Commitment (ACUPCC), 128–29, 130, 216
American Dietetic Association (ADA), 83

Amtrak Downeaster service, 126
Animal and Nutritional Sciences Department, 85, 87–89, 183
Anna and Raymond Tuttle Environmental Horticulture Endowment, 193
Annan, Kofi, 2–3
Aquaculture, 179–81
Architecture, 102–3, 142, 145–49, 151–52
Artistic perspective: building design, 102–3, 142, 145–49, 151–52; Kingsbury mural preservation project, 142, 149–51; The Promise of the Sun, 90–93; Scheier project, 238–40; theatrical response to sustainability, 94–97; wildcat mascot sculpture, 144–45
Arts and Society Program, 90–93, 239
Association for Theatre in Higher Education (ATHE), 97
Atlantic Marine Aquaculture Center, 179–81

B20 fuel, 126
Ban Ki-moon, 34
Barber, Benjamin, 231
Behavioral-change campaigns, 213–14
BEI (Biodiversity Education Initiative), 243
"Being more" vs. "having more" goal for sustainability, 35, 36–38, 45
Burley-Demeritt Farm, 178
Bicycle-safe streets, 125, 126
Biodiversity and ecosystems: agricultural system's impact on, 29–31; and climate change, 13, 18, 158; curriculum and pedagogy, 56, 58–67; degradation of ecosystems, 13–17, 30–31, 47n28, 60; engagement, 198–207; losses from food production, 14; operations, 104–16; overview, 2–7, 12–18;

Biodiversity and ecosystems *(continued)*
    and public health, 61–64; research and
    scholarship, 157–65, 225; undeveloped
    university lands, 111
Biodiversity Education Initiative (BEI), 243
Biodiversity Task Force, 248
Biofuels, 126
Biological Timber Inventory (BioTimber
    Inventory/BTI), 111
Biology, biodiversity and ecosystems applica-
    tion, 59–61
Biometric technology to identify meal plan
    holders, 139–40
Black Heritage Partnerships, 238
Blaha, Denise, 212, 213
Bloom's Taxonomy of Learning, 59
Blue mussel culturing, 180
Bolster, Jeffrey, 237
Botanic garden on campus, 113
Boyer, Ernest, 232
Browne, Ken, 238, 239
Browne, Phil, 202
Bruntland Commission, 8, 11
BTI (Biological Timber Inventory), 111
Building design, 102–3, 142, 145–49, 151–52
Burak, Tom, 218
Burden of disease, defined, 49n59
Bycatch problem for northern shrimp fishery,
    224

CA-CP (Clean Air-Cool Planet), 128, 211
Call to Action (Satcher), 25
Campbell, Robert, 102–3
Campus Master Plan, 104, 124–25
Campus operations. *See* Operations
Cap-and-trade system for greenhouse gas
    emissions, 208
Carbon Challenge (NHCC), 168, 196, 212–15
Carbon Coalition, 208
Carbon footprint, campus, 120–21, 122
Carbon Solutions New England (CSNE), 169,
    196, 209–12, 217–18
Carmona, Richard, 25
Carsey, Marcy, 189
Carsey Institute, 188–92
CAS (Culture & Sustainability Initiative), 243
CEI (Climate Education Initiative), 7, 129, 243
Center for a Food Secure Future (NHCFSF),
    80, 196, 227–29

Central Appalachian Network, 191
CERA (Community and Environment in Rural
    America), 191
Chemical Engineering Department, 68
Children's Garden, 192–93
Child Study and Development Center
    (CSDC), 192
CHP (combined heat and power) plant, 117,
    118–22
CICEET (Cooperative Institute for Coastal
    and Estuarine Environmental Technology),
    158–60
Citizen of the world perspective: and climate
    change, 20, 24; and cultural self-under-
    standing, 12, 36; on food system, 32; higher
    education's role in, 43–44; integration with
    Earth system perspective, 18; introduction,
    2; and liberal education, 41–42
Citizen scientists, engagement with, 199–202
Citizenship, creative, 40
Citizen Volunteers in Environmental Monitor-
    ing, 200
Civic engagement at university, 231–33
Civil engineering, 65–66, 169–70
Classics Department, 91, 92–93
Clean Air-Cool Planet (CA-CP), 128, 211
Clean Air-Cool Planet Campus Carbon
    Calculator, 128
Climate and energy: agriculture's role in, 30–31;
    alternative-fuel vehicles, 117, 125–26; and
    biodiversity, 13, 18, 158; Carbon Challenge
    project, 168, 196, 212–15; co-generation
    power plant, 23, 117, 118–22; curriculum
    and pedagogy, 56, 68–78, 218; engagement,
    208–18; and food system, 29; increased
    concerns about, 208; operations, 23, 117–31;
    overview, 2–7, 18–25; research and scholar-
    ship, 166–74; solar energy, 90–93. *See also*
    Greenhouse gas emission reduction
Climate Change Action Plan, 174, 217–18
Climate Change Policy Task Force, 217–18
Climate Education Initiative (CEI), 7, 129, 243
Clurman, Harold, 94
CNG (compressed natural gas), 125–26
Coalition for Sustaining Agriculture, 220
Coastal Ocean Observing Center, 168
Coastal resource management and habitat
    protection, 158–60
Coastal Response Research Center, 170

Cod-fishing history, 162–63, 179

Co-generation power plant, 23, 117, 118–22

Cohen, Jeremy, 233–34

Collaborative research process, 160

College of Engineering and Physical Sciences, 169

College of Health and Human Services, 62, 192

College of Life Sciences and Agriculture (COLSA): Animal and Nutritional Sciences Department, 85, 87–89, 183; Compost Program, 132, 133–36; food production initiative, 184; Growing a Green Generation Project, 192; Office of Woodlands and Natural Areas, 110–12

College Woods Natural Area, 109

Combined heat and power (CHP) plant, 117, 118–22

Committee for Campus Aesthetics, 141–45

Committee on Real Property Acquisition and Disposal (CRPAD), 111

Committee on Woodlands and Natural Areas (CWNA), 109–10

Community, non-university: and Compost Program, 134, 135; family farm support, 29; introduction, 6; landscape's support of outreach, 106; nutritional health support, 84–85; Sustainable Living courses, 99–100; transportation challenges, 124–25. *See also* Engagement; Extension programs; Outreach scholarship

Community and Environment in Rural America (CERA), 191

Community Based Social Marketing, 214

Community Food, Nutrition, and Wellness Profile (UNH-CFNWP), 182–83

Community Food and Nutrition Profile, 85

Complex Systems Research Center, 212

Compost Program, 132, 133–36

Compressed natural gas (CNG), 125–26

Conferences & Catering, University, 132, 137

Conservation Agriculture, 30

Cooperative Extension, 58, 196, 200, 230, 234. *See also* Extension programs

Cooperative Extension Educators, 84, 85, 221

Cooperative fisheries research, 223–26

Cooperative Institute for Coastal and Estuarine Environmental Technology (CICEET), 158–60

Cooperative Real Education in Agriculture Management (CREAM) course, 87–89

Cooperative Research Partners Program (CRPP), 223

CORE (Curriculum, Operations, Research and Engagement) approach: diagrammatic depiction, 3; ecosystems degradation mitigation, 17; for food systems education, 31; overview, xv–xvi, 2–4, 5, 6; and task force planning, 249

Corn, overproduction of, 28

Cosmopolitan perspective: and cultural understanding, 12, 36, 41; importance for sustainability, 10; rooted cosmopolitanism, 18, 32, 43, 44. *See also* Citizen of the world perspective

Courtyards, campus, landscape planning for, 107

CREAM (Cooperative Real Education in Agriculture Management) course, 87–89

Creative campus movement, 36

Creative Campus Task Force, 249

Creative citizenship, 40

Cross Roads House, 227

CRPAD (Committee on Real Property Acquisition and Disposal), 111

CRPP (Cooperative Research Partners Program), 223

CSDC (Child Study and Development Center), 192

CSNE (Carbon Solutions New England), 169, 196, 209–12, 217–18

Cuellar, Javier Perez de, 9–10

Cultivating Humanity (Nussbaum), 40–42

Cultural self-understanding, 12, 36, 39, 41

Culture and sustainability: architectural expression of, 146–47; consumer culture, 32–33, 39–40; curriculum and pedagogy, 55, 56–57, 90–100; engagement, 230–40; fishing industry, 162–63; historical perspective, 9–12; human rights and cultural rights, 10–11; interdependence of, 36; operations, 141–52; overview, xv, 2–7, 32–39; and quality of life, 11, 33–34; research and scholarship, 159, 185–94; Western/Greek influence, 24, 40–44, 91, 92–93. *See also* Cosmopolitan perspective; Interdisciplinarity

Culture of health recklessness, globalization of, 26

Culture & Sustainability Initiative (CAS), 243

Cunningham, Valerie, 237, 238

Curriculum, Operations, Research and Engagement (CORE) approach. *See* CORE

Curriculum and pedagogy: and agriculture, 58, 176–78, 184; biodiversity and ecosystems, 56, 58–67; climate and energy, 56, 68–78, 218; culture and sustainability, 55, 56–57, 90–100; Discovery Program, 77–78, 97–98; food and society, 57, 79–89, 139; game-based learning activity, 69, 70–71; and Organic Garden Club, 226; overview, xv, 54–57; research contribution to, 185–88, 192–94, 202–4, 205–6; Scheier project's contribution to, 238; student-initiated learning method, 60–61, 68; Sustainability Academy, 246–47

Currier Gallery of Art, 239

CWNA (Committee on Woodlands and Natural Areas), 109–10

Cyclist-safe streets, 125, 126

Dairy farming, 87–89, 176–78

Dairy Teaching and Research Facility, 87–89

DeCarbonizer, 211–12

Democracy Imperative, 233

Democratic role of higher education, dialogue on, 230–33

Department of Environmental Services (DES), 217, 218

Developed vs. developing world on sustainability: climate change challenges, 22; contrasting economic perspectives, 34–35; ecosystem degradation, 13–17; power issues, 9; public health issue, 26–27, 33–34; and unfair agricultural policies, 29

Development: contested nature of concept, 7–12, 34–35; impact on estuarine ecosystems, 157; low-impact development projects, 164; Millennium Development Goals, 11, 34–35, 64; quality of life as alternative goal, 8, 11

Dietetic Internship program, 83–86

Dining halls: Compost Program, 133–35; locally grown food for, 137, 138, 139, 184; organization of, 132; plate waste challenge, 139–40

Direct-market farms, 221–22

Discovery Program, 77–78, 97–98

Disease, 15, 16, 26

Disease Ecology course, 61–64

Disparity, global socioeconomic, 26, 33–34. *See also* Developed vs. developing world on sustainability

Doha round of WTO, 35

Dual major program, 80

Dundorf, Julia, 212, 213

Earth, cosmic perspective on, 44

Earth Charter (1994), 11, 35

Earth Day, 74

Earth Summit (1992), 8, 11

Earth system perspective: and climate change, 20, 21, 23, 24; in curriculum, 69, 76, 155; and ecosystem degradation, 15; on food system, 31–32; and liberal education's benefits, 41; overview, 2; UNH's implementation of, 17, 18

Eberly, Rosa, 233–34

Eckert, Bob, 99

"Eco-cabaret," 94–95

EcoGastronomy, 79–82

EcoLine, 118–22

Ecological Advocates, 74

EcoQuest Education Foundation, 66–67

Ecosystem degradation, 13–17, 30–31, 47n28, 60. *See also* Biodiversity and ecosystems

Ecosystem services, 13, 14–16, 47n28

EEZ (Exclusive Economic Zone), 181

Eggers, Walter, 142

Electric power plant, 23, 117, 118–22

Employee Carbon Challenge initiative, 215

Energy Captains, 72–74

Energy conservation: alternative-fuel vehicles, 117, 125–26; co-generation power plant, 23, 117, 118–22; curriculum and pedagogy, 68–78; landfill energy source, 117, 121–22; operations approach, 23, 117–31; policy formation and reform, 217–18; solar energy, 90–93. *See also* Climate and energy

Energy Star program for appliances, 119, 216

Energy Task Force (ETF), 71, 117, 129–31, 247–49

Energy Waste Watch Challenge, 72–75

Engaged intellectual perspective: and climate change, 20, 25; and culture, 12, 36; and liberal education, 42; overview, 2; UNH's implementation of, 17–18

Engagement: biodiversity and ecosystems, 198–207; climate and energy, 208–18; criteria for successful, 195–96; culture and sustainability, 230–40; definitional issues, 234; food and society, 80, 82, 84–85, 219–29; introduction, 195–97. *See also* Community, non-university; Outreach scholarship

Engineering: chemical, 68; civil, 65–66, 169–70; curriculum for, 64–66, 169; environmental, 65, 76, 169–70; ethics of, 65; for quality of life, 64–66

Environmental Conservation curriculum, 54, 76

Environmental engineering, 65, 76, 169–70

Environmental health, 61–64

Environmental Horticulture Program, 183

Environmental research, UNH's strengths in, 154–55

Environmental Research Group (ERG), 159, 169–71

Environmental Sciences program, 76

Environmental Technology Building, 104

EOS (Institute for the Study of Earth, Oceans, and Space), 69, 154–55, 166–69, 203–4, 213

ERG (Environmental Research Group), 159, 169–71

Ernest, John, 237

Estes, George, 133

Estuarine environmental restoration, 158–60, 165

ETF (Energy Task Force), 71, 117, 129–31, 247–49

Ethics: engineering, 65; global, 10, 11, 12, 21, 35, 39

Examined life, value of, 40, 41

Exclusive Economic Zone (EEZ), 181

Extension programs: community engagement dialogue role, 234; Cooperative Extension Educators, 84, 85, 221; EcoGastronomy program, 79–82; food security, 80; forestry, 58; nutritional health support, 84–85; and outreach scholarship, 155, 196; as part of engagement strategy, 230; water resources program, 200. *See also* Engagement

Extinction rate, species, 13–14

Faculty: and Outreach Scholars Academy, 235–37; and research environment, 153

Fairchild, Tom, 87

Farm Bill, U.S., 28–29

Farmers' market, 84

Farm fields, landscape's support of, 106

Farming. *See* Agriculture

Farm-raised seafood, 179–81

Farm to School Program (NH FTS), 196, 219–22

FAS (Food & Society Initiative), 136, 182, 226, 244

Fishbanks (Meadows) (role-playing game), 69

Fishing industry, 14, 161–63, 179–81, 223–26

Fixed-line entanglement of whales, 224–25

Fleet, university vehicle, 125–26, 127

Food and society: and biodiversity losses, 14; Composting Program, 133–36; curriculum and pedagogy, 57, 79–89, 139; engagement, 80, 82, 84–85, 219–29; food security, 80, 196, 227–29; food sovereignty, 30, 32; operations, 132–40; overview, xv, 2–7, 25–32; research and scholarship, 138, 175–84. *See also* Agriculture

Food & Society Initiative (FAS), 136, 182, 226, 244

Food Task Force, 249

Forested lands, management of, 58, 104, 109–12

Forest Watch, 168, 196, 202–4

Fortress world scenario for culture and sustainability, 37

Four Hands, One Heart (Browne) (film), 239–40

Free-trade agenda, 9, 34

Freshwater supply, 14, 16

Funding: Atlantic Marine Aquaculture Center, 180; CICEET, 158–59, 163; CSNE, 212; EOS programs, 168; ERG programs, 170; Forest Watch, 202, 204; Growing a Green Generation Project, 192; historical support for sustainability, 242; Marine Docent Program, 205; NASA and NOAA as major sources, 154; NHCFSF challenges, 227–28; NH LLMP, 199–200

Future generations, acting for benefit of, 21

Game-based learning activity, 69, 70–71

Gardens, campus, landscape planning, 107

Gastronomy, 79–82

General Agreement on Tariffs and Trade (GATT), 9

Georges Bank fishing grounds, 223
Get Smart Eat Local 10-District Project, 221–22
Global Biological Change course, 59–61
Global change field, origins of, 167
Global Change Research Program, 173
Global consumer culture, 32–33, 39–40
Global Environmental Change course, 69–71
Global ethics and sustainability: climate change
    mitigation, 21; cultural considerations, 12,
    35, 39; United Nations on, 10
Global perspective: climate change mitigation,
    20, 21, 23–24, 78; engagement projects, 198;
    habitat conservation, 94; history of marine
    animals, 161; organic dairy farming, 176–77;
    public health, 25–26, 62; research and
    scholarship, 188; Students Without Borders,
    188, 206–7, 227; and sustainability origins,
    7–10; UNH-EcoQuest program, 66–67.
    See also Citizen of the world perspective
Global Scenarios Group, 37–38
Global trade, increase in, 51n79
Global warming. See Climate and energy
GLOBE program, 155, 168
Gordon, Anita, 95
GRANIT database, 111
Grazing and forage production, 176
Great Bay Estuary Restoration Compendium,
    165
Great transition scenario for culture and
    sustainability, 37
Greenhouse gas emission reduction: cap-and-
    trade system, 208; co-generation power
    plant, 120–21, 122; CSNE, 169, 196, 209–12,
    217–18; in curriculum, 71; dairy farming,
    176; Energy Task Force role in, 130; GHG
    inventory, 128–29; global perspective, 21;
    operational considerations, 117; overview
    of issues, 19; research support, 166; "wedge"
    concept, 68, 211, 212; WildCAP discount
    program, 215–17
Greenhouse Gas Emissions Inventory, 71
Growing a Green Generation Project, 192–94
Gulf of Maine research, 168, 223–26

Hart, Ann Weaver, 129, 144
Hatch, John W., 149
Health issues: Growing a Green Generation
    Project, 192; nutritional health, 25–32, 80,
83–86, 182–83; poor's disproportionate
    share of, 15, 16; YAHRSI, 85, 183. See also
    Public health
Heating, ventilation and air conditioning
    system, 117, 118–22
Heckel, Maynard C., 227
Higher education: and citizen of the world per-
    spective, 43–44; climate change response,
    19, 21, 22–24; community engagement
    dialogue, 233–37; contribution to democ-
    racy, 230–33; culture and sustainability, 36;
    introduction to sustainability role, xiii–xvi,
    1–7; sustainability definitional issues,
    xiii–xiv; sustainable learning community's
    implications for, 39–45. See also Land-grant
    institutions
Hirshberg, Gary and Nancy, 178
History of Marine Animal Populations
    (HMAP), 161–63
HIV/AIDS epidemic, 33–34
Holloway Commons, 134
Horticulture programs and resources, 137, 183,
    184, 193
Hospitality Services, University (UHS). See
    University Hospitality Services (UHS)
Housing, on-campus, 125
Hubbard, Oliver, 242–43
Huddleston, Eric, 141
Huddleston, Mark, 245
Human rights, 10–11, 24
Hurtt, George, 211
Hydrology Program, 154

IAASTD (International Assessment of Agricul-
    tural Knowledge, Science and Technology
    for Development), 27, 30–31
IMF (International Monetary Fund), 9
Income and quality of life, 38
In Defense of Food: An Eater's Manifesto (Pol-
    lan), 79–80
Indoor smoke, 26, 49n60
Inequality, global socioeconomic, 26, 33–34.
    See also Developed vs. developing world on
    sustainability
Institute for Scientific Information (ISI), 154,
    166
Institute for the Study of Earth, Oceans, and
    Space (EOS), 69, 154–55, 166–69, 203–4, 213

Institute of Natural and Environmental Resources (INER), 54–55
Institutional engagement, 195. *See also* Engagement
Integrated Pest Management, 30
Integrity, 3, 5–6, 10, 45n6, 55
Intensive rotational grazing, 176
Intercity rail service, 126
Interdisciplinarity: in curriculum, 75–78; engineering's participation in, 65; EOS, 166–69; ERG, 170–71; as essential to sustainable learning community, 54–57, 155–56, 242; in food production projects, 80–82; Growing a Green Generation Project, 192–93; History of Marine Animal Populations, 161–63; International Environmental Design Contest, 171–73; photovoltaic array for MUB, 91; Sustainability Academy, 246–47; and URC's success, 186–88
Intergovernmental Panel on Climate Change (IPCC), 13, 19, 173–74, 208
Intergroup dialogue method, 233
International Assessment of Agricultural Knowledge, Science and Technology for Development (IAASTD), 27, 30–31
International Covenant on Civil and Political Rights, 10
International Covenant on Economic, Social and Cultural Rights, 10
International Environmental Design Contest, 171–73
International Monetary Fund (IMF), 9
International perspective. *See* Global perspective
Introduction to Sustainable Engineering course, 64–66
IPCC (Intergovernmental Panel on Climate Change), 13, 19, 173–74, 208
ISI (Institute for Scientific Information), 154, 166
It's a Matter of Survival (Gordon and Suzuki), 95

Kates, Robert W., 7–8
Kaye, David, 98
Kellog Commission on the Future of State and Land-Grant Universities, 195, 250
Kellog Foundation Report on Engaged Institutions, 209

Kelly, Tom, 90, 113, 178, 243, 244
Keynes, John Maynard, 38–39
Killer at Large (film), 25
Kingman Farm, 133, 135, 183
Kingsbury mural preservation project, 149–51

Lake Chocura, 200
Lakes Lay Monitoring Program (NH LLMP), 155, 199–202
Landfill energy source, 117, 121–22
Land-grant institutions, mission and culture: food and society, 79; frugality of, 141; land management mission, 58; public health outreach, 63–64; recreating community links, 230; traditional engagement roles, 195. *See also* Extension programs; University of New Hampshire
Landscape, campus, 104–16, 142–45
Landscape Design Guidelines, 107–8
Landscape Master Plan, 104, 105–8
Land-use principles on university property, 58, 104–16, 123–28, 142–45
Lawns, campus, 107, 113–16
Learning community, influence of, 4–5. *See also* Higher education
Leiserowitz, Anthony A., 7–8
Leitzel, Joan, 142, 144
Liberal education, sustainability in, 2, 40–43
LID (low-impact development) projects, 164
Limits to Growth (Meadows), 69
Living Coasts Program, 160
Local action: agricultural systems, 32; building materials, 148; climate change mitigation, 21; food procurement, 84, 132–40, 184, 221–22; and history of sustainable development, 9; nutritional health support for community, 84–85. *See also* Operations
Local Harvest Dinner, 84, 132, 137
Local Harvest Initiative, 84, 132, 136–39
Long-Term Ecological Research (LTER) program, 157
Low-carbon economy, 21
Low-impact development (LID) projects, 164
Lyme disease, 62, 64

MA (Millennium Ecosystem Assessment), 13–17, 47n28, 60
Mallory, Bruce, 238

Marine Docent Program, 204–6
Marine Program, 154
Marine studies, 14, 158–60, 161–63, 179–81,
    223–26
Master of Public Health (MPH) curriculum,
    61–64
Mautz, Bill, 99, 242
McLean, John, 226
MDGs (Millennium Development Goals), 11,
    34–35, 64
Meadows, Dennis, 69
Meadows, Donella, 99
Meadows in landscape, 106, 114–16
Meal plan innovation, student, 139–40
Memorial Union Building (MUB), 90–93,
    112–16
Mentoring relationship, faculty-student, 186,
    187
Methane from landfill as energy source, 117,
    121–22
Microbial fuel cell (MFC) technology, 172–73
Microcellutions, Inc., 172–73
Millennium Development Goals (MDGs), 11,
    34–35, 64
Millennium Ecosystem Assessment (MA),
    13–17, 47n28, 60
Millennium Study, 154
Modern movement in architecture, 147
Monadnock Carbon Challenge, 214
MPH (Master of Public Health) curriculum,
    61–64
MUB (Memorial Union Building), 90–93,
    112–16
MUB Meadow project, 112–16
MyPyramid menu, USDA, 85

Narrative imagination, 42
NASA (National Aeronautics and Space
    Administration), 69, 157, 167, 202
NASA Earth System Science Education
    program, 69
National Assessment of the Potential
    Consequences of Climate Variability and
    Change, 173
National Ecological Observing Network
    (NEON), 157
National Estuarine Research Reserve System
    (NERRS), 159

National Issues Forum approach, 233
National Marine Fisheries Service (NMFS),
    162, 224
National Oceanic and Atmospheric Adminis-
    tration (NOAA), 157, 158–60, 163–64, 180
National Offshore Aquaculture Act, 181
National Sustainable Design Exposition, 207
Native landscapes on campus, 104, 109–12,
    114–16
Natural areas, campus, 109–12
Natural Areas Committee, 109–10
Natural-resource assessment of undeveloped
    lands, 111
Natural Resources and Earth System Science
    program, 76, 155
Natural Resources and Environment Depart-
    ment, 59–61
NEC (Northeast Consortium), 168, 223–24
NECIA (Northeast Climate Impact Assess-
    ment), 174, 208, 217
NECRPP (Northeast Cooperative Research
    Partners Program), 224–26
Neil and Louise Tillotson Fund, 191
NEON (National Ecological Observing
    Network), 157
NERA (New England Regional Assessment),
    173–74
NERRS (National Estuarine Research Reserve
    System), 159
New Clean Water Act Phase II, 163
New England Center, 132
New England character of campus, landscape's
    support of, 106
New England Ecological Garden, 113
New England Regional Assessment (NERA),
    173–74
New Hampshire Agricultural Experiment
    Station, 183
New Hampshire Carbon Challenge (NHCC),
    168, 196, 212–15
New Hampshire Center for a Food Secure
    Future (NHCFSF), 80, 196, 227–29
New Hampshire Climate Change Resolution
    (2007), 213
New Hampshire Coalition for Sustaining
    Agriculture, 220
New Hampshire Farm to School Program (NH
    FTS), 196, 219–22

New Hampshire Lakes Lay Monitoring
Program (NH LLMP), 155, 199–202
New Zealand — UNH EcoQuest program,
66–67
NHCC (New Hampshire Carbon Challenge),
168, 196, 212–15
NHCFSF (New Hampshire Center for a Food
Secure Future), 80, 196, 227–29
NH FTS (New Hampshire Farm to School
Program), 196, 219–22
NH LLMP (New Hampshire Lakes Lay
Monitoring Program), 199–202
NMFS (National Marine Fisheries Service),
162, 224
NOAA (National Oceanic and Atmospheric
Administration), 157, 158–60, 163–64, 180
No Child Left Behind, 206
Northeast Bioneers Conference (2002), 96
Northeast Climate Impact Assessment
(NECIA), 174, 208, 217
Northeast Consortium (NEC), 168, 223–24
Northeast Cooperative Research Partners
Program (NECRPP), 224–26
Nussbaum, Martha, 40–42
Nutritional health, 25–32, 80, 83–86, 182–83

Obesity, 25
ODA (Overseas Development Aid), 34
Office of Sustainability. See University Office of
Sustainability (UOS)
Office of Woodlands and Natural Areas,
110–12
Offshore aquaculture research, 179–81
OGC (Organic Garden Club), 84, 132, 138,
226–27
On Architecture (Vitruvius), 147
Open-ocean aquaculture, 180–81
Open-space planning, 105–8
Operations: biodiversity and ecosystems,
104–16; climate and energy, 23, 117–31;
culture and sustainability, 141–52; food
and safety, 132–40; introduction, 101–3;
overview, xv; transportation system, 107,
117, 123–28, 163–64. See also Physical plant
Organic agriculture, 30
Organic Dairy Research Farm, 176–78
Organic Garden Club (OGC), 84, 132, 138,
226–27

Our Common Future (WCED), 5, 8
Our Creative Diversity, 9–10
Outreach Scholars Academy, 235–37
Outreach scholarship: adjustment to environmental change, 188–92; dairy production
techniques, 177–78; EOS, 168–69; ERG,
171; fisheries research, 161–63, 179–81,
223–26; introduction of, 230; microbial fuel
cell technology, 172–73; organic farming,
176–78; overview, xv, 155; oyster restoration,
164–65; stormwater testing, 163–64; and
successful engagement, 196
Overseas Development Aid (ODA), 34
Oyster restoration research, 164–65
Oyster River Carbon Challenge, 214
Ozone, ground level, 203–4

Pacala, Stephen, 211
Pale Blue Dot (Sagan), 44
Palmer, Matthew Gray, 144
Parking on campus, 107, 123–24, 127, 163–64
Partnership for Pelagic Ecosystem Monitoring,
225
Parris, Thomas M., 7–8
Pasture-based dairy production, 176
Pedagogy, overview, xv. See also Curriculum
and pedagogy
Pedestrian-friendly transportation system, 106,
125, 126
Peer-to-peer education method, 72, 74, 89
Petrini, Carlo, 81
Pettee, Charles, 141
Phaeton, myth of, 92–93
Photovoltaic array, 91
Physical plant: building design, 102–3, 142,
145–49, 151–52; co-generation power plant,
23, 117, 118–22; Energy Waste Watch Chal-
lenge, 74–75; Environmental Technology
Building, 104; housing on campus, 125;
importance of sustainability for, 102;
transportation fleet, 123, 125–26
Place-based orientation: art on campus,
142–45, 239; building design, 102–3, 142,
145–49, 151–52; campus context, 103; curriculum and pedagogy, 97–98; and rooted
cosmopolitanism, 18
Plant Biology Department, 183
PLG (processed landfill gas), 121–22

Policy formation and reform: climate change, 78, 173–74, 217–18; culture and sustainability scenario, 37, 38; public and environmental health courses, 62; transportation, 124; unfair agricultural policies, 29

Pollan, Michael, 79–80

Porous asphalt parking lot, 163–64

Portsmouth Black History Trail, 196, 237–38

Poverty and sustainability, 13–16, 20, 84–85

Privatization agenda, 34

Processed landfill gas (PLG), 121–22

Progress for Children (2007), 33

The Promise of the Sun, 90–93

Psychodramatic techniques, 96

Public art on campus, 90–93, 142, 143–45, 149–51, 238–40

Public health: biodiversity and ecosystems, 61–64; children's status globally, 33–34; developed vs. developing world, 26–27, 33–34; nutritional aspect, 25–32, 80, 83–86, 182–83

Public health practitioner perspective: and climate change, 20, 24–25; and ecosystem degradation, 15; on food system, 32; and liberal education's benefits, 41; overview, 2

Public schools, programs for, 196, 202–4, 215, 219–22, 237

Quadrangles, campus, landscape planning for, 107

Quality of life: as alternative goal to development, 8, 11; and balancing carbon reduction, 210; "being more" vs. "having more," 35, 36–38, 45; vs. consumerism, 38–39; as culturally determined, 11; engineering for, 64–66; and socioeconomic inequality, 33–34; sustainability's contribution to, 44–45

Rail station renovation, 125

The Real Dirt course, 86–87

"The Real Dirt on Farmer John" (film), 86

Recklessness, culture of, 36

Recycled Materials Resource Center, 65, 170

Reefs, oyster, degradation of, 164–65

Regional environment, landscape's support of, 106

Regional Greenhouse Gas Initiative (RGGI), 208, 217

Renewable energy technologies, 172–73

Renewable Portfolio Standard (RPS), 217

Research and scholarship: biodiversity and ecosystems, 157–65, 225; climate and energy, 166–74; collaborative research process, 160; Complex Systems Research Center, 212; cooperative fisheries research, 223–26; culture and sustainability, 159, 185–94; curriculum and pedagogy, 185–88, 192–94, 202–4, 205–6; food and society, 138, 175–84; introduction, 153–56; Marine Docent Program, 204–6; overview, xv; undergraduate participation in, 69, 78, 185–88; UNH's contributions, 153–57, 166; volunteer data collection, 198, 199–202, 204–6. *See also* Outreach scholarship; Water quality

Research-based learning, 185–88, 192–94, 202–4, 205–6

Residential focus of NHCC project, 213–14

Respect in engagement, 196

Responsiveness in engagement, 196

RGGI (Regional Greenhouse Gas Initiative), 208, 217

Rodriguez, Guillermo, 94

Role-playing games, 69

Rooted cosmopolitanism, 18, 32, 43

RPS (Renewable Portfolio Standard), 217

Rural community sustainability, 29, 189–92

Sagan, Carl, 44

Sammons, Mark J., 237

Sanitation facilities, loss of, 14, 16

Satcher, David, 25

Saunders, Wes, 94–95

Scheier, Ed and Mary, 238

Scheier project, 238–40

Schools, programs for public, 196, 202–4, 215, 219–22, 237

Schwab, Chuck, 178

Science, Society and Politics: Exploring Climate Change from Global to Local, 77–78

Science and sustainability, 59–61, 76–78, 169–71. *See also* College of Life Sciences and Agriculture (COLSA); Engineering; Research and scholarship

Science and Technology Studies, 77
Sea Grant Program, 205
Seasonality challenge for local food procurement, 138
SeaTrek Program, 205
SEC (Sustainability Executive Council), 249
Second major for integration of sustainability curricula, 75
Sediment remediation technologies, 159
Self-criticism, capacity for, 41
Shrimp fishery challenges, 224
Single-chamber, open-air microbial fuel cell (MOR-2007), 172–73
Slow Food International, 81
Social justice: environmental perspective, 95; and inequality, 26, 33–34; poverty and sustainability, 13–16, 20, 84–85; and rooted cosmopolitanism, 18; unfair agricultural policies, 29. See also Developed vs. developing world on sustainability
Social Justice Theatre Troupe, 95–97
Societal challenges of 21st century, 2–4. See also Culture and sustainability
Society for the Protection of New Hampshire Forests, 111
Socolow, Robert, 211
Solar energy, 90–93
Somat food-waste pulper, 133–34
Soul of Agriculture conferences, 79, 80
Space Grant Consortium, NASA, 202, 204
Space science research, 167
"Stabilization Wedges" (Pacala and Socolow), 211
Stern Review, 20–21, 23–24
Stewardship of campus, 102, 111–12. See also Operations
Stoneyfield Farms, 178
Stormwater Research Center, 65, 159, 163–64, 170
Streetscapes, landscape planning for, 107
Strickler, Susan, 239
Student-initiated learning, 60–61, 68
Students Without Borders (SWB), 188, 206–7, 227
Subsidies, agricultural, 28–29
Sustainability: definitional issues, xiii–xiv, 7–12, 35–36; future prospects and challenges, 245–50; historical perspective, 7–12, 242–45; learning community's implications for, 39–45; overview, xiii–xvi, 1–7; task force formation, 247–49; UNH program development, 54–57
Sustainability Academy, 246–47
Sustainability Executive Council (SEC), 249
Sustainable development concept, 7–12, 34–35
Sustainable Living course, 99–100
Sustainable Science and Engineering fellowships, 65–66, 171
Sustained dialogue model, 231–33
Suzuki, David, 95
SWB (Students Without Borders), 188, 206–7, 227
Systems Thinking for Sustainable Living course, 99–100

Teaching. See Curriculum and pedagogy
Teaching Excellence Program, 69
Terra Madre, 81
Theatre and Dance Department, 94–97, 98
Thompson, Benjamin, 104–5, 141
Timber harvesting on campus lands, 109, 110
Time affluence, 38
Trade, increase in global, 51n79
Traditional architecture, benefits of, 146–47
Traffic challenges, 124–25
Train-the-trainer method, 203, 215
Transit system, UNH, 124, 125, 126–27
Transportation Demand Management, 117, 123–28
Transportation Policy Committee, 124
Transportation system, 107, 117, 123–28, 163–64

UHS (University Hospitality Services). See University Hospitality Services (UHS)
Undergraduate Research Conference, 185–88
Underground Railway theater company, 94
Undeveloped land, UNH's, 58, 104, 108–12
UNESCO (United Nations Education, Scientific and Cultural Organization), 9
UNH Community Food, Nutrition, and Wellness Profile (UNH-CFNWP), 182–83
UNH-EcoQuest program, 66–67
UNICEF (United Nations Infant and Children Fund), 33

Union of Concerned Scientists, 174
UNISG (University of Gastronomic Sciences), 81
United Nations Development Program, 33
United Nations Education, Scientific and Cultural Organization (UNESCO), 9
United Nations Environment Program, 14
United Nations Infant and Children Fund (UNICEF), 33
United Nations Population Commission, 46n14
University Conferences & Catering, 132, 137
University Dialogue, 72, 97–98
University Hospitality Services (UHS): Compost Program, 133–35; Cross Roads House food provision project, 227; and dietetic intern program, 84, 85; innovative hours project, 139–40; and locally grown food procurement, 136, 137, 138, 139, 184; overview of sustainability role, 132–34
University Office of Sustainability (UOS): aesthetics project, 143; building design, 146; Compost Program, 133; development of, 55, 242–44, 245; food and society initiatives, 84, 136, 182–83; GHG inventory, 128–29; and Global Environmental Change course, 69–70; and Hospitality Services, 132; landscape projects, 113; and Master of Public Health curriculum, 63; Scheier project role, 239; solar energy program, 90–91; and Theatre department, 94–95
University of Gastronomic Sciences (UNISG), 81
University of New Hampshire: agricultural role of, 175; biodiversity and ecosystems focus, 58; as democratic organization, 230–33; historical perspective on sustainability, 54–57, 242–45; historical sketch, 141; as operational community, 101; research contributions, 153–57, 166
University of Tennessee Agricultural Policy Analysis Center, 28

Virtual/web-based integration of sustainability curricula, 75
Vitruvius, Marcus, 147
Volunteerism, importance to sustainability, 198, 199–202, 204–6

Vulnerability, population: to climate change, 19–20, 24; to food system, 29, 32

Walkable campus, 106, 125, 126
Waste management: Compost Program, 133–36; ERG research, 169; plate waste in dining halls, 139–40; Waste Watch Challenge, 72–75; wastewater treatment facility, 133, 135
Waste Management, Inc., 121–22
Waste-Management Education and Research Consortium (WERC), 171–72
Waste Watch Challenge, 72–75
Wastewater treatment facility, 133, 135
Water-extraction system for Niger's Tuareg people, 206–7
Water quality: freshwater supply, 14, 16; Lakes Lay Monitoring Program, 199–202; Stormwater Research Center, 65, 159, 163–64, 170; wastewater treatment facility, 133, 135
Water Resources Research Center, 200
Water Treatment Technology Assistance Center, 170
Watters, David, 237
WCED (World Commission on Environment and Development), 8
Weather disasters and adaptive capacity, 20
Web-based integration of sustainability curricula, 75
"Wedge" concept, 68, 211, 212
Well-being, focusing on, 38–39
WERC (Waste-Management Education and Research Consortium), 171–72
Western/Greek-influenced culture, 24, 40–44, 91, 92–93
Whale population preservation, 224–25
White pine health, school children's monitoring of, 202–4
WHO (World Health Organization), 16, 25, 27
WildActs (theatre troupe), 95–97
WildCAP discount program, 215–17
Wildcat mascot sculpture, 144–45
Wildflower project on MUB Meadow, 114–16
Windrow composting process, 133, 134
Woodlands, management of, 58, 104, 106, 109–12
Woodlands Committee (CWNA), 109–10

Woodlands Managers, 109, 110
Woodman Horticulture Research Farm, 137,
    183, 184
World Bank, 9, 27
World Commission on Culture and Develop-
    ment, 9–10, 35–37, 39
World Commission on Environment and
    Development (WCED), 8

World Decade for Cultural Development, 9
World Development Report (2008), 27
World Food Summit (1996), 27–28
World Health Organization (WHO), 16, 25, 27
World Summit on Sustainable Development
    (2002), 8
World Trade Organization (WTO), 9, 35
Wotton, Sir Henry, 147

Breinigsville, PA USA
27 June 2010
240657BV00001B/84/P